THE SKIN DIVER'S BIBLE

Also by Owen Lee

**THE COMPLETE ILLUSTRATED GUIDE TO SNORKEL
AND DEEP DIVING**

THE SKIN DIVER'S BIBLE

REVISED EDITION

Owen Lee

DOUBLEDAY & COMPANY, INC.,
GARDEN CITY, NEW YORK
1986

Chapters 8 and 9 have been adapted from *The Complete Illustrated Guide to Snorkel and Deep Diving* by Owen Lee, Doubleday & Company, Inc., 1963.

Library of Congress Cataloging in Publication Data

Lee, Owen.
 The skin diver's bible.

 1. Diving, Submarine.   2. Skin diving.   3. Scuba
diving.   I. Title.
GV840.S78L43   1985   797.2'3
ISBN: 0-385-13543-2
Library of Congress Catalog Card Number 82–45522
Copyright © 1963, 1968, 1986 by Owen Lee
All Rights Reserved
Printed in the United States of America

TO
NORA, BECKY, AND ELLEN

Acknowledgments

This book could never have materialized without the generous help and co-operation of many friends and colleagues. Captain Jacques-Yves Cousteau, James Dugan, John Nathan, and John S. Potter, Jr., were instrumental in launching my diving career almost thirty years ago. Jerry Greenberg has been my frequent and favorite diving buddy and took many of the photo illustrations. Commander Jim Williams and Dennis Graver of PADI International made an honest instructor out of me and provided invaluable and material criticism. My students at Camp de Mar in Zihuatanejo, Mexico were uncomplaining models for many of the photographs. *Skin Diver* Magazine, Seahawk Press, and PADI provided help and material. So did Paul Tzimoulis, John Cronin, Chuck Nicklin, Paolo Alfieri, Ramon Bravo, Edwin Corona, Carlos Barreras, Alfonso Barcenas, and Alfonso Arnold. E. R. Cross provided valuable material on altitude diving. The late Dr. Charles Brown provided his expertise for the chapter on diving first aid. T. J. Holub let me use his great dive boat *The Sea Dwellers II* to take pictures. Dr. Hank Frey, Dr. Joe McInnes, Robert Stenuit, Elgin Ciampi, Andre Galerne, Bob Shourot, Pablo Bush, Nora Beteta, Becky Slaton, Leslie Clairidge, Ruth Dugan, Lilia Martinez, Oliverio Maciel, Carlos Duran, and many others contributed invaluably to this publication. Last but not least the patience and forbearance of my lovely editor, Ms. Louise Gault, was truly admirable. To all of you go my heartfelt thanks.

Contents

Introduction

Welcome to the wonderful world of water. You are about to embark upon one of the greatest adventures in learning of our day: the exploration of the last frontier on earth.

Since the beginning of history, mankind has been curious about that vast domain that lay hidden beneath the restless surface of the sea. They explored it clumsily with hook, line, net, and probe, but they could scarcely imagine the wealth and beauty that lay hidden in its depths. Early "hard hat" divers made personal contact with the underwater world, but they were prisoners of the air that they needed to breathe. It was not until Captain Jacques-Yves Cousteau and Émil Gagnan coinvented the Aqua-Lung—the world's first scuba—that men and women won that freedom for which they longed.

Here was the vital key that opened the doors of the sea to everyone. It was our passport to the 71 percent of the earth's surface (and all the riches attendant to it) that lay hidden by water. It allowed us to penetrate the surface and move in three dimensions through the watery realm with all the freedom and agility of a bird in the sky. Now we could deal with it on a personal level. In the process, we not only learned about the sea, but about ourselves, as well.

Among many other things, we learned that certain physiological laws of nature limited our activities underwater. We also learned that the price of breaking these laws was often crippling and sometimes deadly. Consequently, authorities imposed certain minimum standard training procedures on the new diving industry. These standards were set and are now supervised by the American Standards Association (ASA). The enforcement of these standards falls under the stewardship of the various certifying organizations such as those listed on page 16. Many countries have their own certifying organizations, but each belongs to a worldwide confederation. This means that once you are cer-

tified as a diver you can go to any affiliated dive retail store, dive excursion, or charter boat and rent or buy services that are insured and safe. Thus, when you win your "C" card you are joining a huge, international confederation of fellow enthusiasts who seek ways to safely enjoy and enhance the underwater environment.

Diving is like driving a car, flying an airplane, or riding a bicycle. Nobody can tell you how to do it. It is something you must experience for yourself. But once you learn it, the ability never leaves you; it is with you the rest of your life. Thus, this book is not teaching you how to dive and certainly is no substitute for a certified instructor. Rather it is a guide to the fundamental tools and techniques of safe diving that your instructor will teach and practice with you.

Once you are certified as a diver, you are likely to develop a special interest in some particular aspect of diving. It might be underwater photography, commercial diving, spearfishing, research diving, diving for gold, light salvage, wreck exploring, or search and recovery.

In any case, I send you my good wishes for the best in safe diving.

OWEN LEE

The author with Jacques Cousteau aboard the MV Calypso.

Scuba diving can be your entrée to a new profession.

Scuba is your passport to a new, enchanted world.

1

So You Want to Dive!

Small wonder! The sea is the world's last, largest, and most enticing frontier. It covers almost three quarters of the earth's surface and to the more than twenty million who have learned how to dive, it opens up an entirely new world of enchantment, beauty, and opportunity. If only for the duration of your air supply, it enables you to fathom billions of years of evolutionary history—to go back through time and space to the very source and substance of life itself. From each diving experience you return just a little bit wiser regarding the meaning of your own existence in relation to that which surrounds you. Diving can enable you to experience your place in nature in a way that few other sports can, for it is revealed through personal contact and experimental evidence.

There are risks involved in skin diving, as in every sport. The element of risk alone is what attracts some people to skin diving—but they are few and invariably immature. They may even harbor a subconscious desire to end it all. On one of my speaking tours, I encountered a diving organization known as the Forty Fathom Club. One of the entrance requirements was a compressed-air dive to forty fathoms, or 240 feet—far beyond the depth at which nitrogen narcosis overcomes the diver. I tried to discourage this foolhardy defiance, but the Forty Fathom Club went blindly on its tragic course. The inevitable result was a number of needless deaths and the outlawing of skin diving in several counties of Florida.

If you are an avid seeker of danger, please don't become a diver. You will only give diving a bad name and impose restrictions on those who would like to enjoy the sport for other reasons.

On the other hand, if you are a normal, healthy person who enjoys aquatic adventure and wants to live life to its fullest, diving is definitely for you. Indeed, if exercised with all due caution, diving can be one of the most rewarding and thrilling experiences of your lifetime. But to exercise caution in skin diving, you must know what the precautions are and why they exist. You must also know what to do and what not to do, and why. That is the purpose of this book. If you follow the simple instructions in this book and have the guidance of a competent instructor, you can explore the last and most exciting frontier left on earth with safety, joy, and the endless reward of a real pioneer.

WHO CAN DIVE?

To say that everyone can learn and enjoy diving would be an exaggeration. Obviously you must possess certain physical, mental, and physiological qualifications. For example, if you were a chronic heart or respiratory patient, it would be unwise to take up diving, as it would if you happen to be a diabetic, an epileptic, or a tuberculosis victim. An illiterate person would also be disqualified from diving because he or she could not study the physiological principles involved in diving. However, if you possess a mature, healthy body and mind and are endowed with a measure of swimming ability and common sense, there is no reason why you cannot learn to dive with the best of them, regardless of age, sex, or athletic prowess.

A fair swimming ability must be considered a prerequisite if only because it conditions you to be at ease in the water and imparts a certain amount of self-confidence and self-reliance should you ever experience equipment failure. If you are a parent and a bit apprehensive about your teenage children taking up diving as a sport, I suggest you set your mind at ease and join them. Diving is a sport that the entire family can enjoy together, for each member can participate at his or her own pace. In fact, as you associate with more divers, you quickly learn that one of the most important earmarks of an expert diver is the ability to get a maximum of efficiency with a minimum expenditure of energy. If you never allow yourself to get out of breath while underwater, you are likely never to panic. If you always remember to "take it easy,"

you will soon be amazed to discover just how easy it really is!

HOW AND WHERE TO LEARN

Last but not least, even if this were the ultimate in diving books, it could never replace a qualified instructor. You need the personal attention and expertise that only an instructor can give you in order to get the most out of diving with the least amount of discomfort. The place to find such an instructor is at your nearest dive retail store. Your diving pleasure and safety is your dive store's business. All retail dive stores have certified instructors on their staff. In order to obtain the necessary liability insurance, they must be sanctioned by at least one of the following certifying organizations that safeguard the sport of diving by imposing certain standards on diver education and practice. These certifying organizations are the:

> Young Men's Christian Association (YMCA)
> Professional Association of Diving Instructors (PADI)
> National Association of Underwater Instructors (NAUI)
> National Association of Skin Diving Stores (NASDS)
> Skin Diving Schools International (SSI)
> British Subaqua Club (BSC)
> Federación Mexicana De Actividades Subaquáticas (FMAS)
> Confédération Mondiale Des Activités Subaquatiques (CMAS)

CERTIFICATION REQUIREMENTS

In the United States, a certification "C" card is necessary in order for you to rent equipment or buy compressed air from a dive retail store. Without one, the dealers become personally liable for your safety. That is, they could lose their insurance coverage and possibly lose their business.

All certification courses in the United States must conform to certain standards as set forth by the American Standards Association (ASA) in order to be eligible for liability insurance. The

Your local diving retail store can provide you with expert training and advice.

course itself must impose certain standards and requirements for the education of each diver. Before these existed there were so many accidents and so much antidiving legislation attendant to them that diving as a sport almost did itself in. The certification programs are the industry's way to insure its own survival. Therefore all certification programs require you to comply with the following in order to obtain your open water scuba certification:

1. Fill in and sign a student diver enrollment and medical history form.

2. Read, understand, and sign an insurance disclaimer.

3. Swim two hundred yards or more and perform other water skills tests.

4. Attend and understand five to ten sessions of classroom instruction on the equipment, theory, physics, physiology, and practice of diving.

5. Participate in five or more training and practice scuba sessions in a pool or confined shallow water.

6. Participate in five or more training and practice dives in open water.

7. Pass satisfactorily both a practical and a written examination.

2

The Wonderful World of Water

WHAT IS WATER?

Of all of earth's great gifts to mankind, none is so precious as water, for water is synonymous with life. It is the unique substance of our planet that first produced life and now nurtures the entire dynamic system of systems that we call nature.

In its pure form, water is an odorless, tasteless, and colorless chemical compound consisting of two parts hydrogen to one part oxygen (H_2O). Water covers almost three quarters of the earth's surface to an average depth of 10,000 feet. As a solvent and a catalyst, it dissolves and binds together more elements than any other known liquid. As a result, the sea contains every mineral and chemical element known to mankind.

Water has three physical states of being. It constantly changes from a liquid to a gas to a solid with relatively slight variations in temperature and atmospheric pressure. In the warm sunny tropics, water absorbs heat energy from the sun. The spinning of the earth on its axis and other factors set up ocean currents that circulate the solar-heated water throughout the planet. Wherever there is a marked difference between air and water temperatures, there is an interchange of heat and moisture and they tend to equalize. Thus, water makes and regulates our life-giving climate, warming the colder latitudes and cooling the hotter ones. In the process over 100,000 cubic miles of water evaporate into the atmosphere each year. Winds scatter the clouds of water vapor over the earth. When conditions are right, the vapors condense into droplets until they become too heavy to "float" in the atmosphere. Then they fall as rain or snow. Pulled by gravity, they seek the earth's lowest level, the deep sea basins. En route, they feed the plants and animals, turn the dynamos that produce electrical energy and generally promote the amenities of life.

Like a siren from our primordial past, water calls us back to the source and substance of our very being. It entices, threatens, seduces, and cajoles. It challenges both our instincts and our reason. It speaks of adventure, of enchanted islands, of newfound lands and lost horizons. It is our planet's last frontier of both fact and fantasy, and diving is the key that unlocks its door.

MAN BENEATH THE SEA

Ever since mankind evolved from the sea, it has sought ways to return to it. Homer referred to early divers when he wrote the Iliad around 750 B.C. Alexander the Great used the first diving bell in 323 A.D. Leonardo da Vinci had sketches of the first mask, snorkel, and fins among his drawings. In 1819 Augustus Siebe perfected the classical hard hat, flexible dress diving suit. It revolutionized underwater work and is still in common use today. But it was not until Captain Jacques-Yves Cousteau and Émil Gagnan coinvented the self-contained underwater breathing apparatus (scuba) that mankind was given the underwater freedom for which it longed. The scuba is truly our passport to the underwater world. It enables us to leave behind the compressed-air hoses that kept us chained to the atmosphere and to move and work underwater like fish. It enables us to experience the underwater world as a part of it rather than apart from it. At last we discover for ourselves that far from being the forbidden house of horrors that so many had imagined it to be, the sea is a place of enchantment, beauty, and endless opportunity.

THE SECRETS OF LIFE

Diving is an intensely personal experience that can lead to startling revelations. Here we can witness the dynamic interaction of the entire pyramid of life that ultimately nurtures our own life on land. In the warm, sunlit surface of the sea, suspended in limbo like specks of dust, we can see hoards of tiny phytoplankton. These tiny plants use solar energy to convert dissolved minerals and carbon dioxide into chlorophyll, carbohydrates, and oxygen. Reproducing up to 1,000 percent per day, they comprise the pastures of the sea. Among the tiny specks, some appear as translucent globules of organic matter. Others can be observed to move with primitive pulsations or whiplike motions of their bodies. These are the animal plankton or the early larval stages of fish and crustaceans. They graze upon the plants. From out of nowhere a school of tiny silver-sided fish might appear—a massive cloud of individuals so attuned to each other that they seem to think and move as one. As they feed upon the plankton, a school of mackerel encircle them. As fast as bullets, a few mackerel split ranks and dart into the midst of the silversides, shattering the cloud into a million fragments. This incites their companions into a feeding frenzy. It is startling evidence of the eat-and-be-eaten existence of all life in the sea.

Upon surfacing, the diver might find several boats of fishermen trolling baited lines to entice the mackerel onto their hooks. Thus in a single dive, you can glimpse the entire cycle of life from the tiny floating plankton, to small fish, to bigger fish, to man, the ultimate predator. Nowhere else is the whole dynamic picture of life so beautifully explicit.

THE LIMITATIONS OF DIVING

It is the exclusive privilege of divers to share the sea with its natural inhabitants, but such privileges do not come cheaply. Like an astronaut on the moon, the diver in the sea must pay for the privilege with personal sacrifice. First, one must invest time, effort, and money in the research, training, and equipment that is required to get one safely to and from this alien world. Once underwater, the diver's air is compressed while body fluids and tissues remain incompressible. This requires one to abide by a strict code of conduct that is imposed by the physiological laws of nature dealing with the interaction of liquids and gases under pressure.

For example, water is 800 times heavier and therefore denser than air. Consequently the submerged diver must learn to temper one's movement or pay the price in needless exhaustion and air comsumption. Water buoys you up with a force equal to the amount of water you displace, so you must wear weights in order to sink. Sound travels almost five times faster in water (4,800 feet per second) than it does in air, so it is virtually impossible to tell from which direction it comes. If you dive in water that is anything less than normal body temperature (98.6 degrees F.), the water conducts heat directly away from the body surface in direct proportion to the difference in temperatures between your body and the water. (The reverse is also true.) Therefore you must wear a protective suit to insulate your body from the cold. Water molds itself to the curvature of the human eyeball, causing vision to be blurred and confused as in extreme cases of astigmatism. Therefore you must separate your eyes from the water with a flat optical plane—the face mask—in order to restore normal vision. Even then, everything appears nearly a third larger and closer due to the refraction of light passing through the glass faceplate. Water reflects only up to half of the light that hits its surface so underwater light is always less intense. It also filters the color spectrum of normal light according to depth. One by one the colors vanish, until at a depth of 100 feet everything appears to be blue or green. (Blue and green are the only colors in the spectrum that are reflected back into the sky, as well. That is why the surface of clear, deep water always appears to be blue or green.) Rip currents and tidal currents can sweep the diver from his intended destination. If you dive beyond certain depth limits, you become drunk from the nitrogen in your breathing air. If you stay too long beyond depths of 33 feet, your bloodstream absorbs air under pressure and crippling air bubbles can form in it upon returning to the surface.

We will discuss all of these aspects of diving to greater detail later on in this book. For now, let us return to the wonderful world of water and what we can expect to find there.

UNDERWATER TERRAIN

The type of underwater terrain you can expect in a given area almost always corresponds

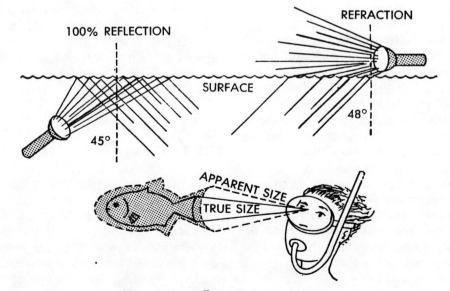

How water affects light and vision.

to the kind of above-water terrain in the area; one is simply an extension of the other. However, the kinds of flora and fauna the area supports vary with the temperature which in turn varies with the latitude and the prevailing currents. In the higher, colder latitudes, you can expect to encounter a wide variety of plant life, such as the giant kelp forests of California, that do not exist in the tropics. In the lower, warmer latitudes you can expect a wide variety of corals that do not exist in the higher, colder latitudes. Each of these, in turn, provides food and shelter for a whole chain of life that is peculiar to the area. Meanwhile, some species—principally the free-roaming pelagic fishes—are common to both.

To date, the evolutionary process that began about 3.5 billion years ago in the sea has produced an incredible variety of living species— over 300,000 species of plants and over a million species of animals. Coliform bacteria and viruses also exist in the sea, but it is interesting to note that the bacteria dies off within forty-eight hours when deprived of its food source— usually sewage or other decomposing matter. It is also interesting to note that practically no insects live in the sea.

UNDERWATER PLANTS

Of the 300,000 varieties of plants on earth, only about 50 species thrive in the sea. Almost all of them are grasses. Of these, only a few species grow off the bottom terrain as land plants do, for only 2 percent of the ocean is shallow enough to transmit enough sunlight to ensure their survival. Those that have no roots rely instead on a stipe or rootlike structure called a holdfast to attach themselves to the bottom. These are the large-leafed plants such as the green, brown, and red algaes that are found in the progressively deeper waters offshore.

The majority of sea plants are comprised of the tiny free-floating plants called phytoplankton. These are the primitive algae, dinoflagellates, and diatoms. Together they comprise the foundation for the entire pyramid of life in the sea.

All sea plants use solar energy to synthesize starches and carbohydrates from dissolved nu-trients and mineral salts in the water. The process is known as photosynthesis. Plants consume carbon dioxide and produce oxygen. Thus they infuse the atmosphere with about 80 percent of its oxygen. Therefore, sea plants are an essential link in the whole ecology of life. They provide the food and oxygen that is essential to animals, just as animals provide the food and carbon dioxide fuel needed by plants. When conditions are right, sea plants can reproduce up to 1,000 percent in a single day and infuse the water with up to ten million living cells per cubic meter. When these plant population explosions take place, the decomposition of dying plants consumes abnormal amounts of oxygen in the water. By blocking the exchange of oxygen and carbon dioxide in the fish's gills this can cause massive fish kills. At night they also produce a blue heatless light known as bioluminescence. When these conditions exist, it is best not to eat shellfish or other filter feeders from the sea because of the possibility of food poisoning. Otherwise, sea plants present virtually no danger to the diver.

Kelp

Of all the plants in the sea, the only one that presents any real potential danger is the *Macrocystis pyrifera*. This is a giant kelp plant, which is common to the West Coast of the United States. Anyone who has dived among the kelp forests of California could not help but be impressed by their giant proportions or their ethereal beauty. Anchored to the rocky seafloor by a rootlike structure (a holdfast) and suspended in the water by bulbous air bladders, they grow to heights of one hundred feet or more. They then spread out on the surface into a giant canopy that may cover several square miles. Diving into such a canopy can be a frightening experience for the novice, but once you are below the canopy it can be like soaring amid the towering spires of a lost cathedral. The kelp presents a potential danger to the diver only in the remote possibility of becoming entangled in it. For this reason, it is always advisable to carry a sharp knife when diving amid kelp. In spite of appearances, however, your chances of entanglement are minimal and a dive in a kelp forest is always an enchanting experience.

Towering kelp like this has entangled divers on the West Coast. (Photo Jack McKenney)

SEA ANIMALS

As I mentioned before, more than a million species of animals live in the sea. Each depends on a delicate interrelationship with the plants and the various geophysical elements of its immediate environment for its existence. Sea animals can be divided into two categories: the protozoa and the metazoa. The protozoa are tiny, primitive, single-celled animals such as foraminifera and *Globigerina.* These comprise the free-floating animal plankton. They are to the animal kingdom what the phytoplankton (algae, dinoflagellates, and diatoms) are to the plant kingdom. They feed directly on the phytoplankton. In turn, they provide food for the metazoa, the larger and more complex animals of the sea.

The seven major kinds of metazoa are the porifera, coelenterata, vermes, arthropoda, mollusca, echinodermata, and chordata. The following outline describes the characteristics of each of these classes of animal species.

PROTOZOA
Single-celled, microscopic, free-floating animals.
1. Foraminifera
2. *Globigerina* (many species that vary with the climate)

METAZOA

Porifera

Pori = bearing and *fera* = holes. Sedentary filter feeders with external skeletons.

1. Sulfur sponge (yellow)
2. Sulfur cliona sponge
3. Siliceous sponge (has siliceous slivers)

Coelenterata

Have holes for stomach.

1. Sea anemones
2. Jellyfish (Have stinging cells called nematocysts that release formic acid when touched or doused with fresh water. Do not attempt to rub cells off skin. Pick them off. Neutralize acid with ammonia, vinegar, papaya, or meat tenderizer.)
3. Corals (Have external skeletons. Live in symbiotic relationship with green algae, which need light to live. Therefore, corals do not grow in deep waters.)
4. Gorgonians, sea fans, sea whips, sea pens, pansies, etc. (Look like plants and grow on coral, rocks, etc. Many grow in two stages: the free-floating larval stage known as medusoid and the anchored or polyp stage.)

Vermes

Wormlike creatures.

1. Flatworms (Platyhelminthes)
2. Roundworms (Nematoda) grow around decomposing matter.
3. Segmented worms (Annelida) tube worms, feather dusters, etc.

Arthropoda

Jointed creatures with external shells that they must shed or molt in order to grow.

1. Shrimps
2. Crabs
3. Barnacles
4. Lobsters
   a. Inflatus = Mexican
   b. Interruptus = Californian
   c. Argus = Caribbean

Mollusca

Soft-bodied creatures, some with shells. Over 80,000 living forms and 50,000 fossil forms exist.

1. Gastropoda (stomach in foot): snails, slugs, nudibranchs, etc.
2. Bivalves (two shells): include Lamellibranchia such as clams, oysters, etc. (also called Pelecypoda)
3. Cephalopoda (shell-less): octopuses, squid, cuttlefish, etc.

Echinodermata

Spiny-skinned animals that are biologically close to man.

1. Starfish
2. Sea cucumbers
3. Sand dollars
4. Sea urchins
5. Brittle stars, etc.

Chordata (Vertebrates)

Sea creatures with bony or cartilaginous spines.

1. Fishes (over 40,000 species)
2. Reptiles such as turtles and sea snakes
3. Mammals such as dolphins, whales, and seals, all of which adapted to the sea after living on land. Most have their nostril (blowhole) on the top of their head and can safely dive by stopping the buildup of carbon dioxide.

Predatory Sea Creatures

In one way or another, all animals that live in the sea are predatory. Whether actively or passively, all subsist on other forms of life that live in the sea. The secret of underwater longevity is simply to eat without being eaten. However, this does not mean that all sea creatures are aggressively hostile or even dangerous. Most feed only when they are hungry. Furthermore, they are selective in their prey. If given a choice, all sea creatures, even sharks, would prefer seafood to terrestrial food, such as man. The smell of human blood does not even start their gastric juices flowing, whereas the mere whiff of fish blood might trigger a hysterical feeding frenzy. Of this you can be sure: if any sea creature attacks a human being in the water, it is a case of mistaken identity, usually due to obscured vision or confusion; revenge for a provocative act of aggression or molestation; or an act of desperation due to the fact that it has become too old or ill to compete for its food on a normal basis.

Although chemically different from our own, the sea is anything but a hostile environment. If approached with a minimum of respect, it can be an amiable place of beauty and endless discovery. Thus you may enter the watery realm with no more apprehension than you might experience when visiting a strange town or taking

Keep a sharp eye out for danger. (Photo Jack McKenney)

your first airplane ride. With the possible exception of the orca and the great white shark *(Jaws),* all sea creatures are basically shy and unaggressive unless teased.

The Orca or Killer Whale

It should immediately be explained that the orca or killer whale is not a fish but an air-breathing mammal, a member of the otherwise friendly dolphin family. Once terrestrial animals like man, the orca's ancestors moved back to the sea eons ago and apparently liked it so well they never came back. Like man, the orca is chained to the atmosphere it breathes. As a result, it lives a nomadic life at the sea's surface. Unlike most humans, however, it has a propensity for cold water. It favors the arctic latitudes, although it ventures as far south as Cape Hatteras on the East Coast and Baja California on the West Coast.

It is fortunate that the orca is relatively rare in U.S. waters, for it is commonly believed that its aggressiveness is not limited to sea creatures but to anything that walks, crawls, or swims. Because of its voracious appetite and its predilection for wanton killing even when not feeding, it has won the reputation of being the "killer of the seas." This and its superior intelligence, cunning, and size make it a most fearsome animal. Nevertheless, its reputation as a wanton killer is probably exaggerated.

In 1976, my friends Ramon Bravo and Bruno Vailati spotted a school of orcas feeding on a pack of seals in the Sea of Cortez. They dove, using a shark cage to protect them. After days of waiting, one of the orcas came close enough to the cage to be photographed. The movement within the cage seemed to excite its curiosity, but it did not appear to be aggressive. Cautiously Ramon left the protective cage to shoot some close-ups. Soon Bruno joined him. Before the whale returned to its school, it provided them with some of the most spectacular film footage of the entire expedition.

Trained orcas are the star attractions of many sea life parks and are highly regarded by train-

Orca or killer whale. (Courtesy of the American Museum of Natural History)

ers for their intelligence and cooperation. Female orcas range in size from ten to twenty feet while males grow up to thirty feet long and weigh several tons. Orcas can be easily recognized by their huge black dorsal fins and their distinctive black and white coloration.

Sharks

Although it is not entirely justified, the shark's reputation as a killer rivals that of the orca. Whenever a real shark attack occurs, it makes such dramatic news copy that practically everybody hears about it and most people believe, erroneously, that sharks attack all human beings on sight. The fact is that the number of shark attacks compared with the number of shark encounters is minute.

If bold and persistent enough, most salt-water divers eventually encounter a shark. The experience invariably marks a milestone in their diving career. Many a shark has turned a hairy-chested diver into a "chicken of the sea." A shark encounter has brought to some a sudden ability almost to run (not walk) on water. Shark encounters are a good test of a diver's enthusiasm. If he ever dives again after his first shark encounter, he is likely to continue diving forever.

Many qualified people, both privately and professionally, have studied sharks to define their behavioral patterns, and a few have met with a certain measure of success. It has been found that all sharks are able to sense the convulsions of a dying fish from distances of over half a mile. This is accomplished by a set of tiny disks and hairlike receptors, called lateral lines, running from the nostrils down the sides of sharks and other pelagic fishes. A diver who spears a fish in shark-infested waters can expect the arrival of sharks in five to twenty minutes unless his spear hits the fish in the brain or backbone and effects an "instant kill." The shark homes in on the vibrations until he picks up the scent of fish blood. The scent of fish blood starts the shark's gastric juices flowing and induces a radical change in behavior. (Note: The shark is basically a fish eater, not a human eater. Since human or animal blood is likely to be a new experience not associated with feeding, it probably will not affect the shark in the same way as fish blood.) Instead of casually circling around in curious perusal, as he usually does, the shark will swim about with abrupt and erratic movements. He is likely to thrash his head from side to side to see where the blood is coming from. He is likely to dart

Great white shark. (Courtesy of the American Museum of Natural History)

up to investigate anything curious. If he sees a fish, he is likely to attack it. If he sees you with the fish or you instead of the fish, he might attack you.

Sharks in pairs or in groups are extremely dangerous when in this "feeding mood." They appear to stimulate each other into bolder acts—probably because they are competing for the same food. If one attacks, the others are almost sure to follow.

But after all their research, scientists can only affirm that a shark's behavior is entirely unpredictable. Shark behavior is rarely the same, even among the same species. All the sharks I have encountered have spent considerable time circling me curiously with only occasional sorties in close for an intimate look at their prospective meal. The one that did attack (after stupid provocation) even stopped and maneuvered into position before he struck. Yet most shark-attack victims report that they never saw the shark before the attack. Almost invariably, however, fish had been caught or speared in the area.

The exception to this is the rogue shark, or, as treasure-diver Teddy Tucker of Bermuda calls it, "the great gentleman." He is an outcast, usually a huge specimen too senile or ill to compete for his food with other sharks and fishes. He is reduced to prowling the more off-beat places where food, though less choice, is more easily come by: sewage outlets, ship and garbage dumps, and sheltered beaches. He may even be reduced to eating something other than the fish he prefers . . . like you!

The best way to avoid attack, of course, is to avoid sharks. Stay away from places that sharks are known to frequent—especially waste disposal areas. Be sure to boat or bag all speared fish immediately, and make sure that the bag has no holes through which fish blood might leak into the water. If you insist on using a fish stringer, tie it to the end of a long, long line. Never tie it close to your body. Fish only during flood tides so that fish blood is washed shoreward. Don't gut or clean fish until all divers are out of the area. Don't dangle your feet in the water from a boat. If you are snorkel diving, return to the surface after each dive, spiraling around in circles as you go to give your eyes a 360-degree sweep of the water. If a shark comes in anyway, don't freeze in fear or splash on the surface. Stay near the bottom and look alive and aggressive as you swim steadily for your boat. If the shark gets too curious, make an aggressive lunge at him. Hit him in the snoot with something solid (other than your fist) if possible. In any case, always swim with a buddy. The shark can only eat one person at a time. Maybe he will go for your buddy first and give you time to climb on the boat! I am only joking, of course, but it does "double the odds."

Barracuda

The barracuda, also, enjoys a highly overrated reputation for viciousness, but it is one of my favorite reef fishes. As fish go, it somehow comes across to me as being much more macho, as the Spanish say, than most. It frequents tropical waters and has a beautiful, streamlined, cigar-shaped body that ranges in size from two to seven feet in length, with a doglike jaw full of razor-sharp teeth. When necessary, it can move through the water with the speed of lightning. However, it usually loafs in the shade beneath boats or piers or lurks practically motionless in the water near coral formations.

Much of the barracuda's ferocious reputation probably stems from its insatiable curiosity. Many divers have been startled out of their wits by the discovery of an unsuspected barracuda peering over their shoulder trying to see what they are up to. When the diver chases it off, it becomes highly indignant, gnashing its teeth and sometimes shuddering in rage like a cantankerous old man. But this is more a bullish show of frustration than a threat. When the diver returns to his business, the barracuda usually settles down and resumes following him curiously but from a greater distance. Finally it gets bored and continues about its fishy business.

Almost invariably, barracuda attacks on human beings have occurred in murky water, where the movement of the hands or feet of a swimmer or diver, being only partially visible, might give the impression of being a small fish moving quickly through the water. Barracudas are easily excited by quick movements or shiny fishy-looking objects and may strike at them impulsively. Therefore, avoid swimming in murky waters, don't wear shiny objects, and swim with slow, steady movements; you then are never likely to feel the barracuda's teeth.

Eels

There are a number of eel species and they range in size from the small spotted moray eel that measures about two feet in length to the South Pacific brown moray that measures up to ten feet. In between there are the slimy green moray that is around six feet long, the stubby black electric eel, around four feet long, and the powerful conger eel and wolf eel that measure up to eight feet in length. They all share a predilection for seclusion, preferring the dark holes and crevasses of the reefs, coral heads, and rock jetties to the open water. They will bother no one unless they are provoked or intruded upon. Most eel bites have resulted from divers reaching into a dark hole for a lobster who happened to share his habitat with an eel. Once the eel bites, however, it clings tenaciously, and severing the back of its head is often the only way to loosen its grip. When under threat of death, it will strike indiscriminately at anything within reach and give you a dramatic demonstration of the meaning of the word writhing.

Look before you poke your head or arm into any dark holes in reefs, wrecks, or jetties. If you spear an eel, hold your spear firmly and keep it at a distance until he is subdued. The eel's teeth are covered with an infectious slime. If you are bitten, your wound is likely to become infected

Barracuda.

Eel. (Courtesy of the American Museum of Natural History)

unless you quickly wash, soak, and disinfect it thoroughly.

Venomous Creatures

Though less dramatic and less consequential than contacts with predatory sea creatures, contacts with venomous animals of the sea are likely to be much more frequent. The Office of Naval Research, in collaboration with Dr. Paul Rom Saunders of the Biology Department of the University of Southern California, compiled a list of the venomous sea creatures so that naval personnel might avoid them. With their permission I quote from their list for your information.

Certain creatures of the sea can inflict in man venomous wounds resulting in serious injury or even death in some cases. In contrast to our extensive knowledge of the venoms of terrestrial animals, relatively little is known about the nature and actions of marine animal venoms. Consequently, the treatment of injuries resulting from such wounds is usually empirical and often ineffective.

Stonefish

The stonefish is one of those animals. It is one of many marine bony fishes that possess venomous spines. When erected the spines penetrate the skin easily. Wounds cause agonizing pain and swelling and in severe cases they can produce cardiovascular collapse and death.

The stonefish is found in shallow water in many parts of the tropical Pacific and Indian oceans. Usually less than a foot long, it is commonly found partially buried in the sand and is extremely difficult to see. Injuries often occur when a person accidentally steps upon the fish.

This fish must be considered one of the most dangerous of the marine animals. Each of the thirteen individual spines of the dorsal fin is covered by a thick sheath of tissue. This sheath is pressed down upon the underlying venom sacs upon contact. The resulting pressure causes the fluid venom to be forced into the puncture wound produced.

Removal of the outer sheath reveals on either side of the spine the two venom sacs, each containing a small drop or less of venom. A duct leads to the tip of the spine.

Lionfish

Another dangerous bony fish found in the tropical Indo-Pacific is known variously as the lionfish, turkey fish, zebra fish, or by other names. This member of the scorpion-fish family reaches a length of about one foot, and is most commonly seen in shallow water swimming about slowly or resting on coral formations or in caves.

The lionfish is readily visible and injuries often result from the careless handling of captured specimens. Wounds are usually inflicted by the long, banded dorsal spines. The covering thin tissue sheath tears when the spine penetrates the flesh, and venom from the underlying spaces enters the wound.

Symptoms produced are similar to those caused by stonefish stings. Serious systemic effects are less common but a marked fall in blood pressure to dangerous levels has occurred.

Like the stonefish, this animal is not known to use its spines as offensive weapons in the capture of prey, but secures its food in the usual manner. The biological function of the venom apparatus in this fish, and in the stonefish, is unknown, although it may play a role as a defensive weapon.

Scorpion Fish

The California scorpion fish also possesses venomous spines on its dorsal fin which can be erected when the fish is disturbed. Wounds, usually due to careless handling by fishermen, cause severe pain and swelling, although serious systemic effects are rare.

Rays

Certain cartilaginous fishes are also venomous, and of this group the most numerous are various rays.

Venomous rays range in weight from less than a pound to hundreds of pounds and are widespread throughout the world. Rays inflict venomous painful wounds by means of a sharp spine on the tail, driven into the victim by a lashing movement of the tail. Rays do not attack man. Stingings usually result from

Stingray.

stepping upon them and are defensive in nature.

Stingrays are most frequently found resting on the bottom, partially buried in the sand. Detection is often difficult. Wounds cause almost immediate intense pain with subsequent swelling and, although serious systemic effects are not common, several fatalities have resulted from stings by very large rays.

Contact of a foot or other object with the dorsal surface of a ray usually results in a rapid lash of the tail with the sharp barb held erected so that it can be forced into the threatening object.

The spine is covered by a layer of tissue that tears easily during entry into the flesh, and the underlying venom is left in the wound after withdrawal.

The sharp barbs along the shaft of a stingray spine produce the lacerated type of wound often seen, although a puncture wound may occur. Immersion of the affected area in very hot water quickly alleviates the pain.

Stings are most apt to occur if a person *runs* in the water, as a result of stepping directly upon a ray lying on the bottom. Rays tend to move away if one shuffles the feet along the sand.

Sea Snakes

A third group of venomous vertebrates are the sea snakes, various species of which are found in the tropical Indo-Pacific. The yellow-bellied sea snake is an example.

The tail is paddle-shaped, and its movements are very effective in propelling the animal through the water.

Although these air-breathing animals are relatively nonaggressive, bites do occur, and the venom is highly toxic. Early symptoms of poisoning are muscle pain .and stiffness, which may be followed by muscle weakness. Death may occur as a result of respiratory failure, renal kidney failure, or other causes.

Bristle Worms

Among the marine invertebrates, certain annelid worms found in the sea and known as "bristle worms" or "fire worms" possess tufts of bristlelike structures called setae along their bodies. Contact with those bristles may result in a somewhat painful wound. It is not known if this response is due to a venom or simply to mechanical injury as a result of the bristles breaking off and penetrating the skin.

In some species the bristles are exceptionally long and cover almost the entire upper surface of the animal. They are present in tufts on both sides of each segment of the worm.

Glycera

Another type of worm, such as the bloodworm, Glycera, possesses biting jaws. The worm is commonly eight to ten inches long and at intervals everts its snout with its four sharp curved terminal jaws, which are black. Wounds may be quite painful and there is some indication that a venom may be present.

Jellyfishes

Another general group of venomous invertebrates are the coelenterates. A great variety of these interesting animals exists throughout the world.

The jellyfishes move by rhythmic contractions of the bell-shaped body. The tentacles

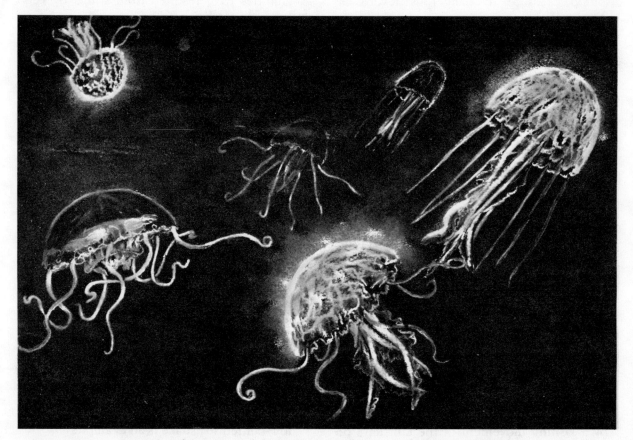

Jellyfish. (Courtesy of the American Museum of Natural History)

and some other parts are armed with specialized stinging capsules known as nematocysts, which range in size from five to fifty or more microns.

Seen microscopically, the nematocysts of coelenterates appear as capsules with a long hollow threadlike tube coiled up inside. Contact with a tentacle can cause an almost explosive eversion of large numbers of the tubes and release of the venom within the capsules.

The extended thread may be several hundred times as long as the undischarged nematocysts and may have numerous barbs by which it becomes attached to the skin.

The thread is believed to turn inside out as it emerges from the capsule.

The effect of coelenterate stings in man due to discharge of venom from the nematocysts is highly variable. Local symptoms range from relatively mild skin irritation to severe pain and welts. Contact with the tentacles in some cases has caused marked systemic effects, and deaths have been reported following stings by some species.

Stings can also result from contact with the tentacles of dead specimens washed up on the beach.

The animals vary greatly in appearance and size, and the bell of some species may have a diameter as great as six feet, with tentacles trailing downward for perhaps a hundred feet.

Lion's Mane

Like other representatives of this class of coelenterates, the lion's mane captures animals that blunder into the mass of tentacles and are stung by the venom-containing nematocysts.

A fish may be captured after only slight contact with the tentacles and held tightly in spite of vigorous struggling. As the venom exerts its effect, the victim is eventually subdued and eaten.

Portuguese Man-of-war

The Portuguese man-of-war is another type of coelenterate possessing nematocyst-bearing tentacles that may trail fifty or more feet below the float.

The float is a gas-filled bag, and the pressure of the wind upon the sail-like crest of this structure causes the animal to move slowly through the water. In contrast to the jellyfishes, movement of the man-of-war is controlled only by the wind and the ocean currents.

Man-of-war stings are not uncommon in some areas. Severe burning pain and local weal formation are the most common effects produced. Some individuals experience nausea, respiratory difficulty, and other systemic symptoms, but available data do not support the popular view that man-of-war stings are often fatal.

Persons touching the tentacles of dead specimens may also be stung. Fish and other animals may be captured after contact with a tentacle and soon subdued and eaten.

The long tentacles have a beaded appearance due to the presence of batteries of nematocysts. They shorten and lengthen periodically, and the muscular elements can contract and bring captured prey up to the region of the digestive structures.

Hydroids

Hydroids, which are often found attached to rocks or other objects, may also cause painful stings. The tentacles possess the nematocysts characteristic of coelenterates.

Coral

The stinging or fire coral found in warm waters is another coelenterate which can cause a painful sting. Not a true coral, it is in the same animal class as the Portuguese man-of-war and the hydroids. It exists in a great variety of shapes ranging from upright columnar or fanlike structures to incrustations on rocks and other objects. The hard calcareous external skeleton is laid down by the innumerable individual polyps making up the colony.

If one brushes up against living fire coral with its multitude of tiny polyps, an almost immediate burning, stinging pain is produced by the venom of the discharged nematocysts.

The true corals, in contrast to the stinging corals, do not in general produce venomous wounds in man, although they can cause severe cuts that exude fluid and often take

Sea urchins and stinging (fire) coral. (Courtesy University of California, Scripps Institution of Oceanography. Photo Willard Bascom)

weeks to heal. However, if you wash your skin with meat tenderizer or a weak ammonia and water solution as soon as possible after contact, the effects can be greatly reduced.

Anemones

Sea anemones also capture small animals by means of nematocysts. The small anemone fish is exceptional in that it lives in close association with certain anemones and is not stung; on the contrary it serves to attract larger fish into the anemone's grasp. If other fish brush up against the tentacles of these coelenterates, however, they may be captured and eaten by both. This is an act of symbiosis between two different species.

If a person touches the tentacles of most sea anemones, the finger may become stuck lightly, but usually no symptoms are produced. Certain tropical anemones, however, can cause quite a painful sting.

Fish that even slightly touch one of the extended tentacles may be captured. After the initial capture, additional tentacles are then brought into action and escape becomes almost impossible.

Struggling may continue as the fish is drawn into the mouth of its captor.

The fish is finally consumed and digested in the internal cavity of the anemone.

Sea Urchins

Another general group of animals, of which some are venomous, are the echinoderms, comprising, among others, the sea urchins and starfishes. Certain warm-water sea urchins possess venomous spines that may puncture the flesh and cause an extremely painful wound.

The animals move about by means of the spines and also the tube feet which attach to rocks and other objects.

Many species of urchins are found throughout the world, but only a few appear to be capable of inflicting a venomous wound. Venomous sea urchins possess both long primary and shorter, thinner secondary spines. Only the thin spines are believed to possess a venom. Symptoms produced in man are local pain with variable amount of swelling.

Some short-spined sea urchins possess quite a different type of venom apparatus— small grasping organs known as pedicellariae which range in diameter from a fraction of a millimeter to several millimeters.

Starfish

Another type of echinoderm is the starfish, most species of which are not venomous. However, certain species with stout spines may be capable of inflicting a venomous wound, although this has not been clearly established.

Contact with the spines has been reported to cause painful wounds but nothing is known about the nature of any venom.

Octopus

Certain mollusks are also venomous. The salivary secretions of the octopus contain toxic substances believed to be of importance in the capture of prey. Bites in humans by most species do not cause symptoms other than those due to the trauma produced by the animal's sharp beak. Some species, however, may cause severe local pain, swelling, and sometimes systemic effects.

Cone Shells

Some of the most interesting of the venomous marine animals are the mollusks of the genus conus, known commonly as the cone shells. These animals, found throughout much of the world, possess a unique and highly developed venom apparatus. Stings produce effects ranging from local pain to paralysis and death.

The animal usually withdraws into its shell when picked up but may occasionally sting a person if handled carelessly.

Following contact of the tip of the thin red-

Cone shell. (Courtesy of the American Museum of Natural History)

dish orange snout, a hollow dartlike radula tooth is discharged into the flesh, and venom is injected through the lumen of the tooth. The prey of these gastropods are other snails, small fish, or various worms.

PHYSICAL DIVING HAZARDS

It is axiomatic that water constantly seeks its own level. The only rub is that it never finds it. Even the smallest body of water never rests. It is always in some degree of motion, due among other things to the speed and rotation of the earth and the magnetic attraction of the moon and sun. The effect of these forces varies directly with the size of the body of water, producing tides in oceans and slighter motions in smaller bodies of water. Added to these is the awesome force of the unhampered winds. These forces are transmitted to water, which is eight hundred times denser than air. Nothing in water can withstand its movement in currents, tides, and waves, and that includes you, for by comparison to the forces involved, you are nothing but an overgrown grain of sand on the beach.

When dealing with forces of such magnitude, one has little choice but to "swim with the current," and a diver should never forget this. To fight against such odds is to invite exhaustion and disaster. In relatively still bodies of water, surface currents are generated almost entirely by the wind. The results are surface waves, chop, or swells. When wind and water are moving together, the force of the wind is combined with the force of the moving water. Together, they can move a diver much farther than he can swim in the same amount of time. Or they can crush him against the shore with devastating effect. When working against each other, their forces tend to cancel each other out, but the two are rarely, if ever, in perfect balance.

Therefore, you should learn to cope with these forces and use them to your own advantage. How do you learn? Experience is the only teacher, but perhaps I can warn you about what to expect.

Tidal Currents

The oceans slosh back and forth in their basins every six hours like clockwork, as a result, primarily, of the gravitational pull of the moon. In the process, as the water piles up on one shore it recedes from the opposite shore, in what are called high (flood) tides and low (ebb) tides. As the tides encounter the narrow passages that separate the many bays, inlets, harbors, or estuaries from the open sea, a venturi effect is created and the flow of water becomes much more extreme than normal. Bottom contours such as shoals and reefs can effect the same results. Thus there are always certain spots where divers simply should not dive except at brief periods between tides (that is, diving slack tides), and then only if necessary. These places and periods can easily be determined by consulting local experts or local charts and tide tables, which can be obtained at most boat marinas or from the U.S. Coast and Geodetic Survey in Washington, D.C.

If you are caught in an adverse current, swim diagonally with it to the closest shore point, even if it is not the one you want. Better a long walk than being swept out to sea. If the shore point is close enough and speed is essential to avoid missing it, swim diagonally against the current but anticipate the exhausting effort that will be required and pace yourself accordingly. If you are swept out to sea, don't panic. Inflate your life vest and float with it until the current turns and dissipates; you then can summon help or hop on your float and paddle ashore.

Surf Undertow

Seawater that continuously rolls ashore from the sea must return offshore to the sea, or our lands would soon be flooded. On sloping beaches the surface waves pile up relentlessly until they finally crest and topple over onto themselves in the form of surf. The water seeks the easiest return route to the sea, which is close to the bottom. The "bottom current" thus created is called undertow. It can be extremely strong, especially close to shore. If a strong wind is blowing parallel to shore or if there is a rip current present, the undertow may not run directly offshore but diagonally off in the direction of the wind or rip current. All undertows are very easy to avoid, however. All you need to do is stay on the surface.

Surf Breakers

All breakers are not of equal magnitude. The return flow of a particularly big wave tends to flatten out succeeding waves. Therefore only every third to seventh breaker is a really big one. When entering the water through surf, you should time your entry to begin just after a big breaker begins to wash offshore and go with it. When succeeding breakers approach, go to the bottom and let them roll over you, until you are beyond them.

When returning ashore through surf, good timing is essential. If the surf is light, you can pick a wave and ride it in. Then try to make it to the beach before the next wave breaks. If the surf is heavy or you are wearing heavy tanks, stay near the bottom as you approach shore, hanging on to something solid if possible during the backwash. When the water becomes so shallow that you cannot avoid the breakers, choose a nice one and let it take you in. Then get high and dry before the next one hits.

If you are wearing fins, enter and exit the surf walking backward, so that the fin blades won't buckle under and trip you. If you have a float, tow it behind you on entering and let it tow you on leaving. In both cases be sure all loose equipment is securely fastened.

Approaching a rocky shore in surf requires special skill and caution. If possible, exit in the lee of a shallow cove or big rock. As you approach your chosen point of exit, face the breakers (not the shore) and swim through or dive under the breakers until you see one that suits your taste. Then turn and pick out your foothold or handhold underwater as the breaker carries you in. Grab it, hold fast until the breaker recedes and then scramble ashore before the succeeding breaker gets to you. And good luck!

Rip Currents

Rip currents are caused by surf rolling over a shallow sandbar or reef into a lagoonlike basin and then exiting through widely separated channels that it cuts through the reef or bar as it escapes seaward. The rip current might run parallel to the shore until it reaches the channel, where it cuts sharply out to sea and then turns shoreward again.

Rip currents are usually so strong that they

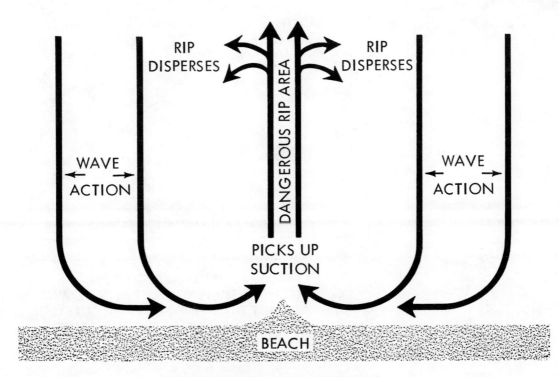

How rip currents are produced.

carry a heavy burden of silt or sand and tend to flatten out the breakers as they rush seaward. They can easily be detected by looking for the discolored water and flattened surf. If you get caught in a rip, swim at right angles to it. If it is carrying you seaward already, it is sometimes easier though less reassuring to let it carry you until it dissipates and turns shoreward again.

A similar kind of rip tide is caused when tides roll into a deep cove. The water rolls off the surrounding shores and returns seaward in the form of a rip current through the middle of the cove. Here again, swim crosscurrent to shore or be swept out to sea. Always use a float or emergency flotation gear when diving where currents or rip currents are present.

Boats

When you are diving or snorkeling in popular boating areas, you always run the risk of being run over by a boat or injured by a whirling pro-peller. Avoid heavily trafficked areas and always display the "diver down" flag. This is a red square with a white bar running diagonally from the upper staff corner to the lower free corner. Theoretically, at least, this warns boatmen to stay clear of the area because of the underwater activity. But take no chances. Always look and listen first, then surface with your hand or spear gun fully extended above your head. As for your own boat, stop the motor before allowing divers to enter or exit the water.

Spear Guns

Spear guns are lethal weapons and should always be treated with the respect due all firearms, whether ashore or underwater. Never point a loaded spear gun at anybody, no matter where you are. If your diving buddy carries a gun and you don't, let him lead. Always keep the trigger safety locked when stalking fish until you are ready to fire, and always fire or unload

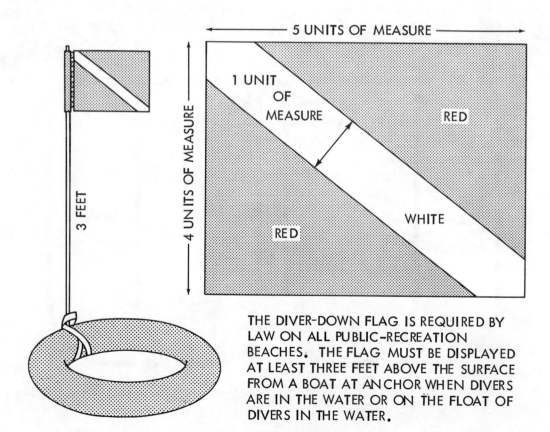

THE DIVER-DOWN FLAG IS REQUIRED BY LAW ON ALL PUBLIC-RECREATION BEACHES. THE FLAG MUST BE DISPLAYED AT LEAST THREE FEET ABOVE THE SURFACE FROM A BOAT AT ANCHOR WHEN DIVERS ARE IN THE WATER OR ON THE FLOAT OF DIVERS IN THE WATER.

"Diver down" flag.

"Diver down" flag.

it before boating it. Then cover the barbed end with a large sheath or piece of cork, and set it out of the way and flat on the deck.

With experience, I think you will find that of all the dangerous creatures that frequent the sea, a careless man is by far the most dangerous.

Temperature

Water—especially the still water of lakes, ponds, quarries, and estuaries—stratifies itself into layers according to temperature. In summertime the bottom layers of water can be as much as 30 degrees colder than the surface layers. (In wintertime it is the reverse.) Therefore, know the character of the water before you dive. If you are going to need a diving suit, do not dive without one. It could only be a drudgery if you did, for nothing is more miserably uncomfortable than to get to the bottom on a long-planned dive only to begin trembling with the cold. Once shivering begins underwater, it is almost impossible to stop it until you return to the surface and restore your body warmth with a hot shower or a warm fire and hot liquids. Meanwhile, you exhaust yourself and overtax your heart. Your breathing pace triples and you consume most of your limited air supply in a futile but involuntary effort to produce enough heat to keep your body temperature up to normal. Furthermore, you become jittery and bumbling. You become dangerous to yourself and everyone near you. Worst of all, the joy is gone from diving. Insulated with a good wet suit, your body needs only a minute to warm the volume of trapped water before you can venture into even the coldest depths with great pleasure and relative comfort.

3

The Physics and Physiology of Diving

A COMPROMISING POSITION

Scientists are now experimenting to find ways by which men will be able to breathe oxygen from the water like a fish. If and when they achieve this goal, we will be able to remain submerged in the sea for unlimited periods. Meanwhile, however, we are chained to the atmosphere by the necessity for breathing air. When we venture underwater, we must take our atmosphere with us. We must either hold our breath or carry tanks of compressed atmosphere on our backs. Either way, we place ourselves in a kind of compromise environment. Although we are living and functioning in the aquasphere, we are still dependent on the atmosphere. Accordingly, we must make a number of

psychological and physiological compromises in order to cope with it. For this reason, it is absolutely essential that we understand the limits and demands that will be imposed upon us.

AIR VERSUS WATER

The air that you breathe at sea level consists of 79.02 percent nitrogen (N_2), 20.94 percent oxygen (O_2), and .04 percent carbon dioxide (CO_2). Pure air is colorless, odorless, and tasteless, but it is by no means weightless. A column of air covering only one square inch at sea level and extending all the way to the outer limits of the earth's atmosphere (about seven miles) weighs 14.7 pounds. The same column cover-

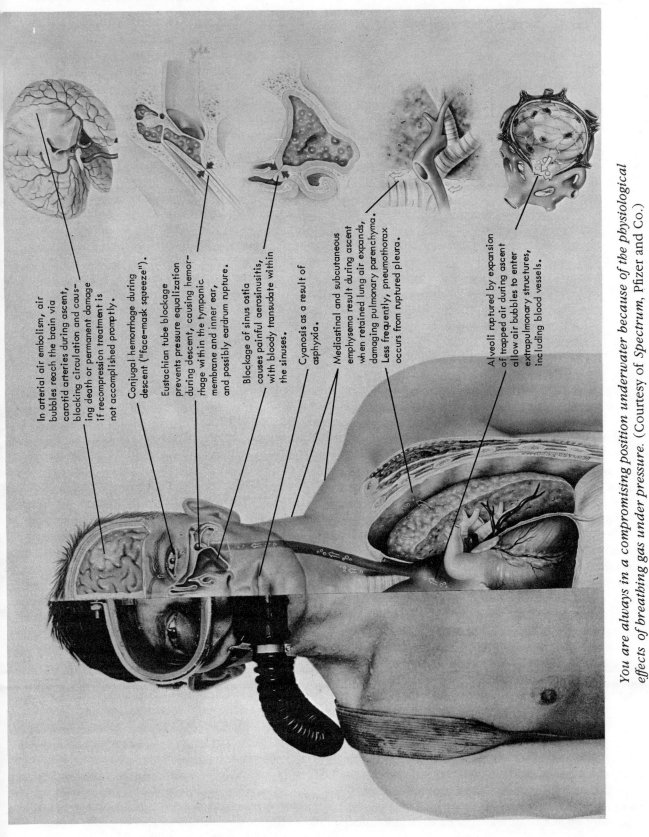

In arterial air embolism, air
bubbles reach the brain via
carotid arteries during ascent,
blocking circulation and causing death or permanent damage
if recompression treatment is
not accomplished promptly.

Conjugal hemorrhage during
descent ("face-mask squeeze").

Eustachian tube blockage
prevents pressure equalization
during descent, causing hemorrhage within the tympanic
membrane and inner ear,
and possibly eardrum rupture.

Blockage of sinus ostia
causes painful aerosinusitis,
with bloody transudate within
the sinuses.

Cyanosis as a result of
asphyxia.

Mediastinal and subcutaneous
emphysema result during ascent
when retained lung air expands,
damaging pulmonary parenchyma.
Less frequently, pneumothorax
occurs from ruptured pleura.

Alveoli ruptured by expansion
of trapped air during ascent
allow air bubbles to enter
extrapulmonary structures,
including blood vessels.

*You are always in a compromising position underwater because of the physiological
effects of breathing gas under pressure. (Courtesy of Spectrum, Pfizer and Co.)*

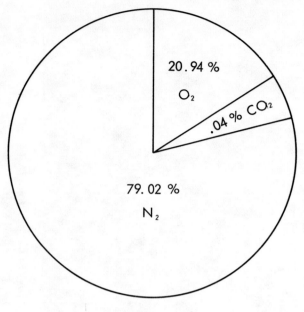

20.94 %

O₂

.04 % CO²

79.02 %

N₂

Components of air.

ing a square foot at sea level would weigh 2,116.8 pounds. And if your body occupies an area of ten square feet, the column of air above you at sea level weighs 21,168 pounds! But don't get exhausted at the thought. You are not actually supporting such a tremendous load. You are simply living in it. Air is a mixture of gases and, like all gases, its weight is transmitted equally in all directions in the form of pressure. Therefore, since the weight of our atmospheric air at sea level is 14.7 pounds per square inch, so the air pressure at sea level is 14.7 pounds per square inch. Since our planet is, for all practical purposes, spherical in shape and since seawater always seeks its own level, the weight and pressure of our atmospheric air remain constant all over the world. Thus it is used as a standard of measure by which we can express such things as heights, depths, and (by measuring the very slight changes in atmospheric pressure with a barometer) even the weather. Unlike air pressure, water pressure increases with depth at a very rapid but constant rate, so the atmospheric pressure at sea level provides an appropriate standard. You will often hear any kind of pressure measurement used in diving referred to in terms of so many atmospheres—that is, in units of 14.7 pounds per square inch (or 14.7 p.s.i., its abbreviated form).

When you leave the gaseous realm of our atmosphere and enter the liquid realm of our aquasphere, you enter a physiologically distinct world. Water is 800 times denser (thicker) than air. That is, the molecules in a given volume of water are 800 times more numerous and closer together than the gas molecules in air. Pure air weighs less than one twelfth of a pound per cubic foot at sea level, the densest level of our atmosphere. Pure water (H_2O) weighs 62.4 pounds per cubic foot. A column of water only 33 feet deep weighs the same as a column of air of the same size that extends from sea level over seven miles to the outer limits of our atmosphere. Since the molecules of water are about as close together as they can get and cannot be squeezed (compressed) closer together, unlike gas molecules, the weight of a given volume of water remains constant, regardless of how many volumes of water you stack on top of it. Thus you have the first example of how this atmospheric term of measure can be applied to the underwater world. Water increases *one atmosphere* (14.7 p.s.i.) in pressure for every 33 feet of depth. Thus, a diver swimming at a depth of 33 feet could be said to be at a depth of one atmosphere gauge.

GAUGE PRESSURE VERSUS ABSOLUTE PRESSURE

But is the diver actually swimming under the pressure of just one atmosphere of 33 feet of water or is he actually swimming under two atmospheres of pressure—that is, the pressure of one atmosphere (or 33 feet) of water *plus* one atmosphere (or the seven miles) of air above him? To be accurate in your measurements, you must differentiate between measurements of pressure by specifying *gauge pressure*—that is, the pressure of the water alone—or *absolute pressure*—that is, the total pressure of the water plus the pressure of the atmospheric air above the water as well. To facilitate this, all diving pressure gauges read zero (0) at sea level, and pressures are expressed as so many atmospheres or pounds per square inch *gauge* (p.s.i.g.) or so many atmospheres or pounds per square inch *absolute* (p.s.i.a.). Thus the diver swimming at a depth of 33 feet is under a pressure of one atmosphere gauge (14.7 p.s.i.g.) or

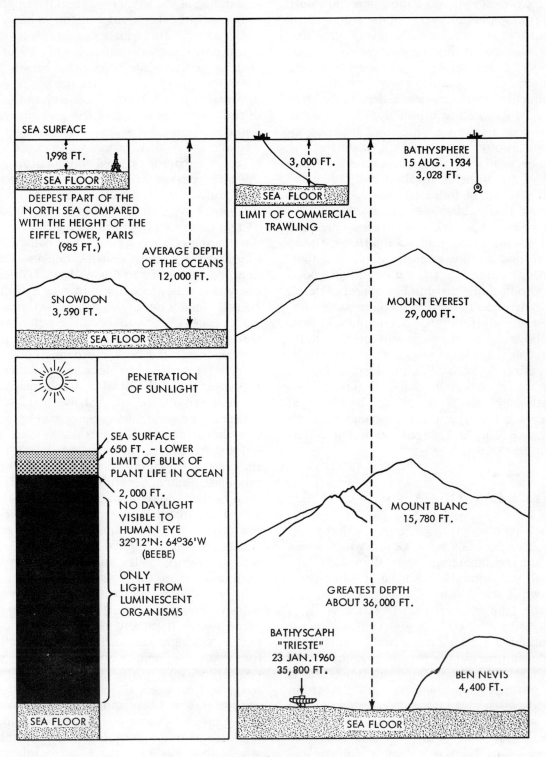

Depths of the ocean.

under a pressure of two atmospheres absolute (14.7 p.s.i.g. plus 14.7 p.s.i. of the atmospheric pressure = 29.4 p.s.i.a.). However, since seawater increases at the constant rate of one atmosphere gauge (14.7 p.s.i.g.) for every 33 feet of depth, or .445 p.s.i. for every foot of depth, the same diver swimming at a depth of 66 feet would be exposed to a pressure of two atmospheres gauge (29.4 p.s.i.g.) and three atmospheres absolute (44.1 p.s.i.a.). At 99 feet the pressure would be three atmospheres gauge and four atmospheres absolute, at 132 feet the pressure would be four atmospheres gauge and five atmospheres absolute, and at 297 feet the pressure would be nine atmospheres gauge and ten atmospheres absolute, *ad infinitum*. Therefore, to find the pressure of the ambient (surrounding) water at any given depth, you need simply to multiply the number of feet of depth by .445. In order to find the absolute water pressure at any given depth, you simply add onto the above figure the pressure of the atmospheric air at sea level (14.7 p.s.i.). Conversely, the depth in feet can be figured by dividing the gauge water pressure in p.s.i. by .445 p.s.i. Thus a depth gauge that reads zero on the surface at sea level is simply a pressure gauge with the last-stated formula (gauge) calibrated on its dial, in feet of depth.

BOYLE'S LAW OF GASES

The phenomenon of gas compression is expressed in Boyle's Law of Gases, which states that "at a constant temperature, the volume of a gas will vary inversely with the absolute pressure, while the density of a gas varies directly with the (gauge) pressure." In other words, if the pressure exerted on a given volume of gas is doubled, the gas is compressed to one half its original volume but the density is doubled. It is essential that you understand this law of gases, for it governs the conditions that exist within the body when a man breathes compressible air while submerged in noncompressible water. To illustrate how Boyle's Law of Gases applies to diving, let us borrow a flexible rubber diaphragm from a friend and a quart glass cylindrical beaker from another friend and conduct an experiment.

Standing at sea level, let us seal the open end of the quart beaker (which is full of air at 14.7 p.s.i.) with the rubber diaphragm and let us say that it now represents the lungs of a diver who is about to dive while holding his breath. If we invert the quart beaker so that the sealed end is down and plunge it 33 feet beneath the surface of the water, we note that the pressure of the water has pushed the flexible diaphragm halfway into the beaker. According to Boyle's Law, we can see that the original volume of air inside the quart beaker has been cut in half to one pint, and we surmise that the density has been doubled. If we plunge the beaker an additional 33 feet deep to a depth of 66 feet, we see that the volume of air is again cut in half to half a pint and we surmise that the density is again doubled. According to Boyle's Law of Gases, we know that this process would repeat itself for every 33 feet of depth. Now, if we withdraw the glass beaker to the surface of the water, we see that the reverse of this procedure takes place. The air inside the beaker expands until, once more at the surface, the air has assumed its original volume and the flexible rubber diaphragm has returned to its original shape.

Exactly the same phenomenon takes place inside the diver who dives to the bottom while holding his breath. Because the diver's lungs, rib cage, and diaphragm are flexible, like the rubber diaphragm covering the open end of the glass beaker, the water pressure compresses the air volume inside his lungs (and other air cavities such as his throat sinuses and inner ears as well) to half of its original volume every 33 feet. When he returns to the surface the air expands until, once more on the surface, his lungs, rib cage, and diaphragm have resumed their original shape and volume. From the experiment above we see that there is always a balance between the air pressure inside the diver's air cavities with the ambient (surrounding) water pressure, thanks to the compressibility of the lungs and rib cage. (The diver's body tissues, such as muscle, bone, and skin, are of about the same density as water and are therefore incompressible by water. For this reason, only the relatively hollow air cavities are subject to "squeeze" by ambient water pressures.) We also see that for every change of air pressure within the diver's lungs and air cavities (result-

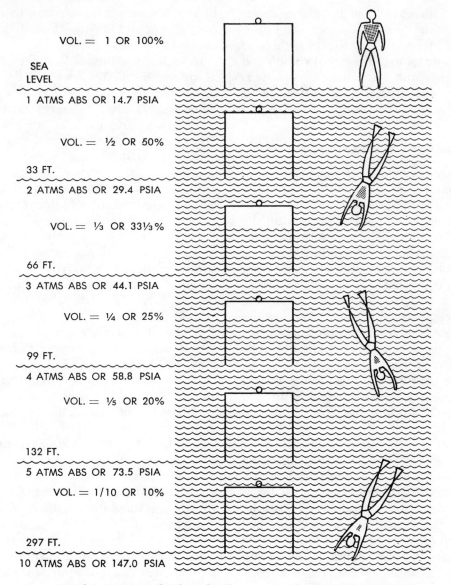

VOL. = 1 OR 100%

SEA
LEVEL

1 ATMS ABS OR 14.7 PSIA

VOL. = ½ OR 50%

33 FT.

2 ATMS ABS OR 29.4 PSIA

VOL. = ⅓ OR 33⅓%

66 FT.

3 ATMS ABS OR 44.1 PSIA

VOL. = ¼ OR 25%

99 FT.

4 ATMS ABS OR 58.8 PSIA

VOL. = ⅕ OR 20%

132 FT.

5 ATMS ABS OR 73.5 PSIA

VOL. = 1/10 OR 10%

297 FT.

10 ATMS ABS OR 147.0 PSIA

Boyle's Law applied to depth versus volume and pressure.

ing from a change in ambient pressure) there is a corresponding change of volume.

However, when a diver breathes from a scuba tank full of compressed air, not only does the air pressure within his lungs and air cavities remain in constant balance with the ambient water pressure, but the volume of air within his lungs and air cavities remains constant as well. As explained in the chapter on scuba equipment, when a diver inhales, he creates a slight vacuum that displaces a flexible rubber diaphragm separating the air chamber from the water chamber (which is exposed to ambient pressure) in his breathing regulator. As the diaphragm moves, it presses against a spring-loaded lever that opens a valve and permits high-pressure air from the tank to flow into the air chamber (and the diver's lungs). The flow continues until the air pressure on one side of the diaphragm is again equal to the water pressure on the other side. At this point, the diaphragm returns to its normal position, shutting off the air flow in the process. Then the diver exhales through a one-way valve and repeats the process with each new breathing cycle. Thus, thanks to the constant balance of air pressure and ambient pressure, his lungs are able to expand and contract to their normal volume, regardless of depth, and with such ease that he is hardly aware of the mechanism that makes it possible.

Boyle's Law and Scuba

Now let us return to our original experiment to see how Boyle's Law of Gases applies to the diver breathing from a scuba.

With the quart beaker still representing the lungs of a diver and still sealed and full of air from our first experiment, let us equip it with an imaginary scuba and take it underwater to a depth of 33 feet again. Since the scuba permits the pressure to increase in proportion to the ambient water pressure without affecting the volume, we notice that the flexible rubber diaphragm is not displaced at all but remains in its original position, regardless of depth. Thus, we know that the pressure both inside the beaker and outside the beaker is in perfect balance at 14.7 p.s.i.g. or 29.4 p.s.i.a. But now let us suppose that for some obscure reason the beaker (and the diver it represents) is suddenly deprived of its supply of compressed air from the scuba. The diver's first instinct in such a case would be to hold what air he has in his lungs and return to the surface as quickly as possible. So, with the beaker full of compressed air equal to the ambient pressure of 33 feet firmly sealed (as the lungs of a diver holding his breath would be), let us withdraw the beaker quickly back to the surface and see what happens.

Since the ambient water pressure decreases .445 p.s.i. for every decreasing foot of depth, the air trapped inside the beaker expands and displaces the flexible rubber diaphragm proportionately. Since the ambient water pressure decreases 100 percent between 33 feet and the surface, it follows that the volume of air sealed inside the beaker doubles in the same distance. Thus on the surface we see that the rubber diaphragm bulges out.

But what about the poor diver whose lungs the beaker represents? The human lungs, when full of air, cannot be stretched more than 15 to 30 percent without bursting. Since a diver under threat of drowning can easily will himself to hold his breath, it is obvious that under such circumstances his lungs could burst like an overinflated balloon.

In such a case he would suffer what is known as *air embolism.* This is without doubt the worst thing that can possibly happen to a diver, for air embolism is almost always fatal unless recompression and medical aid are immediate. Therefore, it is most essential that you remember never to hold your breath during ascent while diving with compressed gas. You should rehearse this fact in your mind so well that whenever you think of *ascent,* you automatically think to breathe normally while doing so. Even if you have the unlikely experience of being suddenly deprived of your air supply while on the bottom, you must purge your lungs of all compressed gas during ascent or you will run a grave risk of suffering air embolism.

When air embolism occurs, air bubbles are forced into the bloodstream through the ruptured capillaries in the lungs. Any bubble too large to pass through constricted areas will form an "embolus" (blood clot) that obstructs the circulation of life-giving blood. And the dependent body tissues quickly die. If an embolus lodges in the brain, death or severe brain damage is sure to result within a few minutes.

In addition to air embolism, there are other maladies that might result from failure to equalize the pressures inside and outside the lungs during ascent.

Mediastinal emphysema occurs when compressed air escapes from a ruptured lung and accumulates inside the chest cavity. The pressure of this air hampers the function of the vital organs such as the heart, blood vessels, esophagus.

Subcutaneous emphysema results when air from the ruptured lung lodges in the tissues beneath the skin, usually ballooning the skin around the neck and collarbone. It is usually associated with mediastinal emphysema.

Pneumothorax results when compressed air from a ruptured lung forms in a pocket between the lung covering and the chest wall. This air can hamper the function of the vital organs or even collapse the lung as it expands during ascent.

Although these last-described maladies alone are much less serious than true air embolism,

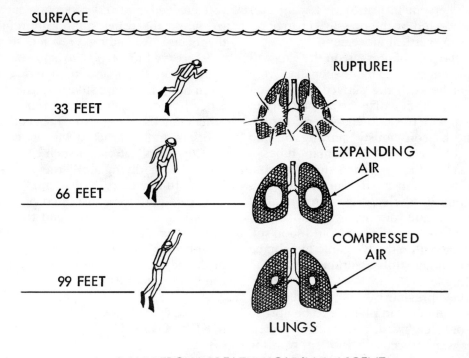

SURFACE

33 FEET

66 FEET

99 FEET

RUPTURE!

EXPANDING
AIR

COMPRESSED
AIR

LUNGS

DANGEROUS BREATH-HOLDING ASCENT
CAUSES COMPRESSED AIR IN SCUBA DIVER'S LUNGS TO EXPAND
AS WATER PRESSURE DECREASES. RUPTURE RESULTS.

they frequently accompany air embolism and are the only obvious signs and symptoms of its presence. Thus, with these as with air embolism, an ounce of prevention is worth almost all the possible cure you can muster.

Whenever you dive with compressed gas, *remember to:*

1. Exhale all the way to the surface during emergency ascents.
2. Breathe normally throughout all normal ascents.

Other Applications of Boyle's Law

According to Boyle's Law, as we have seen, any air cavity such as the lungs whose interior air pressure is not in perfect balance with the ambient pressure is distorted in direct proportion to the pressure differential. But Boyle's Law does not apply to the lungs alone. Whenever the mask, diving suit, sinuses or any kind of semirigid mechanical apparatus or housing that

depends upon a gas pressure to counteract the ambient water pressures fails to equalize, Boyle's Law comes into play. The ears, for example, are acutely affected by the slightest differential between the air pressure in the inner ear and the water pressure on the outer ear. Furthermore, because of their peculiar physical structure, you must learn a certain technique to "equalize" or "clear" them. All the other air cavities in the body "equalize" and vent themselves automatically as long as breathing remains normal.

The ears. The eardrum divides each ear into two parts, the inner ear and the outer ear. The eardrum is so sensitive to pressure differentials that sound waves are powerful enough to make it vibrate (otherwise you could not hear!). Any displacement of the eardrum greater than that caused by normal sound waves is likely to cause acute pain. Most people have experienced this descending for a landing in an airplane or descending from a mountaintop in a car. Thus, submerged in a liquid in which the pressure changes 100 percent in just 33 feet, your ears are severely affected by the pressure change resulting from any vertical movement.

Normally, the pain of pressure in the ears will prevent you from diving any deeper than from 10 to 15 feet beneath the surface unless you "clear your ears" or equalize the air pressure in your inner ear with the ambient water pressure. This is done by consciously snorting air into your inner ears via the Eustachian tubes—small, mucus-lined tubes connecting the nasal passages with the inner ears—until pressures inside and outside the eardrums are equal. If you were to continue your dive without "equalizing," the chances are that you would soon suffer hemorrhage within the tympanic membrane and inner ear and possibly eardrum rupture and sinus bleeding.

As mentioned previously, it requires a certain amount of technique and practice to be able to "equalize" or "clear" your ears. For the professional diver who is accustomed to it, working the jaws, wiggling the nose, swallowing, yawning, or chewing on the mouthpiece is usually enough to facilitate the equalizing process. If you are a beginner or an occasional diver, however, it is sometimes difficult. You must try to snort air through your nose while pinching off your nostrils to force the air through the Eustachian tubes. Many of the better face masks are molded with indentations that fit on either side of the nose or with some other nose-pinching device to facilitate "equalizing" or "clearing." You frequently must try several times before you succeed, and very often one ear will equalize while the other stubbornly refuses. When this occurs, ascending a few feet to relieve the pressure (which tends to squeeze the Eustachian tube shut) and then trying again will often help. If you are suffering from hay fever or a head cold, the Eustachian tubes (along with other mucus membranes) become irritated, swollen, and obstructed with mucus, thus preventing equalization. In such cases it is best to refrain from diving until the condition is relieved. In any case, "equalizing" or "clearing" your ears must be considered one of the basic skills required in diving, and the chances are that you won't enjoy diving until you learn to do it with ease. However, practicing at home can be dangerous, for if you snort too forcefully, you can blow out an eardrum.

METABOLISM

If you are a normal person, the billions of tiny cells in your body are continually combining food calories with oxygen and burning them up by a chemical oxidation process called metabolism. This combustion process gives off a waste material comprised of carbon dioxide, water, and heat. If any body cell is deprived of its share of fuel, the fires in its furnace slowly die. Also, if the exchange of fuel for waste does not take place at the same rate, the cell becomes suffocated. It is clear, therefore, that metabolism requires several exchanges of gases

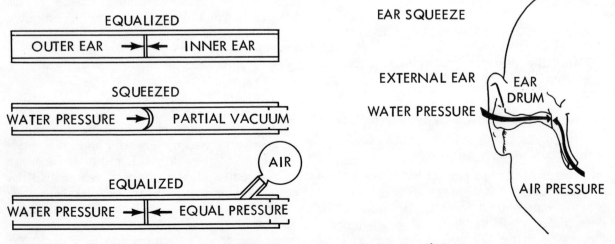

Effects of unequalized pressure on the ears and sinuses.

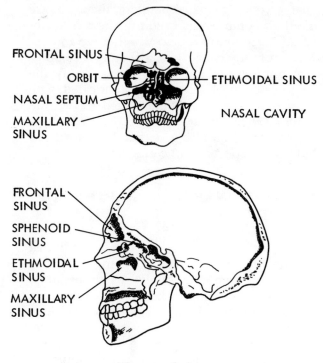

FRONTAL SINUS
ORBIT
NASAL SEPTUM
MAXILLARY SINUS
ETHMOIDAL SINUS
NASAL CAVITY

FRONTAL SINUS
SPHENOID SINUS
ETHMOIDAL SINUS
MAXILLARY SINUS

The nasal sinuses.

during each breathing cycle: first, between the blood and the oxygen in the lungs; second, between the oxygen-carrying blood and the tissue fluids; third, between the tissue fluids and the cells. The procedure is then reversed. The cells exchange oxygen for wastes (including CO_2). The waste gases are returned to the lungs by the bloodstream, and the lungs exhale the waste gases. With inhalation the cycle begins again.

When the diver holds his breath, his body cells do not drop dead like proverbial flies. They continue to burn the residual oxygen in the bloodstream. The exchange continues but not without a build-up of waste content (CO_2) within the bloodstream. When you pant after holding your breath, it is just nature's way of purging your bloodstream of excess wastes. What happens is this: inside the main arteries, tiny censors called chemoreceptors monitor the oxygen content of the bloodstream. When the oxygen content gets too low or the waste CO_2 content gets too high, chemoreceptors send impulses to the respiratory center in the brain to increase the breathing rate. This involuntary urge to breathe drives every snorkel diver back toward the surface for air.

By supersaturating the bloodstream with ox-

ygen, the diver can greatly increase the amount of time before this urge to breathe occurs. This is done by hyperventilation: repeatedly inflating and deflating the lungs to the fullest extent for periods of from one to three minutes before diving. Purging the bloodstream of carbon dioxide (CO_2) waste accompanies this procedure. Thus the diver beginning his dive under almost ideal physiological circumstances can easily double his breath-holding time.

SHALLOW-WATER BLACKOUT

Hyperventilation is used by almost all champion snorkel divers and spearfishermen. However, it has probably caused more diving deaths than all other factors combined, for a diver can consciously repress the urge to breathe until he is overcome with oxygen starvation or anoxia. After the diver represses the first few urges delivered by the chemoreceptors, the urge to breathe seems to subside. This is obviously a very dangerous point. The diver can lose consciousness in what is known as "shallow-water blackout" and not remember anything when he is by chance revived by artificial respiration. Thus, such competitions as breath-holding contests should be avoided at all costs. There have been several recorded incidents in which divers have continued swimming underwater even after blacking out, and so it is difficult to detect for both practitioner and observer.

Another fact to remember when hyperventilating is that the deeper you dive, the longer you can stay at the bottom. When you are on the bottom the ambient water pressures compress the air in your lungs according to Boyle's Law. The bloodstream finds it easier to absorb oxygen from compressed air than from air at normal sea level pressures. Thus you are able to consume almost the total amount of oxygen in your lungs before having to "break for the surface." When at last you do ascend, the air in your lungs expands and the partial pressure of the oxygen in your lungs—already low—decreases sharply. Thus it is theoretically possible to starve yourself of oxygen to the point of "blacking out" during the ascent, even though you feel no discomfort while at the bottom. In addition, any excess of carbon dioxide in the bloodstream is extremely taxing on the cardiovascular system, especially when combined with great exertion. When consistently repeated, excessive breath-holding like that done by professional spearfishermen, for example, has even been known to cause some brain damage, which causes some divers to act slightly punch-drunk. But carbon dioxide (shallow-water) blackout and oxygen starvation are not limited to the breath-holding snorkel divers. So let us now consider how they affect the compressed air scuba diver.

DALTON'S LAW OF PARTIAL PRESSURES

Dalton's Law of Partial Pressures states: "The total pressure exerted by mixture of gases is the sum of the pressures that would be exerted by each of the gases if it alone were present and occupied the total volume." Thus, air containing only 2 percent carbon dioxide by volume at 132 feet or 5 atmospheres absolute has the same partial pressure of CO_2 and produces the same results (that is, blackout or loss of consciousness) as air at sea level containing as much as 10 percent carbon dioxide.

CARBON MONOXIDE (CO) POISONING

Exposure to only slight amounts of carbon monoxide (CO) can also cause blackout, anoxia, and oxygen starvation, although by an entirely different physiological process from that described above. The red corpuscles of the blood and the tissues they serve absorb carbon monoxide almost two hundred times more rapidly than they absorb oxygen. Therefore, any carbon monoxide in the air you breathe will quickly supersaturate the red corpuscles of the blood and render them incapable of absorbing anything else, including oxygen. Thus, body tissues are deprived of the oxygen on which they depend for life and soon die.

Carbon monoxide poisoning can cause unconsciousness with little or no warning. However, carbon monoxide is not a normal component of air. It results only from fuel combustion, and the only way it can contaminate your air supply is through the air compressor used to charge your air tanks. Therefore, the air intake of all air compressors used to compress air for breathing should be placed well away and upwind from the exhausts of all internal combustion engines, including its own. Ideally the compressor itself should be lubricated with some nonpetroleum products such as soap and water or vegetable oil. If you buy your air from a commercial air-filling station, be sure its air has been inspected and certified pure.

NITROGEN NARCOSIS: RAPTURE OF THE DEPTHS

The partial pressure of nitrogen in the air that you breathe imposes limits on the depths to which you can dive safely. When breathed under pressure, the normal amount of nitrogen in the air induces a narcotic effect on the diver that deprives him of his senses and renders him incapable of logical reasoning. This phenomenon is called nitrogen narcosis or "rapture of the depths." It begins at a depth somewhere around 100 feet and gets worse the deeper you go and the longer you stay. The effect is the same as getting sloppy drunk on alcohol. Some people want to cry, some people want to laugh. It depends upon the individual. In each case the person is robbed of his good judgment. He is indeed drunk with the depths, and the simplest task can become more than he can cope with. I once tied and untied an overhand knot at least a dozen times before I finally caught on to what was happening to me and struck out for the surface. On my return to the topside of the 100-foot mark where nitrogen narcosis begins, it vanished mysteriously and left no hangover. Sometimes the diver can, by sheer willpower and concentration, overcome nitrogen narcosis long enough to get a job done, but even then he can never be sure if and how he actually did the job. Obviously, under such conditions the diver becomes dangerous not only to himself but also to the people with whom he is working. Since the most interesting diving depths are less than 100 feet where nitrogen narcosis begins anyhow, it makes sense to limit the depth of your dives to 100 feet. There is no other way of avoiding it so long as you are breathing compressed air.

Together with decompression sickness or

"the bends," nitrogen narcosis is the greatest limiting factor of compressed-air diving. Within the Navy and sophisticated commercial diving organizations, compressed air has been replaced with exotic mixtures of various inert gases such as helium and oxygen. With the nitrogen removed, so is the threat of nitrogen narcosis. These exotic mixtures may allow men to dive to depths of as much as three thousand feet someday. Meanwhile, however, helium is rare and very costly, and its availability is controlled by our government. Deep diving on artificial atmosphere is far beyond the reach of the sport diver.

HENRY'S LAW OF GASES

Henry's Law of Gases states that "the amount of gas that will dissolve in a liquid at a given temperature is almost directly proportional to the partial pressure of that gas." In other words, a liquid will tend to absorb the air (gas) to which it is exposed until the pressure of the air both within and without the liquid is equal. For example, the surface water of the sea is saturated with air at sea level pressure. Similarly, our bloodstream is saturated with air at sea level pressure (or the pressure of whatever altitude you happen to live at), and the compressed air in the diver's bloodstream tends to become saturated with the air that he breathes at the pressure of whatever depth he happens to be working at. If he is working at a depth of three atmospheres, or 99 feet, his bloodstream tends to become saturated with air at a pressure of three atmospheres. The same thing happens in reverse to pilots who fly into the lower pressures of the atmosphere. The bloodstream of the test pilot who takes off from sea level and rockets through our atmosphere to the edge of space (where the absolute ambient pressure is zero) would tend to become desaturated with air at sea level pressure until there was no air left in his bloodstream if he did not wear a pressure suit. But this process does not take place instantaneously. It requires nearly twelve hours to thoroughly saturate or desaturate a liquid.

You can see Henry's Law of Gases in action every time you open a bottle of soda pop. Before the soda water was sealed inside the pop bottle at the factory, it had been saturated with a gas (usually carbon dioxide) at a pressure of at least one to several atmospheres. So long as the bottle cap remains tightly sealed over the bottle, the pressure within the bottle—both inside and outside the liquid—remains the same, and no bubbles appear in the liquid. But when the bottle is uncapped, the liquid within is exposed to a very sudden drop in ambient pressure. The gas within the liquid and outside it immediately tends to equalize in pressure. That is, the liquid begins to give off its excess pressure of gas in the form of bubbles. And that's what gives your soda pop all its fizz and sparkle. (Since it takes twelve hours to thoroughly saturate or desaturate a liquid, the soda water will continue to give off some bubbles for twelve hours before it becomes thoroughly "flat.") If a diver whose bloodstream had been saturated at a depth of from at least one to several atmospheres of pressure were to suddenly shoot to the surface, the effect of the sudden decrease in pressure would be identical to that which happened to the uncapped soda water. The air in his bloodstream would immediately tend to equalize with the sudden drop in ambient pressure. As the gas came out of solution in his blood to rejoin the ambient atmosphere, bubbles would form. Blood corpuscles form clots around air bubbles. These clots usually lodge at constricted areas like joints of the limbs and generally pinch off and damage the nerves, resulting in paralysis. If they don't lodge there, they may travel to the brain where they can cause brain damage or even death. Thus, when you open a bottle of your favorite soda pop and watch the bubbles fizz, you are watching a case of decompression sickness (commonly known as the bends) take place before your very eyes.

However, if you were to cover with your thumb a freshly uncapped bottle of soda water, bubbling and fizzing for all it's worth, and take it underwater, you would not have to dive very far before the soda water would stop fizzing and the bubbles would vanish, for the ambient pressures of the water would soon overcome that of the soda and the transfer of gas would soon be reversed. Likewise, if you were to send the stricken diver back underwater to a depth where the ambient pressure of the water would at least equal or be greater than the pressure of the gas dissolved in his bloodstream, the bubbles would vanish. As a result the blood clots

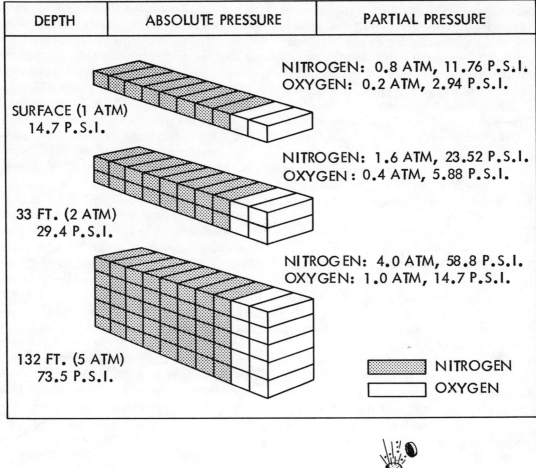

DEPTH	ABSOLUTE PRESSURE	PARTIAL PRESSURE
SURFACE (1 ATM) 14.7 P.S.I.		NITROGEN: 0.8 ATM, 11.76 P.S.I. OXYGEN: 0.2 ATM, 2.94 P.S.I.
33 FT. (2 ATM) 29.4 P.S.I.		NITROGEN: 1.6 ATM, 23.52 P.S.I. OXYGEN: 0.4 ATM, 5.88 P.S.I.
132 FT. (5 ATM) 73.5 P.S.I.		NITROGEN: 4.0 ATM, 58.8 P.S.I. OXYGEN: 1.0 ATM, 14.7 P.S.I.

NITROGEN
OXYGEN

Henry's Law in action.

would break up and no further nerve or tissue damage could be done. For this reason, if no re-compression chamber—a kind of man-size pressure cooker in which surface decompression can take place—is convenient, a diver suffering the bends is sometimes sent back underwater at least as deep as he had been in the first place, or deeper. Then he is brought back to the surface very slowly according to a strict depth schedule known as the Recompression Tables, so that the pressure differential never becomes so great that the gas comes out of solution before the lungs can pass it off. However, since the diver may have already suffered some irreparable nerve damage, he may not be in control of all his faculties. Therefore, whenever possible, equivalent measures are taken by placing him under pressure in the controlled environment of a recompression chamber.

However, recompression chambers are fairly rare, and much invaluable time is often lost in transporting the victim to the site, during which irreparable damage can be done. Before making any decompression dives, it is best to learn the location, telephone number, and the quickest mode of transportation to all nearby recompression chambers. These can be found by calling your local U.S. Coast Guard or Naval Station.

INTRODUCTION TO DECOMPRESSION DIVES

The modern Decompression Tables for diving were born in 1907 when an English scientist, J. S. Haldane, discovered that a liquid could hold a gas in solution until its partial pressure amounted to about twice the ambient pressures. Therefore, according to Boyle's and Henry's laws, a diver saturated with air at 33 feet could come all the way to the surface without stopping regardless of duration of the dive, while a diver saturated at 100 feet could come all the way up to 33 feet without stopping regardless of the duration of the dive. From these findings, scientists who were concerned with diving and caisson work were able to compute the depths and duration of "decompression stops" that

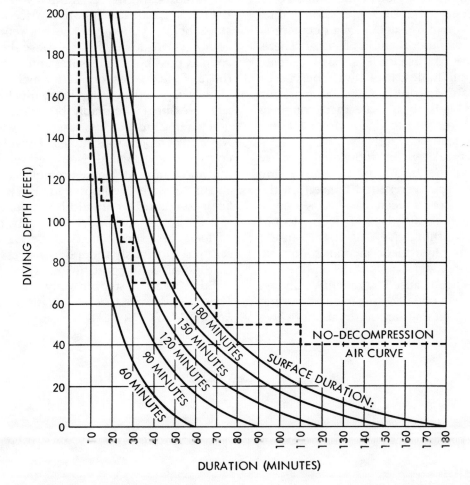

Depth-time ratio for compressed-air tanks at various depths for constant volumetric use (work) rates, giving surface durations indicated with relation to the no-decompression air-diving curve. Average air consumption at surface is about one cubic foot per minute (.9 cfm). Thus, a standard 71.2-cubic-foot tank should last about seventy minutes at the surface (depending more or less on the individual's breathing habits and exertion), about half that at 33 feet, about a third at 66 feet, etc.

would enable a diver to return to the surface in stages without the threat of decompression sickness. These findings were reconfirmed by the U.S. Navy Experimental Diving Unit and the U.S. Navy Medical Research Laboratory in New London, Connecticut. The U.S. Navy Standard Air Decompression Tables are a result of these efforts (see Chapter 10). They have been tested and retested by thousands of divers, but it does not necessarily follow that even strict compliance with the tables will guarantee you immunity from a case of the bends. Susceptibility to decompression sickness varies with the individual. It even varies in the same individual on various days and under various conditions. To be 100 percent safe, the Decompression Tables would have to require such a long decompression time as to render them impractical. Therefore, whenever you use the U.S. Navy Standard Decompression Tables, it is always best to be conservative in figuring your decompression time. That is, it is always safe to decompress longer but never safe to decompress for less time than the tables call for.

Generally speaking, the individual is more susceptible to the bends, or decompression sickness, if he has overexerted himself on the dive, or suffers from a recent case of the bends, or from senility, obesity, lack of sleep, alcohol hangover, or anything else that might cause a generally poor physical or mental condition. However, most modern cases of decompression sickness have been caused by repetitive diving: that is, more than one dive in a twelve-hour period. Bear in mind that it requires about twelve hours to desaturate a liquid of gas. When a diver makes more than one dive during any twelve-hour period the effect on the amount of gas in solution within the bloodstream is cumulative. The diver must follow an entirely different set of decompression tables called the Repetitive Dive Decompression Tables. These tables figure in his "surface interval time" in relation to his total "down time" on both dives and spell out the safe decompression procedure for the second dive.

Because of the gravity of decompression sickness, you must plan all dives, especially those in which decompression becomes a factor, with the utmost care. Be certain that you have more than enough air to support any decompression stops before you dive. The one cure for decompression sickness is to expose the victim as soon as possible to pressures at least as great as those of the deepest depth to which he was previously exposed and then bring him back to surface pressure—preferably breathing pure oxygen when 25 feet or less—according to the U.S. Navy Recompression Tables. However all recompression procedures are grave matters of life and limb. All are extremely complicated and in-the-water recompression is especially difficult to control. It should be undertaken only as a last resort and under the guidance and/or advice of an expert who is trained in such procedures. Obviously then, decompression dives have no place in sport diving. They should be avoided at all costs, but only you can do so. Therefore, always carefully PLAN YOUR DIVE AND DIVE YOUR PLAN.

Snorkel and Scuba Diving Equipment and How It Functions

I like to divide diving into two categories: snorkel and scuba (*self-contained underwater breathing apparatus*). The basic equipment of the snorkel diver consists of a mask, snorkel, and fins. The basic equipment of the scuba diver consists of the snorkel equipment plus a compressed-air tank, a breathing regulator, a weight belt, and a buoyancy compensator (B.C.).

It is difficult to say which item in the basic equipment list is the most important, for without any one of them your efficiency in the water would be greatly impaired. Therefore each item should be given equal consideration. The first job of your instructor will be to familiarize you with this equipment. Pay close attention to his recommendations, and try the equipment out in the instruction pool before you invest in your own.

FACE MASK

Your face mask is your magic window to the sea. Without one, the water forming around the curvature of your eyeball creates an optical sur-

The skin diver's basic equipment. (Courtesy U.S. Divers Corporation)

face that distorts vision and focuses it some-where behind the eyeball, as in a case of ex-treme astigmatism. The enchanting world be-neath the sea becomes a ghostly place full of vague blurs and shadowy outlines. In the old days, pearl divers discovered that by placing a pane of transparent tortoise shell between the eye and the water, the shadowy outlines sud-denly took on sharpness and definition, and so the divers devised a pair of goggles by setting panes of transparent tortoise shell in bone cups that fitted over the sockets of the eyes. Unless the panes were adjusted so as to be on the same geometrical plane, however, the divers saw double visions of everything and became dizzy

and confused. They devised the single-plate face mask to allow both eyes to share the same vision through the same geometrical plane.

The modern face mask consists of a shatter-proof-glass faceplate seated usually in a soft neoprene or rubber skirt and made watertight by a stainless metal band surrounding the edge. The skirt is flexible enough to conform to the contour of the face. Masks made out of material that is less pliable (such as hard rubber) should be avoided, for they usually allow some water to enter through smile and eye wrinkles on the face. Face masks whose *plates* are made of plas-tic or tinted glass should also be avoided. Plas-tic has a nasty habit of fogging and obscuring vision, and tinted glass diminishes the intensity of light that is transmitted to the eye. Light normally decreases in intensity the deeper the diver goes, and the diver needs all the light he can get.

The mask should be an unencumbered piece of equipment, without any attachments ·or appendages. Masks that feature built-in snorkels are clumsy and dangerous. They are sure to give the beginner a good case of claustrophobia and might discourage him from skin diving forever. If you place the face mask in position and inhale slightly through your nose, the mask should stay in place without the help of the head strap. This is a good way to test your mask for proper fit or leaks before you buy. With the strap on, the mask should sit comfortably on your face without binding and without leaving red marks. The straps on most masks are adjustable, and a good fit can be accomplished with

Face mask. (Courtesy U.S. Divers Corporation)

relative ease. The faceplate lens should be made of totally transparent, shatterproof tempered or safety glass. The glass plate should permit the widest angle of view possible. However, it should have no curvature or "wraparound" feature, since distortion occurs wherever there is curvature in the lens. The added peripheral vision is not worth the disorientation resulting from the distortion.

Many masks feature molded-in cavities or squeezing devices that fit on either side of the nostrils and facilitate pinching the nose shut to help "clear the ears." Others feature a one-way valve that facilitates draining the mask of water. Both features are highly desirable but not essential. There are many diving masks available on the market.

SNORKEL

The snorkel is a J-shaped tube made of plastic or hard rubber. One end is equipped with a soft-rubber bit that fits in your mouth, and the other end pokes into the air, allowing you to breathe air from the surface while your face is partially submerged. After inhaling, you exhale sharply through the same tube to blow out any accumulated water. However, try as you may, it is almost impossible to clear the snorkel tube completely of all water. The wise diver inhales very slowly, so that residual water remains in the snorkel, and he exhales sharply. With a little practice you will find this procedure very easy and rhythmic, because no energy is wasted in raising your head out of the water for air. You can cruise on the surface for miles without becoming tired or winded.

A few snorkels come equipped with closure

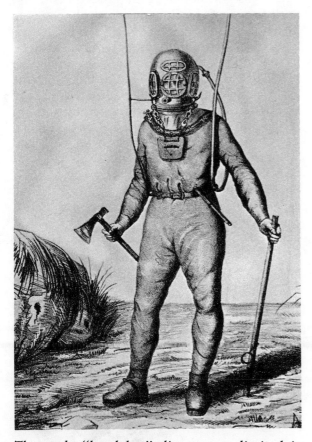

The early "hard hat" divers were limited in movement and remained tied to the atmosphere with air hoses. (Courtesy Musée de la Marine, Paris)

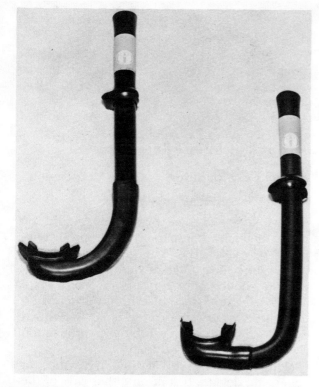

Snorkels (with different mouthpieces) (Courtesy U.S. Divers Corporation)

devices that fit on the open end. They usually consist of a ping-pong ball in a cage. Other snorkels are equipped with a purging valve that is supposed to keep the tube dry. However, it has been my experience that these contraptions never work properly and are more hindrance than help. The ideal snorkel is the simple J-shaped open-end tube, fitted with a soft-rubber mouthpiece that will not chafe the gums. The tube should not be longer than sixteen inches, for anything longer makes proper breathing extremely difficult. The diameter should be wide enough to allow the free passage of air adequate for your needs—at least the size of a nickel. The larger you are, the larger the diameter should be. If the diameter is *too* wide, however, you will find it difficult to clear the snorkel of water. The rubber mouthpiece should fit comfortably between teeth and lips when the teeth are closed over the two small rubber bits.

FINS

A fin or flipper can be described as a rubber shoe with a rubber paddle attached. A good pair of fins can increase your swimming efficiency as much as 60 percent, enabling you to move with the speed and agility of a fish while leaving your hands entirely free for useful work.

There are two general types of fins: The full-foot fin and the open-heel fin. The full-foot fin fits over the entire foot like a shoe and is superior to the open-heel fin that simply fits over the front of the foot and is held on by a heel strap. Because black-rubber products tend to hold up longer than rubber products with color pigment, and because fins should be as lively as possible, I recommend that you select black-rubber fins. The blades should be canted slightly downward for maximum thrust and should snap quickly back into place when bent.

Swimming with fins requires considerably more leg effort than swimming without them. Therefore, beginners should avoid the so-called "giant fins" (sometimes called snorkel cruisers) until they have developed the muscle power to match the size of the fin blade. The bigger the blade the more muscle power required to move it. If you don't happen to have the muscle, the blades (and you) remain motionless in the water while your knees pump up and down like mad. Even if you succeed in getting the big blades to move, the chances are that they will soon cause your leg muscles to knot up and cramp, especially in cold water. This is a very painful experience that will force you to abort the dive unless you can manage to stretch the effected leg and massage the cramp out with your hands. It is better that you start with a small but highly resilient blade. This will per-

Fin (Courtesy U.S. Divers Corporation)

mit you to increase your speed by simply increasing the number of your kicks per breathing cycle.

It is extremely important that the fins fit the feet properly. If the fins are too small they will bind, bruise, and cause pain. On the other hand, if they are too large, you may lose them while swimming underwater. Try them on and, if possible, try them out before you buy.

AIR TANKS

Although many pertinent research projects are currently underway, man has not yet devised a way of breathing underwater. In fact, the modern scuba diver never fully relinquishes his liaison with the surface atmosphere. He carries his atmosphere on his back inside a heavy steel or aluminum cylinder containing air under pressure. In fact, the air pressure inside the tank is so great that the tank constitutes a potentially dangerous piece of equipment, and tanks are manufactured under strict regulations of the U.S. Department of Transportation (DOT). By law, the "pressure rating" of each air tank is stamped on its shoulder near the valve, together with the date of the last hydrostatic pressure test, the serial number, and the manufacturer's trademark.

It is a legal offense to charge an air tank beyond 10 percent over the pressure rating stamped on the shoulder and with good reason. If a tank is charged far enough beyond its rated capacity, it can explode like a bomb. Furthermore, the strength of the cylinder weakens with time and use, because of corrosion and oxidation. The oxidation process is almost never discovered until it is too late, because it is concealed inside the tank. For this reason, the DOT further requires that all high-pressure air tanks be subjected to a hydrostatic pressure test every five years and receive a new pressure rating if required. Further, because of the weakening of metal through oxidation, it is wise to purchase air tanks made of anodized aluminum or galvanized steel.

Compressed-air tanks come in various sizes, capacities, and pressure ratings. The most popular tank as of 1985 is made of anodized aluminum. When fully charged, it contains 80 cubic feet of air under 3,000 pounds per square inch (p.s.i.) of pressure. As you will soon learn, the average person consumes approximately one cubic foot of air per minute at sea level. Therefore "the aluminum 80," as it is called, will last the average person about eighty minutes at the surface or about half that time at 33 feet of depth. This tank permits the diver to easily surpass the U.S. Navy No-Decompression Limits (see Chapter 10) and requires the user to pay close attention to depth and bottom time in order to avoid decompression sickness (the bends).

Before aluminum tanks arrived on the market, the standard tank was made of galvanized steel and held 71.2 cubic feet of air at 2,250 p.s.i. In theory, a tank of this capacity is large enough to provide a diver with about forty minutes of bottom time at 33 feet but not so large that he or she could surpass the U.S. Navy No-Decompression Limits. In actual practice, however, the bottom time can be stretched beyond those limits and there are thousands of these tanks still in use, so you must pay attention to your depth-time limits regardless of which of these tanks you use. When empty, both tanks weigh around 40 pounds and tend to float in water. When fully charged they are 6 to 8 pounds heavier and tend to sink in water.

Steel tanks are also available in 50-, 24-, and 18-cubic-foot capacities, but they are rarely used any longer.

Since all air tanks made for diving are manufactured to the strict specifications of the Department of Transportation (DOT), it makes little difference what brand name of tank you choose. They are all good. Therefore, it is best to select your tank on the basis of its weight, pressure rating, capacity, the type of air valve it has, the type of harness, the protective finish, and the price. Tank interiors should be visually inspected once a year and hydrostatically tested every five years.

TANK VALVES

Like a chain, the air tank is no stronger than its weakest link. The valve, which opens and closes the flow of air, must be able to withstand the pressure of the air inside the tank. Furthermore, the DOT requires all air valves to have a safety-release plug which will blow off at a pressure considerably lower than that at which the tank would explode.

Today only two kinds of air valves are commonly used with air tanks. They are the straight K valve and the constant-reserve J valve. The K valve is a simple open-and-close valve mechanism that provides air to the breathing regulator straight from the cylinder. There is no built-in air-reserve mechanism. When the air pressure inside your cylinder becomes low, it gradually becomes harder for you to breathe. When at last the air pressure inside the cylinder becomes almost equal with the water pressure surrounding it, it becomes impossible to breathe. But the moment the diver begins to ascend toward the lesser pressures of the surface, the residual air in the tank expands and provides a few more breaths, which are adequate to get you safely to the surface. You cannot, however, go any deeper before starting your ascent.

If an air tank is equipped with a J valve, a spring-loaded shutoff device stops the air flow automatically when the air pressure drops to about 300 pounds per square inch. At that point the diver pulls a lever that releases the remaining 300 pounds per square inch of air pressure for breathing, and the diver knows that he has from five to fifteen minutes (depending on his depth) of air remaining in order to reach the surface. If necessary, the diver can still swim deeper to free himself from entanglements or to leave the interior of a sunken wreck or cave before heading toward the surface. Since the straight K valve does not permit going deeper once the air flow stops, the J valve is highly recommended when diving in caves or wrecks. Otherwise, the standard K valve and an underwater pressure gauge are all you need for standard diving safety.

BACKPACKS AND HARNESSES

A large variety of custom-made harness and backpack assemblies are available to hold the air tank on your back. However, the assemblies that are sold with an air tank as standard equipment are usually the best. In any case, the harness and backpack assembly should be made of material such as plastic, nylon, and stainless steel, which resist the corrosive and deteriorating effects of salt water. Make certain that your

Tank and pack assembly. (Courtesy U.S. Divers Corporation)

harness assembly includes a quick-release buckle so that you can easily ditch your gear should the occasion arise. If you acquire more than one tank in your diving locker, then it might be wise to consider one of the new clamp-on backpacks, which permit changing air tanks in only seconds.

BREATHING REGULATORS

There are two radically different kinds of underwater breathing apparatus that fall under the all-inclusive term scuba. They are the compressed-air, open-circuit scuba and the closed-circuit, oxygen-rebreathing scuba. The closed-circuit, oxygen-rebreathing scuba is not available on the open market except in Army and Navy surplus stores, for it was designed primarily for military use. Since oxygen becomes toxic to the diver when breathed under pressures greater than those of one atmosphere (14.7 pounds per square inch; a depth of 33 feet is equal to one atmosphere) and requires constant adjustment, it is potentially a very dangerous

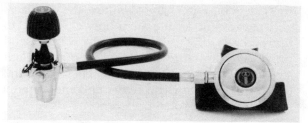

Single-hose regulator. (Courtesy U.S. Divers Corporation)

piece of equipment. Therefore, it should clearly be understood that whenever the term scuba is used in this book, it refers to the compressed-air, open-circuit rig and not to the oxygen rebreather.

The open-circuit, compressed-air scuba in popular use today was coinvented by Captain Jacques-Yves Cousteau and the French engineer Émile Gagnan in June 1943. Gagnan had developed several kinds of gas-flow demand regulators that were in common use on automobiles and in hospital operating rooms during World War II. Cousteau figured that with slight modification, these demand regulators could be used to provide underwater swimmers with air from a tank strapped to the back. Gagnan liked the idea and, after a few false starts, their experiments worked perfectly. In fact, the device was so simple, safe, and effective that it opened the doors of the sea to intimate investigation for the first time in history. When Cousteau filmed and wrote about his experiences in the enchanting underwater world, thousands clamored for the chance to try it for themselves. Cousteau persuaded Gagnan's parent company, Air Liquid of France, to manufacture the breathing regulators for the consumer market, and thus the sport of scuba diving was born. The basic single-stage, double-hose regulator that introduced thousands to scuba diving differs very little from the original prototype model that Cousteau and Gagnan first produced in France.

The single-stage scuba regulator consists of a noncorrosive housing divided into two chambers by a very flexible rubber diaphragm. On one side of the diaphragm is a watertight air chamber and on the other side a water chamber that is open to the sea. A corrugated rubber hose leads from the air chamber to the diver's mouth, and from his mouth it returns to the water chamber. Within the regulator, the air pressure on one side of the diaphragm is always equal to the pressure of the water on the other

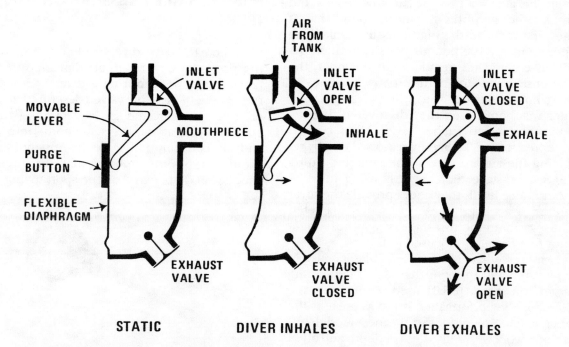

Cross section of the second stage of the two-stage, single-hose breathing regulator. (Courtesy PADI International)

side. When the diver inhales he creates a slight vacuum in the air chamber. To fill this vacuum, the water must push against the flexible diaphragm, which in turn activates a lever that opens and closes a valve. The valve regulates the flow of air from the air tank. When the diver's lungs are full, the vacuum ceases to exist, the water and air pressure are instantly equalized, and the diaphragm returns to its normal position. Thus it releases the pressure on the valve-actuating lever, and the valve closes. At this point, the pressure of the air inside the regulator air chamber (and inside the diver's lungs and throat and nasal passages as well) is in perfect balance with the pressure of the water that surrounds him, regardless of depth. For this reason, the diver is never aware of any squeeze from the pressure of the water. (The solid body tissues are of approximately the same density as water and are therefore virtually incompressible by water.) When the diver exhales, the exhausted air passes through the hose into the water chamber of the regulator via a nonreturn valve that keeps the water from entering. From there the exhalation rises to the surface in the form of bubbles.

The disadvantage of this kind of single-stage regulator (providing the diver with air directly from the tank) is that the air flow begins and stops rather abruptly. Engineers found that, if they first reduced the high-pressure tank air to approximately 100 pounds per square inch before it entered the regulator air chamber, the abrupt start-and-stop of the air flow becomes almost imperceptible. Thus, the two-stage regulator was born. Later, they discovered that the bulky corrugated rubber hoses often created water resistance. Then they reasoned that by reducing the air pressure at the tank and fitting the second-stage diaphragm housing into the mouthpiece itself, they could provide the diver with air via a single hose of smaller diameter. Thus was born the two-stage, single-hose regulator that is commonly used today.

Compressed-air breathing regulators vary in price from $90 to more than $200, depending largely on the materials used. Fortunately the difference in performance is not as great as the price range. Except for the cheapest models, all of them work well regardless of depth and all of them provide the same fail-safe safety features that assure a constant supply of air. Should there ever be a mechanical failure, the regulator will never shut off the air supply abruptly. On the contrary, the valve will remain open and provide a continuing supply of air that will not stop until the tank is empty. Therefore, the breathing regulator you select becomes largely a question of personal preference.

Octopus Regulators

Almost all single-hose regulators have three openings or ports built into the first stage which fits onto the tank valve. One is a high-pressure (H.P.) port, giving direct access to the high-pressure chamber. The submersible pressure gauge attaches to this port so that you can get a continuous reading on the amount of air remaining inside your tank. The other two are low-pressure (L.P.) ports to which a hose and second stage (mouthpiece) can be attached. A regulator to which two second stages and hoses are attached is called an Octopus regulator. Octopus regulators permit two people to breathe simultaneously off a single tank of air. It thereby provides an added safety measure in case one's diving buddy runs out of air when submerged.

SUBMERSIBLE PRESSURE GAUGE (SPG)

In the early days, divers had no way of knowing precisely how much air remained in their tanks at any point during a dive. They had to rely on the "J" reserve valve (described earlier) or make an educated guess according to the elapsed time at depth (see depth–time ratio and air consumption table in Appendix III). Around 1960 the submersible air pressure gauge (SPG) appeared on the sport diving mar-

Submersible pressure gauge (SPG). (Courtesy U.S. Divers Corporation)

Octupus regulators (dangling) at the ready. (Courtesy U.S. Divers Corporation)

ket. Simply put, it is a visual-reading air pressure gauge that fits into the high-pressure (H.P.) port on the first stage of your breathing regulator. It can give you a continuous reading of the amount of air in your tank up to 5,000 p.s.i. It is an invaluable adjunct to diving safety and is now considered an indispensable aid to safe diving practice.

The submersible pressure gauge works on the principle of the bourdon tube. This is a curved piece of tubing, one end of which is closed while the other end is exposed to the air pressure in the high-pressure port of your breathing regulator by means of a short length of high-pressure hose. As the air pressure inside the tube increases, the tube tends to straighten or uncurl. This movement is mechanically translated into movement of the needle on the dial of your SPG. The dial readings are usually accurate to within 50 p.s.i.

There are two kinds of bourdon tubes used in SPGs. One is short and relatively fat and shaped like a C. The other is longer and thinner and wound in a spiral. Of the two, the second is slightly more rugged and dependable, although both are good. The SPG you choose should have an easy-to-read dial with a low-pressure warning zone clearly marked at the low-pressure end of the scale. Some SPGs come with a capillary depth gauge incorporated into the housing of the dial. These are handy accessories, as they give you both depth and pressure readings at a glance. However, the depth gauge should not interfere or be easily confused with your pressure readings.

Your SPG is a precious instrument that needs tender loving care. You should protect it against hard blows by encasing it in a rubber housing and keep it from dangling by using a retaining strap that attaches to your tank harness.

BUOYANCY COMPENSATOR (B.C.)

In the course of every dive your normal buoyancy is constantly changing. The tanks become 5 to 7 pounds lighter as the air inside them is consumed and expelled into the water. Meanwhile your wet suit becomes heavier as the tiny bubbles in the neoprene rubber compress with depth. In the early days, this required divers to weight themselves very carefully—the ideal being to slowly sink on exhalation and slowly rise on inhalation. Once on the surface, the diver had to use kick power to keep himself there. Then a few divers started using the old Mae-West-style inflatable life vests. Finally someone put a purge valve on the oral inflator of his life vest so he could inflate it or deflate it at will. This marked the birth of the buoyancy compensator device. Now it is commonly referred to simply as the "B.C."

The B.C. revolutionized buoyancy control in diving. It is the most innovative contribution to diving since the invention of the regulator. When properly used it takes the kick out of all vertical movement and can function almost like an elevator. Thus the diver can conserve both energy and air supply while vastly increasing his or her personal safety in the water. Although most B.C.s still resemble the prototype Mae West aviator's life vest, there are also those that are worn like a jacket. These attach to your backpack or tank or come over the shoulder. However they all function in the same way and have several things in common. They all consist of one or two rubberized air bags that fit inside an outer shell much like a tube fits inside a tire. All have an oral inflator that consists of a corrugated rubber tube with a rubber mouthpiece mounted near the left shoulder and a manually operated valve that permits you to orally inflate the air bag or deflate it while in or under the water. They also have a one-way, nonreturn, low-pressure (one or two p.s.i.) relief valve. This allows any excess pressure to escape and thus prevents "ballooning" on ascent. They also attach with straps of soft webbing and noncorrosive fittings. Most front-mounted B.C.s also include a pocket suitable for carrying a small writing slate and other goodies. Optional equipment includes a whistle that one can use on the surface to call for help, a CO_2 cartridge that is a carryover from the old life-vest days and

Buoyancy Compensator (B.C.) device. (Courtesy U.S. Divers Corporation)

seldom works well enough to warrant the extra expense, a manual dump valve for emergency purging, and a power inflator that eliminates the necessity of removing the regulator from your mouth in order to inflate the B.C.

Of all the optional equipment, the power inflator is the only one worth its price and then some. It consists of a simple nozzle fitting that attaches to the standard oral inflator mouthpiece and an air hose that simply plugs into it at one end and attaches to the low-pressure port of your breathing regulator at the other end. With it you can rise or sink simply by pushing a button.

When selecting a B.C. for your equipment inventory, try before you buy. The back-mounted models are quite different from the front-mounted models in that they place the flotation behind you rather than in front. You had best get the feel of both and select the one that is most comfortable for you. The bigger you are, the more lift you will need. The normal range for most divers is between 25 and 50 pounds of total lift. If you are super big or carry heavy equipment you may need more. Be sure your

B.C. will accept a power inflator if it does not already have one.

Follow instructions on the use and care of your B.C. It is an expensive piece of equipment. After every dive, rinse it thoroughly in fresh water. Run water through the oral inflator, letting it drain through the overpressure relief valve or back out through the oral inflator. After rinsing, hang it upside down to dry partially inflated. When it is dry, squeeze out the remaining air and water in the inner bag through the oral inflator. Then partially inflate it again. Store it in a cool, dry place.

DIVING AND EXPOSURE SUITS

Water is one of the most effective cooling agents known. About three thousand times more heat calories are required for warming a given amount of water than for warming the same amount of air to the same temperature. Furthermore, water tends to stratify itself into layers, according to temperature and density. These well-defined temperature layers are called thermoclines. The deeper you go, the colder they become, regardless of what the water temperatures are on the surface. When a diver becomes cold, the small blood capillaries near the surface of the skin open up, so that the blood can carry heat to the extremities. Since the head has less fatty protection than other parts of the body, heat loss through the head is especially rapid. To produce this heat, the body burns greatly increased quantities of food and air to maintain metabolism. For this reason, the cold diver, whether he is holding his breath or breathing from a tank of compressed air, will in-

Diving suit. (Courtesy U.S. Divers Corporation)

crease his air consumption greatly. The diver who is cold will consume a tank of compressed air almost twice as fast as one who is comfortably warm. Body warmth becomes not only a question of comfort but a question of diving economy as well. If the body ever becomes so cold that shivering begins, then cold has become a health hazard, for shivering is simply the body's desperate attempt to produce heat by friction as a last resort.

There are two basic types of diving suits available to keep the diver warm: the "wet suit" and the "dry suit." However, it is such a costly process to manufacture a dry suit that really keeps the diver dry that most manufacturers have stopped making them. We shall discuss only the wet suit, the more effective, cheaper, and easier to maintain of the two suits.

Almost all wet suits are made of gas-filled unicellular neoprene rubber about ³⁄₁₆ to ¼ inch thick. Because neoprene rubber tears easily, the better wet suits also have a backing of synthetic nondeteriorating cloth such as stretch nylon for added strength. The properly tailored wet suit should fit skintight, but as the name wet suit implies, it does not keep the diver dry. A thin layer of water seeps inside the suit. For this reason, the moment of water entry is always the most traumatic as far as comfort is concerned. But once the suit fills, the water is trapped there. It cannot circulate and carry off body heat, and the body very quickly warms the thin layer of water almost to body temperature. Thus insulated not only by the neoprene rubber but by the thin layer of body-warmed water as well, the diver can go in the coldest of waters in relative comfort. Because of the free passage of water, the pressures inside and outside the wet suits are always the same. Therefore there are never any problems of suit squeeze with wet suits as there are with dry suits. The ¼-inch neoprene suits, being thicker, are slightly warmer than the ³⁄₁₆-inch varieties. Because of the required skintight fit, the wet suit should be equipped with zippers at the arm, leg, and chest openings. Even then, entry is difficult unless you sprinkle the interior of the suit with talcum powder before donning it, so that the material will slide over the skin without binding or tearing.

Neoprene wet suits require a certain amount of postdive care. After each ocean dive, they should be rinsed thoroughly in fresh water and allowed to dry in the shade, because sunlight tends to deteriorate neoprene. Then they should be sprinkled liberally with talcum powder and stored in a cool, dark place. This preserves the rubber and keeps the suit in readiness for your next dive.

Wet suits come in many fancy colors and patterns; however, as I have said, color pigment tends to weaken some rubber products, and I recommend that you stay with the standard black neoprene material. A few diving stores offer do-it-yourself suit kits at a considerably lower price.

For temperate waters that are cool but not cold, or around coral reefs where skin protection is as important as thermal protection, a snug-fitting suit of woolen or thermal underwear or other street garments will often provide all the protection you need. If just one layer is not enough, try two.

WEIGHTS AND WEIGHT BELTS

Archimedes' Law states that "any object wholly or partly immersed in liquid is buoyed up by a force equal to the weight of the liquid it displaces." In other words, if an object placed in water weighs more than the water it displaces, it will sink and, conversely, if it weighs less than the water it displaces, it will float. If it weighs exactly the same as the water it displaces, it neither floats nor sinks but rather has neutral buoyancy. If the human body were all solid tissue, it would have neutral buoyancy, as body tissue is of about the same density and weight as water. However, because of the air cavities in the human body, such as lungs,

Weights and weight belt (with quick release buckle). (Courtesy U.S. Divers Corporation)

throat, nasal passages, and sinuses, the body tends to float. A diver wishing to descend to the bottom could not do so without exerting an effort to propel him or without weights to counteract his natural buoyancy. If the diver happened to be wearing a neoprene wet suit, the suit itself might displace up to twenty pounds of water, depending upon its thickness. Therefore, the diver would have to carry twenty pounds of additional weight in order to counteract the buoyancy of the suit alone.

In the old days, pearl divers used to plunge to the bottom carrying huge stones so that they could reach their destination without effort. The modern diver wears a belt with a number of lead weights attached. By adding and subtracting the number of weights, he can adjust his buoyancy so that it is almost perfectly neutral; that is, he will tend to sink when he exhales and float when he inhales. He is able thereby to rise or sink with minimum effort. Because salt water is denser and therefore more buoyant than fresh water, the diver will need slightly more weights when diving in salt water.

All commercially produced weight belts are made of nondeteriorating synthetic fiber such as nylon. They are equipped with a quick-release safety buckle so that the weight can be quickly and easily ditched in case of emergency. The weight belt should be worn over all other equipment so that it can be released without tampering with other equipment in an emergency.

Commercially produced weights are almost always made of lead, which is the cheapest and heaviest material available. The standard-size weight units are one, two, three, and five pounds. A weight belt with pockets for sand is also available.

KNIVES

A sharp, sturdy diving knife is an indispensable safety aid and tool, not a weapon. Only a fool would pit his diving knife against a shark the way so many "Hollywood divers" are depicted doing. A knife is a safety precaution against the possibility of becoming entangled in underwater lines or kelp. It is a tool used to pick and probe. Since the knife is constantly exposed to the corrosive effects of salt water, it

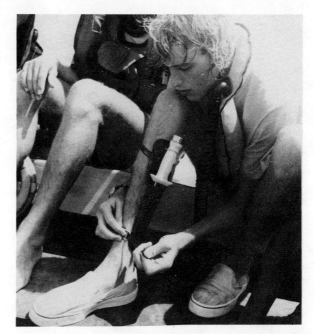

Diver's knife. (Courtesy U.S. Divers Corporation)

should be made of noncorrosive materials, such as plastic or rubber and stainless steel. In addition the blade should be fairly short, sturdy, and serrated on at least one edge to facilitate cutting fibrous material like rope. It should be kept handy at all times, worn on the belt or strapped to the calf of the leg.

DEPTH GAUGES

If you plan to use scuba gear beyond depths of 33 feet, you will also need a portable depth gauge to determine depth and the possible need for decompression stops. There are three basic kinds of depth gauge: the Bourdon tube gauge, the diaphragm gauge, and the capillary gauge. Since water pressure increases at a constant rate (one atmosphere or 14.7 pounds per square inch for every 33 feet), all depth gauges measure depth in terms of water pressure. The Bourdon tube gauge measures the pressure by the tendency of a crescent-shaped tube to straighten out when subjected to water pressure. The diaphragm gauge measures the pressure by a hydrostatic principle. The capillary gauge measures pressure by the compression of a column of air entrapped within the gauge by the water.

Depth Gauge. (Courtesy U.S. Divers Corporation)

UNDERWATER COMPASSES

There is no sun, moon, or stars to guide you underwater. Sometimes, if the water is murky, it is difficult to tell which direction is up, much less which is north. A wrist compass is usually worn by divers who expect to have to navigate underwater. The compass rose card is usually suspended in a liquid-filled housing for easy visibility. The dial face should be as large as possible, have a lubber line to mark the diver's line of motion, a course marker, and be printed in large letters, for it then makes for more accuracy and easier reading. The combination depth gauge and compass should be avoided, for it is a compromise instrument that gives compromise data. Underwater wrist compasses range in price according to precision and ac-

The depth gauge is worn on the wrist like a watch, and the pressures are calibrated on the dial face in terms of depth. In each case the gauge is equipped with a small port through which water enters and leaves. Since salt water corrodes, it is important that the depth gauge be rinsed thoroughly in fresh water after each dive and that the entry port be kept free of salt and corrosion if you are to get accurate depth readings. Since the depth gauge helps to determine your depth-time limit and thereby your susceptibility to decompression sickness, it should be treated as the delicate instrument it is and not subjected to undue shock. The diaphragm depth gauge is the most accurate but the price makes it prohibitive in most cases. The Bourdon tube gauge is the most popular and sells for less. The capillary gauge is extremely simple, consisting solely of a sheet of plastic with a channel cut into it. It sells for very little, but it seldom gives an accurate reading.

Underwater compass with lubber line and course setter.

curacy. The better they are the more they cost. Often the compass is incorporated into an instrument console. This is something of a diver's dashboard comprising a depth gauge, temperature gauge, bottom timer, and underwater pressure gauge as well as the compass. It gives you the whole story at a glance and is highly recommended.

UNDERWATER WATCHES

The underwater wristwatch is often an imposing instrument that is worn like a badge. It signals you are a diver and opens the possibility of striking up a conversation. But as well as being a fraternal symbol, it is an indispensable tool in planning your dive and diving your plan safely. Depth and time are your only limits underwater and you must always know one to determine the other's limit of safety. A sport dive should not be allowed to slip over the no-decompression

Underwater wristwatch. (Courtesy U.S. Divers Corporation)

time limit, so the diver's watch or bottom timer—an underwater stopwatch that measures elapsed time—is an essential piece of equipment. Since all underwater watches are pressure proof, often to depths of several hundred feet, many people never remove them. Whether dial or digital, the big, bold luminous numbers tell you the time no matter where you are, night and day, wet or dry. Accuracy and dependability are what you want to look for in a diver's watch. The better they are the more they cost.

PORTABLE DECOMPRESSION TABLES AND METERS

As far as deep diving goes, knowing the time and depth will do you little good unless you have a copy of the U.S. Navy Standard Decompression Tables with you (see Chapter 10). These tables tell you the number and duration of the decompression stops you must make, if any, during your ascent to the surface. Leaving the Decompression Tables at home or in the car has cost some divers a serious case of the bends. Always carry a copy of the tables with you when diving beyond 33 feet. A few of the more advanced diving shops also offer the Decompression Tables silk-screened on a plastic card that can even be taken underwater. I repeat: Always take the Decompression Tables with you if you expect to dive beyond depths of 33 feet.

Three companies have an automatic decompression meter on the market that simulates the reaction of the bloodstream to compressed-air breathing and records the amount of time and depth of any decompression stops that may be necessary. It also considers the amount of interval surface time between dives if you are doing more than one in the same day. Though very accurate, the meter is a delicate instrument capable of error and should not be relied on to the exclusion of a well-planned dive or repetitive dive.

UNDERWATER FLASHLIGHTS

Most diving-equipment manufacturers offer an underwater flashlight that is pressure proof up to 250 feet. The flashlight comes in very

Underwater flashlight.

Most come equipped with a plastic strap that can be worn around the wrist or attached to your belt.

The sealed beam dry cell units offered in most automotive supply stores also work well underwater especially if you coat the exposed wires with silicone rubber. In a pinch, an ordinary flashlight will give adequate vision for most jobs for a short period of time before the salt water robs the batteries of their power. After exposing the ordinary flashlight to salt water, you should remove the batteries immediately and wash the flashlight thoroughly in fresh water, otherwise it will corrode and become useless overnight.

HOOKAH GEAR

These gas-powered, low-pressure compressor units provide air for two divers to depths of 25 feet via two plastic hoses. They are perfect for the occasional and weekend divers who like to go to out-of-the-way places where heavy air tanks are clumsy and air-filling stations inaccessible. You won't break any depth records, but who wants to? The most enchanting sights are

handy when you are working in murky water, for invisible objects will often show up quite clearly when a source of light is held close by. For night diving, it is indispensable. The pressure-proof housings of most underwater flashlights are made of noncorrosive plastic or metal.

A hookah diver emerges from the water. One hose carries air, the other hot water.

in the first 25 feet of water anyway. Most units include: float collar that can be inflated on the spot, Fiberglas housing for a two-horsepower gasoline engine and an air compressor, two lengths of vinyl hose and two full-face diver's masks. A "diver down" flag is mounted to the engine's exhaust stack on most models. It operates from boat deck or pier as well as in calm water.

Typical party boat for divers.

DIVING BOATS

Good diving boats are costly, but if you want to reach the best diving areas, they are almost indispensable. Anything from a pram to the *Queen Mary II* will serve as a diving launch. For the person of average income, the open-type skiff powered by an outboard motor can be perfectly adequate for all but the heaviest work in the open sea. Since it is a cardinal rule always to dive with a buddy, the boat must easily carry at least three men and all their equipment. It should measure sixteen to twenty-four feet in length, be of wide beam for stability, and be sturdily constructed of wood or, better yet, Fiberglas. It should have a wide, spacious cockpit with lots of deck space to hold the huge clutter of diving gear. The double- and triple-hull skiff known as the Boston whaler is ideal for such purposes, for it provides extra stability for entering and leaving the water. Ideally, diving boats should be equipped with a glass panel in the floor so that you can inspect the bottom for good diving areas. A good sturdy boarding ladder is almost a necessity. If the water is murky or very deep in your area, an echo sounder is also a great aid for finding sunken reefs and wrecks as well as for measuring depth. Portable battery-driven echo sounders are available at various prices depending on their power. Incidentally, an echo sounder can be encased in an underwater housing, just as a camera might, and used to measure horizontal as well as vertical distances.*

* The chapter "Search and Recovery" in my *The Complete Illustrated Guide to Snorkel and Deep Diving* gives more information concerning underwater echo sounding.

UNDERWATER TRANSPORTATION

There are six types of underwater transportation available to the diver: tow sled, tow scooter, push scooter, aqua ped, wet submarine, and dry submarine. A diver can at least double his speed, distance, and the duration of his air supply by conserving energy through the use of any one of these.

The *tow sled,* sometimes called an aqua plane, is by far the cheapest and most practical mode of underwater transportation. It consists simply of a paravane with handles on it. It is towed behind the boat at the end of a long line. The diver holds onto the handles as the boat pulls the sled through the water. Merely by pointing it upward or downward he can ascend or descend.

The tow sled can be used with either snorkel or scuba. Its primary purpose is to facilitate underwater visual searches and for this it is almost perfect. One big disadvantage of the tow sled is that the arms tire after the diver has been hanging on for a while, but this can be remedied by rigging up a harness between diver and sled with quick-release buckles.

Effective use of a tow sled requires a certain amount of practice and skill. One's rate of descent and ascent is much faster with a tow sled than without one. Therefore the diver runs the risk of popping an eardrum should he descend too quickly to clear his ears, or of incurring an embolism should he ascend too quickly without purging his lungs of compressed air.

If possible, you should rig an electric buzzer signal system between the tow sled and the boat operator. Boat operators tend to pull divers with tow sled too quickly, and any speed of more than three miles an hour is likely to tear the diver's face mask off. The tow line should measure three feet or more for every foot of depth that you expect to descend. Otherwise you have to fight to keep the sled on the bottom.

You can buy a tow sled ready-made or make one yourself for half the price.

Electric-powered tow scooters are of either the push or pull type and are commercially available. They consist of a pressure-proof battery housing with a separate housing containing an electric motor that drives the propeller. In most cases the motor is activated by a hand pressure switch that stops the motor automatically when released. Most of the push-type electric motor scooters clamp onto the diver's air tank. The push-type scooter offers some advantages over the tow-type scooter because it leaves the diver's hand free for useful work and for protecting himself from underwater obstacles. Furthermore, there is no propeller wash in the diver's face as there is with the tow-type

scooter. With the tow-type scooter the diver must hang on by two handles, much as with the tow sled.

The big disadvantage of most electric-powered scooters, whether tow- or push-type, is the maintenance. Most of them are underpowered and, unless the batteries have a full charge, are likely to go only half as fast and half as far as the manufacturers say they can.

There are several kinds of *wet submarines* available to divers at various prices. Most of them consist of a Fiberglas hollow tube in which one or two divers may acquire a certain amount of protection from the onrush of water. The submarine is towed through the water, much like the tow sled. It is equipped with two paravanes, one on either side, usually near the bow, which are controlled separately. As with the tow sled, you point them upward and up you go; if you point them downward, indeed down you go, and very rapidly at that. If you point them in opposite directions, you can do barrel rolls as if you were in an airplane. A few of the wet submarines can be fitted with a battery-powered electric propulsion system. However, as stated previously, these propulsion systems tend to be underpowered and we must await the invention of a reasonably priced battery that will deliver adequate power for prolonged periods.

5

Learning to Snorkel Dive

WHERE, WHEN, AND WITH WHOM

Although most instructors now bypass snorkel diving in favor of the scuba experience, I include this chapter here for you who might want to experience diving without yet enrolling in a formal scuba course.

One of the cardinal rules of skin diving, whether it be with snorkel or scuba equipment, is **Never Dive Alone.** It is best to choose a diving buddy right at the outset, so you can begin your lessons and dive together as much as possible. Every person has his own peculiarities, and when you stick with the same diving buddy, you both soon get to know each other's abilities and limitations and can spot trouble the instant it approaches. Having a good diving buddy, however, is no substitute for having a good instructor when you are learning. Your instructor should be a qualified teacher as well as a good diver. He should be certified by the National Association of Underwater Instructors (NAUI), the YMCA, the Professional Association of Diving Instructors (PADI), or one of the other international certifying organizations.

A baby must learn to crawl before he can walk or run, and the same slow beginning applies to diving. After requiring you to pass a test in basic swimming skills, your instructor will almost invariably teach you diving physiology first and will start you out in the shallow end of a swimming pool, or the shallow water of a protected beach. He will then, most likely, lead you through the following steps to snorkel and then scuba diving. It is best to do the entire training with a single instructor. Inquire at your local dive retail store.

STEP 1: EQUIPMENT FAMILIARIZATION

As described earlier, the basic equipment of a snorkel diver consists of a mask, snorkel, and fins, and, in open water, a buoyancy compensator (B.C.). When you are preparing to dive, the first thing you must do is attach the snorkel to the mask. Most snorkel tubes are equipped with a small rubber tab for this purpose. The tab loops around the strap on the left side of your face mask and thus holds it in place. Whether you affix the snorkel high or low is immaterial; so long as the mouthpiece fits comfortably in your mouth, it is only a matter of personal preference. Your instructor or your local dive retail store can advise you on your selection of equipment and enroll you in a snorkel or scuba certification program.

STEP 2: DEFOGGING THE MASK

In the water, the warm moist air from your exhalation will condense on the inside of the faceplate of your mask unless you properly defog it before putting it on. This is done by simply spitting on the inside of the faceplate and rubbing the saliva around the glass. In some mysterious way, the chemicals in your saliva prevent moisture from condensing on your faceplate and obscuring vision. (There are commercially produced defogging solutions, but nothing is so handy as spit and you can't beat the price, either.)

STEP 3: TESTING FOR LEAKS

After defogging the mask, place it over your eyes and nose and inhale sharply. The mask should stay in place without the strap, because of the slight vacuum created by your inhalation. With the mask in place, put the strap over your head, adjust for comfort, and remove any hair, wrinkles, or buckles. Make sure no hair protrudes from under the mask so as to prevent any water from leaking into your mask. Then adjust the snorkel so that the mouthpiece fits comfortably. Place the two rubber bits between your teeth and the flanges between your teeth and lips. Practice breathing through the snorkel for

Defog your mask by spreading saliva around the faceplate.

a while so that you become accustomed to it before getting in the water. Some people find it difficult to breathe only through their mouths, but this feeling quickly passes when the mask is in place.

STEP 4: DONNING THE FINS

With the mask and snorkel in place, the prospective diver wets both feet and both fins; this permits the fins to slip easily over the foot without binding or catching. Insert your foot into the fin as far as it will go and then pull the heel of the fin up with your thumb. The fins should fit comfortably without binding or hurting in any way.

STEP 5: ENTERING THE WATER

When you have all your equipment on, the instructor teaches you how to enter the water. First, you will notice that walking with your fins on is very awkward. You must lift your feet high off the ground to prevent the blade of the fin from buckling and possibly tripping you. When you begin walking into the water, you will notice that the blade of the fin constantly buckles beneath your foot from the resistance of the water. Therefore instructors teach their students to walk backward in order to prevent buckling and tripping.

STEP 6: SNORKEL BREATHING

Your instructor will ask you to lower your head into the water when the water is a few inches above your waist to accustom you to breathing through the snorkel while your face is submerged. This in itself is a new experience. Bend at the waist and submerge your face to the level of your ears. Then practice breathing. You will notice that, even though you are only partially submerged, the pressure of the water presses the mask against your face, creating a tight seal. You will also notice that no water leaks in around the snorkel in your mouth. While you are practicing breathing, develop the habit of inhaling very slowly and exhaling sharply. The "blast" of air clears the snorkel tube of any water that might leak into it from the open end above your head. Now, try it floating on the surface of the water while pressing lightly against the bottom or hanging onto your buddy's hand to keep yourself afloat.

STEP 7: CLEARING THE SNORKEL

Once you have mastered this, try ducking your head beneath the water, allowing your

Clearing the snorkel by the blast method.

Clearing the snorkel by the displacement method.

the ascent however or the air will escape. A little practice makes perfect.

STEP 8: CLEARING THE FACE MASK

If some water leaks into your mask during a snorkel dive, it is a simple matter to lift the bottom edge of your face mask when you surface and then drain it. Next try to replace the mask so that it has a better seal. Once you have committed yourself to the underwater world for longer periods with scuba gear, clearing your face mask of water becomes a different problem, but we shall deal with that when the time comes. If your mask has a one-way purge valve, you can purge water from it by remaining face-down and simply exhaling into your mask.

STEP 9: SNORKEL CRUISING

Once you accustom yourself to breathing through your snorkel, hang onto the edge of the pool or your buddy's hand or swimsuit and stretch out so that your body lies flat on the surface. Keep your face submerged in the water and practice kicking with your fins, using the flutter kick just the way it is used in swimming the crawl. The flutter kick can be used equally well while swimming on your back or on either side. Keep your knees as straight as possible, point your toes, and kick from the hips. Because of the greater surface area of the fins, much more energy is required to move the fins through the water than to move your bare feet. You will notice that your kick is much slower and that your legs tire much more quickly as a result. This is natural. With a little practice, you will develop your leg muscles so that they can sustain kicking with the fins for long periods of time without tiring. Meanwhile avoid using the oversized "giant" fins until you have developed the muscle to handle them.

When practicing kicking, remember that the fins can do no good unless they are completely submerged in the water. Therefore, be sure to kick so that only your heels, not the entire fins, break the surface of the water. If the fins leave the water, you lose a good percentage of the power and efficiency of your kick. By raising your head slightly you lower your feet so that

snorkel to fill. Then bring your head back to the surface and clear your snorkel. You will notice that, if you do not exhale with enough force, water will remain in the snorkel and you might choke on it when you inhale. This unpleasant experience quickly teaches you the proper technique for clearing the snorkel, and you will soon be snorkel breathing like a pro. The displacement or "downhill" method provides an easier and surer way to clear the snorkel. At the end of a surface dive, the normal ascent procedure is to "look up, reach up, and go up" to the surface. If you release a little air into the snorkel tube as you begin your ascent that air will expand as you ascend and displace the water inside the snorkel so that you can immediately inhale upon surfacing without having to "blast" the water out. It is important that the open end be kept lower than the mouthpiece throughout the fins will remain submerged with each kick. You will also learn that it is not necessary to kick as rapidly with fins as you would without them. A strong steady kick at a pace of no more than twenty per minute will drive you through the water at a good cruising rate without exhausting you. As you improve your technique you will notice that the fins are so efficient that it becomes superfluous to use your arms. Any movement of your arms through the water while snorkel cruising simply creates added drag that slows you down. It is best to keep your arms glued next to your sides so as to streamline your body as much as possible. Later you will see that it is very convenient to have both hands free to spear fish, take pictures, or do some other kind of practical underwater work.

If you use a buoyancy compensator (B.C.) while snorkeling, it should be partially inflated while cruising on the surface, but you must purge it of air if you want to dive.

STEP 10: SURFACE DIVING

Once you have developed the technique of snorkel cruising on the surface, it is time to learn to dive from the surface. There are three basic kinds of surface dives: the cannonball tuck, the pike tuck, and the "kelp" or feet-first dive. In each case, it is best to plan each dive. If wearing weights, check your quick release buckle and deflate your buoyancy compensator (B.C.) before diving. Now, lie flat and still on the surface of the water as you breathe deeply and plan your dive.

You can build up your supply of residual oxygen by breathing deeply several times while thinking about what you want to do. Pick a target on the bottom so that you have some specific thing to look at on your way down; otherwise it is very easy to become disoriented once you get underwater. After you have planned your dive and hyperventilated a few times, ex-

Snorkel cruising: note that only the heels break the surface.

hale as much as you possibly can. Then inhale as much as you possibly can and hold it. Then go into your dive.

Cannonball Tuck

From a horizontal position on the surface, the easiest and most frequently used dive is the cannonball tuck. As you take your last breath, give a powerful backward stroke with both hands while you tuck both knees up under your chest and roll your head and shoulders forward under the water. When your hips are directly over your head, lift your legs out so that they stick straight up above the surface. The weight of your legs will drive you straight downward. Then reverse the stroke of your arms by bringing them in front of you sharply down to your sides. This helps to propel you to the bottom. Once your arms are by your sides keep them there until you reach the bottom by kicking. Any arm movement will create drag and possibly throw you off course.

As explained in the chapter on diving physiology, the deeper you go the longer you can stay without apparent discomfort or lack of air. Because of the danger of shallow-water blackout during ascent, never willfully stay on the bottom more than a few seconds after you experience the first compulsive urge to breathe. By the time the second compulsive urge to breathe rolls around, you should already have pushed off the bottom on your ascent toward the surface. This is best done by crouching on the bottom and then pushing hard toward the surface with your feet while extending one arm above your upturned head. At the same time exhale a bit of air into the snorkel so it will expand and displace the water as you ascend. For the average depths of most beginning dives, this should bring you back to the surface without much more kicking. The moment you break the surface, exhale sharply through your snorkel tube. This will clear (purge) any residual water from the tube so that you can inhale immediately afterward.

Remember: "Look up, reach up, and go up."

Pike Tuck

The pike tuck is executed much like the cannonball tuck, except for the initial rollover maneuver. While floating on the surface in a spread-eagle position, bring your hands fully

Cannonball tuck dive.

Pike tuck dive.

Underwater view of pike tuck dive.

down to the sides. Then, while backstroking your hands, bend at the waist, keeping your legs straight. When your hips are directly over your head lift your legs up into the air just as in the cannonball tuck and begin to descend. The rest of the dive and recovery should be executed as in the cannonball dive.

Feet-First (Kelp) Dive

The feet-first dive is used almost exclusively in spearfishing, when the splashing from the tuck or cannonball dives might frighten a prize fish out of spear range. Begin this dive from a vertical position in the water. With a powerful kick of your flippers, rise out of the water up to your chest. When the weight of the exposed portion of your body overbalances the thrust of the kick, reverse the direction of your movement, and you will begin to sink. At this instant, bring your arms sharply upward in a reverse kind of breast stroke, driving yourself farther beneath the surface. Once beneath the surface, roll over, so that you can continue the descent head first throughout the remainder of the dive. The ascent is made exactly as in the tuck and cannonball techniques.

Let the weight of your legs and fins drive you under.

The feet-first kelp dive.

STEP 11: EQUALIZING YOUR EARS

During your initial dive, you will experience such ear pain from the rapidly increasing water pressure that you will not be able to dive much deeper than ten or fifteen feet. Certainly you could will yourself to proceed in spite of the pain, but this is inadvisable, for you would run the risk of rupturing an eardrum if you did. Once you learn how to equalize or clear your ears, however, the only limit to the depth you can dive will be your ability to hold your breath.

The basic technique for "clearing" the ears is described in the chapter on diving physiology. It involves pinching off your nostrils and pushing air through the Eustachian tubes that lead from your nasal passages into your inner ear. This equalizes the air pressure in your inner ear with the surrounding water pressure. Many modern face masks are molded with cavities that fit on either side of the nose to facilitate pinching off your nostrils for the ear-clearing procedure. If your face mask does not have this built-in facility you must press the bottom of the mask up against your nose before "snorting" in order to prevent the air from escaping into the mask. When you succeed in clearing your ears, you will actually hear the air rush through your Eustachian tubes and feel instant relief of any pain and pressure.

You will be able to descend until the ear pain begins to bother you again, at which point you must repeat the ear-clearing procedure. If one ear clears and the other does not, do not try to force it. Ascend a few feet to relieve the pressure and then try again.

If you are a beginner or have not dived in a long time, it is best to open your Eustachian tubes by clearing or equalizing your ears in a couple of practice sessions before you reach the water. This can be done by simply pinching off

Clearing your ears underwater.

your nostrils and gently pushing air into your inner ear as you normally would in the water. However, this must be done with great caution, for it is possible to burst your eardrum if done too forcefully. If you have difficulty in clearing your ears, try swallowing or working your jaws up and down at the same time you "snort." Once having gotten the air inside your inner ear, you need not worry about getting rid of it. The pressure in your inner ear will equalize automatically during ascent, for the air exits from your Eustachian tubes much more easily than it enters.

One other word of caution—head colds cause the Eustachian tubes to swell and fill with mucus. This sometimes makes it virtually impossible to clear your ears. For this reason, it is often best not to dive if you suffer from a cold.

Off you go now . . . Have fun!

6

Learning to Scuba Dive

WHERE, WHEN, AND WITH WHOM

After you pass the required test in diving physiology, your instructor will probably return you to the shallow end of the swimming pool or protected beach and introduce you to the techniques of scuba diving. He will then, most likely, lead you through the following 15 steps:

STEP 1: EQUIPMENT FAMILIARIZATION AND PREDIVE CHECK

In addition to the basic equipment of the snorkel diver—that is, mask, snorkel, and fins—the scuba diver must have a tank of compressed air, a breathing regulator with a submersible air

pressure gauge, and a buoyancy compensator (B.C.). If the temperature of the water warrants it, he must also have a rubber exposure suit and a quick-release belt of lead weights to counteract the buoyancy of the suit.

In the chapter on snorkel diving you have already learned how to check and adjust your mask, snorkel, and fins. Once you have them properly adjusted for fit, they should remain that way. Since your life will depend upon your scuba equipment while you are submerged, you must also be certain that it functions properly. Therefore, before you enter the water, spread your equipment out before you, inspect it for flaws and damage, and then proceed as follows:

a. Attach your regulator and check the air pressure in your tank with your pressure gauge,

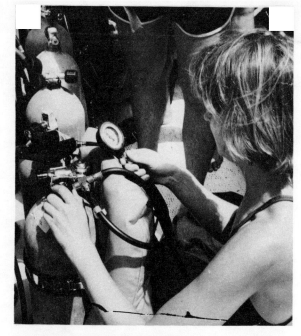

The predive check.

Check air pressure and no-decompression limits.

even though you may have just filled it. Make sure it is at least 70 percent full before you enter the water.

b. Check the position of the air reserve lever, if any. Make sure it is in the closed or "up" position.

c. Check the backpack and harness assembly of your air tank. Make sure the tank is securely fastened and that the harness straps do not have dangerous worn spots. Adjust the harness straps for a comfortable fit and see that all couplings are made with quick-release hitches.

d. Check the breathing regulator for leaks by inhaling strongly through the mouthpiece while the protective cap still seals the high-pressure stage. If you receive air, check the hose for leaks, especially around the connecting joints. If you cannot find any in the hose, remove the regulator housing and check the rubber diaphragm for leaks. *Do not dive with a leaking regulator.*

e. With the regulator attached to the air tank, check the sealing by opening the tank valve and listening for leaks. If you are not sure, submerge the valve and regulator in water and look for bubbles.

f. Check the air flow by inserting the mouthpiece and breathing from it. Air flow should start easily and stop completely after each exhalation.

g. Check your rubber suit for tears or weak spots. Repair if necessary while the suit is still dry.

h. Check your weight belt. For neutral buoy-

Check your regulator.

ancy, the average nude diver needs about six pounds of weight in salt water and about four pounds in fresh water and about double that if using a full wet suit. (Once in the water, you can add or subtract weights until you are perfectly weightless. When at this point you would slowly sink after exhaling and slowly rise after inhaling.) On the surface, when fully dressed you would float vertically with the surface at eye level.

i. With your instructor and/or your buddy, determine the objective of the dive. Decide now what direction you will move in, what you will do, what signals you will use, and what emergency ascent procedures will be used if needed.

STEP 2: DONNING EQUIPMENT

If everything checks out, the equipment should be donned in the following sequence: 1. The wet suit (if any). 2. The buoyancy compensator (B.C.). 3. The tank and regulator assembly. 4. The weight belt. 5. The face mask (either over your eyes or around your neck—never on your forehead where you can easily lose it). 6. The fins.

If needed, you can sprinkle talcum powder or its equivalent over the inside of your wet suit (if any) to prevent the rubber from binding on your skin when you dress. Slip the B.C. on, making sure the straps are not entangled or twisted. Now inflate it only slightly. After putting on your cap and adjusting it for comfort, you are ready to don your tank.

The easiest way to get into your scuba harness is to ask your buddy to hold it for you while you slip into it as if it were a coat. Otherwise you can set it on a seat, spread the straps and slip into it yourself. Then buckle on your weight belt with a quick-release hitch or buckle, making sure it is unencumbered by straps, etc. Once you have donned your tank you are likely to feel clumsy and top-heavy, so sit down or lean against a bulkhead before you attempt to don your fins.

If your fins bind, wet your feet so they will slip on easily. Then reach down and draw the heel or strap over the heel of your foot with your fingers. If you are seated on a deck or a beach, you can put on a pair of fins as you would put on a pair of shoes. (If you must walk with your fins on, walk backward while looking over your shoulder, or you are likely to trip over the blades of your fins.)

STEP 3: ENTERING AND LEAVING THE WATER

The proverbial fish-out-of-water is only slightly more pathetic than the diver fully suited up and ready to dive. He is awkward, hot, and uncomfortable. But once he enters the water, he can be as free and as graceful as a fish. Therefore, once you are suited up and ready you should head for the water as soon as possible, with the least possible last-minute dilly-dallying around.

Climbing up or down a ladder or walking backward on a beach is the easiest and most practical way to enter or leave the water. This is, no doubt, how your instructor will have you enter and leave the water for your first scuba lesson. However, entering and leaving the water are often the most taxing parts of a dive. Most divers like to get it over with as soon as possible, so they usually enter by either jumping in or rolling in—they *never dive head first.*

I should mention here that the sudden pressure change resulting from jumping in is hard on the sinuses, but occasions arise when you have little choice in your method of entry, so it is best to learn the jump entries. The most commonly used entry is the feet-first jump or giant stride entry. Stand erect on the boat gunwale or the pool deck and make sure that you have a clear landing area and enough water beneath. Protect your face mask with one hand. Then simply step out into space, entering the water vertically.

Standing on the gunwale of a pitching boat poised to jump feet first is not easy. In choppy water, divers usually use the back roll-in entry. Execute this by facing the middle of the boat and sitting, back to the water, as close to the edge of the gunwale as possible. Steady the mask and tank as described above and simply lean back over the water until the weight of the tank pulls you in. It is important that the tank be completely clear of the gunwale or pool deck and your feet completely clear of your buddy's chin before you begin your roll in.

The side roll-in entry, a variation of the back

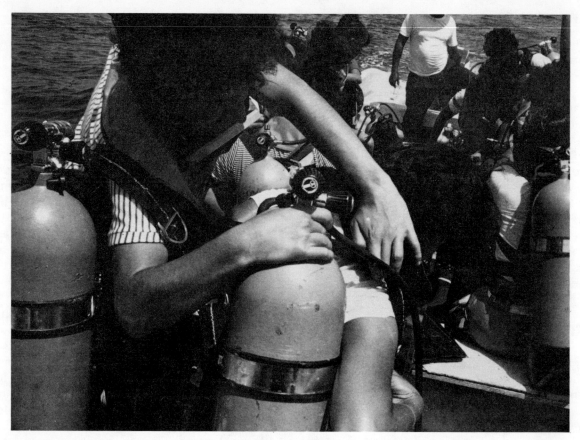

Help your buddy . . .

. . . then help yourself.

Check your buddy and review your plan.

Take compass bearings and set your course.

roll-in, is often used in very rough water. Instead of sitting on the gunwale (or edge of the pool deck), crawl up to it on all fours. Then, fall sideways over the edge of the boat, steadying your mask and tank before you hit the water.

Leaving the water is not quite so simple as entering it. After the dive, you will usually be exhausted, and pulling yourself onto a boat or deck while wearing heavy diving equipment is a herculean task. A deep, sturdy boarding ladder is the obvious solution. A boatswain's chair, Jacob's ladder, cargo net, or knotted rope hung over the side will also facilitate exit from the water. But even when these are available, it is always best to remove your heavy, cumbersome equipment before you attempt to leave the water. Hanging onto a ladder or a rope, first remove your weight belt and hand it to a helper on deck. Do the same with your tank and regulator. If you exit onto a beach, swim in as far as you can go. Then remove your fins and simply wade or crawl ashore.

Use the giant stride entry.

STEP 4: SCUBA BREATHING

Standing in waist-deep water, your instructor will ask you to put your face mask and mouthpiece in place and then accustom yourself to breathing through the scuba above water. Then he will ask you to submerge your face in the water and continue breathing through the scuba while you hang on to him or to your buddy. If you are like most people, you will feel that it is impossible to either inhale or exhale the moment your face hits the water. After years of believing that it is impossible to breathe underwater, this is normal. However, I assure you that it is all in your mind. Your scuba will permit you to breathe normally underwater just as soon as you begin to believe it will.

Once you overcome this hurdle, the sensation of being able to breathe underwater will be so thrilling that you will want to go spinning off in all directions. Resist this urge for a while and content yourself with ducking your head deeper underwater by walking your hands down your instructor's or buddy's leg until you reach his ankles. Then just hang on and

Preparing for the back roll-in entry.

The back roll-in entry.

breathe. When you are thoroughly convinced that your scuba really works, you can let go and begin to swim along the bottom, feeling it out very cautiously. If you pop to the surface in spite of yourself the moment you let go, your instructor will give you enough weight to keep you neutrally buoyant. Swim side by side with your buddy back and forth along the bottom until you are thoroughly accustomed to the sensation. Then return to the surface, and practice making surface dives to the bottom just as you learned to do in snorkel diving. As you gain proficiency, try diving deeper and deeper until at last the pain in your ears tells you that you had better clear your ears before proceeding any farther.

Caution. Always remember how Boyle's Law of Gases applies to you. Never hold your breath while changing depths if you are breathing compressed air, for you will run the risk of suffering squeeze (barotrauma) or, worse yet, air embolism. Always breathe normally especially when changing depth levels, as during ascent.

Purge your B.C. when you're ready to dive.

STEP 5: EQUALIZING YOUR EARS

Equalizing your ears is much easier when you are diving with scuba than with a snorkel, because you have a supply of precompressed air to do the job. Unlike snorkel diving, if at first you don't succeed, simply take another breath and try again. The compressed air supply also allows you to begin clearing earlier in your descent so that your Eustachian tubes will not be squeezed shut by the pressure before equalization can be completed. For this reason, it is advisable to begin clearing the moment you dive and to continue snorting, swallowing, or wiggling your jaws throughout your descent to the bottom. Do not hesitate to gently pinch your nostrils closed if needed.

Clearing the ears during repetitive dives is sometimes more difficult because of an accumulation of mucus in the Eustachian tubes from previous dives. However, generally speaking, the more you dive, the more easily you can equalize.

Equalizing your ears.

STEP 6: CLEARING YOUR MASK

Regardless of how well your mask fits over your face, some water is bound to leak inside sooner or later. This causes discomfort and distorted vision. Furthermore, it would be sense-less to return to the surface every time you needed to clear your mask of water as you might normally do while snorkel diving. Therefore, clearing the mask while underwater is a basic skill of the scuba diver.

To understand the principle of clearing your mask while underwater, try this experiment: plunge an ordinary drinking glass into a tub of water, and allow it to flood. Then hold the glass vertical in the water, open end down. Now bend the end of a drinking straw so that it is shaped like a fishhook and hook it around the open end of the glass so that one end emerges from the water far enough to permit blowing through it. Blow through the straw and you will see air accumulate at the top of the glass. It quickly drives the water inside the glass out the bottom until the glass is filled with air down to the level of the opening and the air bubbles out the bottom.

In clearing your mask of water, you follow the same "diving bell principle." However, instead of using a straw, you simply roll your head backward so that your faceplate is parallel with the surface of the water. Then holding (not pressing) the mask in place you exhale air into it through your nose. The air rises and pushes the water out the bottom of the mask. You will find, with practice, that one exhalation is all you need to completely clear your mask of water. However, if one exhalation is not enough to do the job, you can take another breath and repeat the procedure until your mask is clear of water. The salt in seawater may cause a slight stinging sensation in your nose and eyes, but it can't hurt you and water cannot enter through your nose unless you inhale through it.

As you gain proficiency, you will find it unnecessary to roll all the way back to make the faceplate absolutely parallel with the surface. By holding the top of your mask in place and gently lifting the bottom of the mask with your fingers, you can roll your head back or to either side until the faceplate is just slightly off vertical and accomplish the same thing. The important thing is to maintain a tight seal at the upper edge of the mask to prevent the air escaping from under the upper skirt of the mask.

Many of the more expensive face masks are equipped with a one-way purge valve. This allows water to exit the mask but prevents it from entering. With a purge valve you need not roll

Clearing your mask of water (top purge).

Clearing your mask of water (side purge).

over on your back or side and utilize the "diving bell principle." By simply exhaling through your nose into the mask, you can keep the mask clear and dry. While you are learning, it is best to practice the mask-clearing process by diving to the bottom, removing the mask, and then replacing and clearing it while underwater. When you have mastered this, you can try this exercise: throw your mask into the water several yards away from you, then swim underwater, retrieve it, put it on, and clear it, all the while breathing normally from your regulator. This will teach you that it is not necessary to be wearing a face mask in order to breathe underwater with a scuba regulator.

STEP 7: CLEARING THE MOUTHPIECE

It is a common practice for experienced divers to remove and replace their scuba mouthpiece while underwater. To inflate a B.C. at depth, to replace a camera strap around the neck, to fill a lifting bag with air from the air tank, or to give air to a buddy in distress (buddy breathing)—these are just a few reasons you might want to remove a mouthpiece. However, there is also the possibility of having your regulator yanked from your mouth accidentally by catching your air hose on an unseen object. Therefore, it is essential that you learn how to remove and recover a lost mouthpiece and clear it of water while totally submerged.

The mouthpieces of all modern breathing regulators are equipped with a nonreturn valve that prevents water from entering the air chamber of the regulator while it is in your mouth. Water can enter only the small confines of the mouthpiece itself—usually only about two ounces—and this is easily cleared by inserting the mouthpiece and exhaling sharply. All modern single-hose, two-stage regulators are equipped with a purge button which, when pressed, mechanically opens the intake valve and allows a free flow of air to escape from the feeder hose. This automatically clears the regulator mouthpiece of water, so that the diver can then inhale almost pure air. I say "almost pure air" because a few drops of water are likely to remain in the mouthpiece after direct exposure to the water. Therefore, after clearing the

Purging your scuba regulator.

mouthpiece of water, the diver's next inhalation should be executed slowly and cautiously as he faces the bottom, so that the few remaining droplets of water will fall away from the mouthpiece and be blown out through the exhaust valve with the next exhalation. If a small amount of water is inadvertently drawn into your mouth, don't fight it. Swallow it. If you should accidentally lose your scuba mouthpiece while diving, simply reach over your right shoulder to your tank valve and find the regulator hose. Then slide your hand along the hose until you find the regulator mouthpiece, reinsert it, and clear it. The need to clear face mask and mouthpiece while diving is very common, so you should practice both procedures until they are second nature to you. If you persist in having difficulty with them, ask your instructor for assistance.

STEP 8: BUOYANCY CONTROL

Underwater you will become slightly heavier as you descend and slightly lighter as you con-

sume your air supply or ascend, but with help from your weight belt, your buoyancy compensator (B.C.) can provide you with push-button buoyancy control. If you do not have an automatic inflator on your B.C., it is only slightly more bothersome to control it manually.

When you enter the water, your B.C. should be inflated just enough to keep your head above water without kicking. To submerge, raise the B.C. inflator tube over your left shoulder and depress the purge button so the air in your B.C. can escape. When your B.C. is completely deflated, you should begin to sink, feet first. You can carry out your entire descent in this vertical feet-first posture (and save a good deal of wear and tear on your sinuses) or you can double over and continue your descent headfirst.

Once on the bottom you can readjust your B.C. until you attain neutral buoyancy—that is until you tend to rise with each inhalation and tend to sink with each exhalation. This will enable you to move in any direction you choose with perfect ease. If you change depth by more than a few feet, however, you will probably need to readjust your B.C. for neutral buoyancy again. When you are ready to ascend, "look up, reach up, and go up." As you ascend, your B.C. will tend to balloon because of the diminishing

Inflating your B.C.

Purging your B.C.

STEP 9: UNDERWATER SWIMMING

Swimming underwater requires a different technique than that normally used in surface swimming. For example, you should avoid using your hands except when changing directions, for excessive stroking may actually work against you. For maximum efficiency, use moderate size fins. Your body should be kept as streamlined as possible and your flutter kick should be slower and deeper and more powerful. You should avoid "bicycling" the knees and kick from the hip. Count on the flex of your fin blade during the downward thrust for most of your power. You should also utilize most of the glide from each kick cycle before beginning another. For cruising underwater, your kick cycles and your breathing cycles should be slow, easy, and coordinated.

STEP 10: BUILDING CONFIDENCE

Once you have gained proficiency in the above-mentioned water skills, your instructor will also test your knowledge of the various theories involved with diving. Then he will require you to execute some underwater drills that you may find rather difficult. These drills were not invented to haze or harass you. They were conceived in order to improve your skills and build your confidence in handling both your equipment and yourself under adverse conditions underwater. Every open water dive is a new experience under new conditions. Unexpected dangers can crop up at any time. It is the instructor's job to prepare you to meet and overcome the worst conditions that can possibly confront you underwater. The only way he can do that is to simulate those conditions while still in the safe and controlled environment of the instruction pool or beach. These drills are for your benefit, not the instructor's. So bear with him as he puts you "through the ropes" and learn as much as you can. As your personal repertoire of diving experiences grows, you will be glad you did. Herein follow a few of the exercises most commonly used by instructors.

pressure of the water. This will make you more buoyant as you approach the surface. Therefore, it is advisable to hold the purge button of your B.C. above your head throughout your ascent in order to maintain control. If your buoyancy becomes such that you begin to exceed the recommended ascent rate of 60 feet per minute (about the speed of your smallest exhaust bubbles) purge your B.C. of air until your ascent rate returns to normal. If need be, you can help slow down your ascent rate by flaring your body out horizontally so as to increase the drag. If, in spite of these efforts your B.C. continues to expand, you will be running the risk of accelerating beyond these normal means of control. In such cases you will have to activate the "dump valve" on your B.C. This will enable the air to escape from your B.C. at a much faster rate and allow you to quickly regain control of your ascent. Above all, remember to never hold your breath during ascent in order to avoid the dangers of an air embolism.

Underwater cruising.

STEP 11: BUDDY BREATHING AND EMERGENCY SWIMMING ASCENTS

In the unlikely event that you are suddenly deprived of air, you have three possible choices: (1) You can drown. (2) You can swim for the surface or (3) You can go for your buddy's air supply. Rejecting the first alternative as impractical, your best bet, if you are in water less than 30 feet deep, is to swim for the surface. As you ascend, the residual air in your tank will expand and thus provide a couple more breaths—enough to get you there even at the normal rate of ascent (60 feet per minute).

If in water deeper than 30 feet, your next best bet is to make an emergency ascent using a buddy's octopus (extra second-stage) regulator. If no octopus regulator is immediately available, you have no alternative but to share the same regulator with your buddy. Consequently it is advisable to learn and practice buddy breathing techniques under supervision of your instructor before you venture into open water.

All of these techniques are described in detail in Chapter 9, "Emergency Procedures."

If you see this "recall flag," return to the boat.

STEP 12: DONNING AND DOFFING

Donning and doffing is a drill designed to develop skill and confidence in yourself and your equipment. In practice, most instructors require students to place all their scuba equipment, including mask, snorkel, fins, and tank under a weight belt in 8 to 10 feet of water. Then the students are required to swim underwater to their equipment, don the equipment, swim some distance with the equipment on, then return to the point of departure, doff the equipment, and return to the starting point—all

without breaking the surface. Here's how:

As you approach your equipment, the first thing you must do is drape your weight belt over your thighs so that you won't have to fight to stay down. Then open the air valve of your tank, insert the mouthpiece, clear it, and begin breathing. Now place your face mask and clear it of water so that you can see. Don your air tank with an overhead lift and buckle up your harness. Buckle your weight belt and put on your fins. Then begin to swim.

At the end of the drill, simply reverse the procedure. First unbuckle your weight belt and drape it over your thighs. Then remove your fins. Unbuckle your harness and doff your tank by pitching forward and swinging the tank over your head. Do not let go of the mouthpiece until you doff your face mask, take a last deep breath of air, and shut the tank valve. Then take off for the shallow end, being careful to exhale slowly as you gradually ascend toward the surface.

A variation of the above is the "bail-out" drill in which the diver jumps into the water not wearing but carrying all his equipment with him. Once on the bottom, you proceed to don the equipment as above and then return to the surface fully "dressed." The secret here is to organize your equipment well before you jump.

STEP 13: BLIND DIVING

Many instructors put their students through a blind-diving drill to acquaint them with the inevitable underwater experience of being weightless without being able to see. I say "inevitable" because the slightest disturbance underwater can raise a cloud of silt that will suddenly turn your underwater environment as dark as night. In addition you may be asked to perform in water so murky that your sense of sight becomes useless. Therefore, it is advisable that you learn to "see" underwater through your sense of touch.

You begin this drill by first placing a piece of cardboard or foil over the inside of the faceplate of your face mask. Then your instructor asks you to submerge, swim several lengths of the pool, find some object that is placed on the bottom, and perform some minor task with it before returning to the surface.

Needless to say, blind diving is a weird sensation. In your weightless state, it is difficult to tell which direction is "up" unless you feel the direction of your bubbles or note which way you tend to float when inhaling deeply. When you are swimming blind underwater, it is best not to break contact with the bottom. By dragging one hand along the bottom and swimming along the edge of the pool, you can maintain direction. However, always protect your head by extending your other hand out in front of you.

Surface procedure: Inflate your B.C.

Pass up your weights, then your tank to helper.

If there's no boarding ladder, hoist yourself up on the gunwale . . .

. . . and twist into sitting position.

STEP 14: EXHAUSTING YOUR AIR SUPPLY

You should never remain submerged until your air supply is totally exhausted but at least once during your early training, you should experience how it feels to run out of air. This can be done without causing condensation within the tank by using an air tank equipped with a constant-reserve "J valve." This is an experience that you are likely to encounter if you continue diving, and it will demonstrate the following characteristics of air exhaustion: You will note that the airflow never stops abruptly. Breathing becomes gradually more difficult until you either ascend toward the surface or, if your tank has a J valve, you release your air reserve. As you ascend, the decreasing ambient water pressure will allow the residual air in the tank to expand and thus provide you with a few more breaths of air—at least enough air to get you back to the surface.

STEP 15: POSTDIVE CHECK

When the dive ends the work begins: first log your bottom time and determine your repetitive dive classification—even if you think you do not need to. Then all equipment should be rinsed in fresh water and gathered in one place. Check it off a list to make sure it is there. As you rinse it off in fresh water, inspect it for damage or necessary repairs. Be sure to close the valve on your air tank and purge the last bit of air from your regulator to release the air pressure before detaching the regulator. Otherwise the escaping air might damage the "O" ring in the valve seat. Drain the water from the mouthpiece by shaking it with the mouthpiece opening pointed downward. Dry and store the regulator in your equipment bag. Dry your rubber goods out in the shade. (Drying them in direct sunlight will eventually cause rubber goods to deteriorate.) You can sprinkle talcum powder or rubber preservative on the rubber goods before you store them to prolong their life. When you reach home base, dry them again and store them in a cool, dry place. Your B.C. should be dry and partially inflated and hung on a coat hanger together with your wet suit, if any.

7

Underwater Communications

UNDERWATER SOUND

Few sounds can be heard underwater as we hear them on land, and audio communications between submerged divers is virtually impossible without aids. The diver's ability to articulate underwater is sharply limited by the fact that he must hold a snorkel or breathing regulator clenched between his teeth. Since sound travels much faster underwater (4,800 feet per second), it is almost totally nondirectional. Thousands of dollars and man-hours have been spent in various attempts to develop an electronically amplified voice communications system for divers, but with limited success. Most scuba divers must rely solely on the old tried and true media of visual hand and line-pull signals. But even these have their limitations. You are left little choice but to settle on some basic kind of visual sign language with your diving buddy before each dive or else adjust to the idea that you are going to be practically incommunicado while underwater. If you dive often enough with the same diving buddy, you will find that your own private sign language will evolve of its own accord. Indeed, a kind of basic visual communications system has already evolved on an international level. With the kind permission of PADI International, I am reprinting herewith their national standard hand signals from the PADI Standards and Procedures Manual. The first ten hand signals are internationally used in over fifty countries that are affiliated with the Confédération Mondiale des Activités Subaquatiques (CMAS).

An underwater writing slate . . .

. . . is the clearest means of communication.

HAND SIGNALS

I'M OK.

I'M OK.

I'M OK.

HELP!

STOP!

LOOK!

SHOW ME YOUR GAUGE.

LEVEL OFF. ADJUST BUOYANCY.

BUDDY UP

JOIN HANDS.

COME HERE.

WHAT IS YOUR DEPTH (OR TIME)?

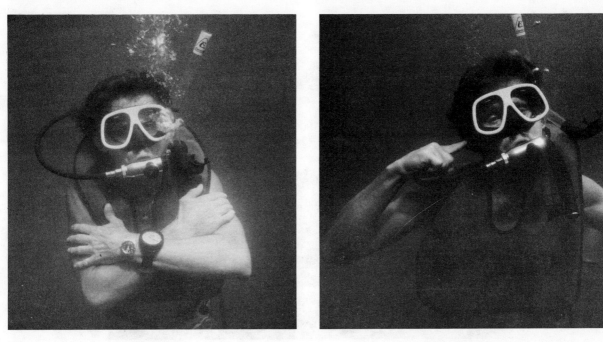

I'M COLD.   EAR TROUBLE.

YOU LEAD, I'LL FOLLOW.   GROUP UP (HERE).

I DON'T UNDERSTAND.

STAY WHERE YOU ARE.

I AM LOW ON AIR.

I AM OUT OF AIR.

I NEED TO BUDDY BREATHE.

U.S. NAVY LINE-PULL SIGNALS

ASCENT AND DESCENT (CODE: 4–2 PULLS)

Tender to Diver		**Diver to Tender**	
1 pull	OK?	1 pull	OK! Proceed.
2 pulls	Going down or stop and redescend.	2 pulls	Lower away or give slack.
3 pulls	Stop. Stand by to come up.	3 pulls	Stop. Take up slack.
4 pulls	Come up.	4 pulls	Take up.
2-1 pulls	I understand but wait a minute.	2-1 pulls	I understand but wait a minute.

SEARCHING (CODE: 7 PULLS)

1 pull	Stop and search there.	1 pull	I am stopping and searching here.
2 pulls	Follow where the life line leads you or (if using circle search) circle around.	2 pulls	I am following the line (diver must keep line taut) or circling.
3 pulls	Move to right.	3 pulls	I am moving to my right.
4 pulls	Move to left.	4 pulls	I am moving to my left.
5 pulls	You are there.	5 pulls	I have found objective.

EMERGENCY SIGNALS (NO CODE)

2-2-2 pulls	(Answer only.) I acknowledge you are fouled and need assistance.	2-2-2 pulls	I am fouled and need assistance from a diver.
3-3-3 pulls	I acknowledge you are fouled but are safe.	3-3-3 pulls	I am fouled but can clear myself.
4-4-4 pulls	Come up immediately!	4-4-4 pulls	Haul me up immediately!

LIFTING AND LOWERING (CODE: 2–4 PULLS)

1 pull	Stop.	1 pull	Stop.
2 pulls	Slack off.	2 pulls	Slack off.
3 pulls	Take up slack.	3 pulls	Take up slack.
4 pulls	Haul away.	4 pulls	Haul away.
5 pulls	Line coming.	5 pulls	Send me a line.

NIGHT DIVING SIGNALS
(Buddy at Distance)

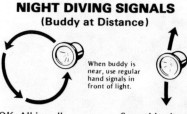

When buddy is near, use regular hand signals in front of light.

OK. All is well.
Large, slow circles with light.

Something is wrong.
Large, rapid up-and-down motions with arm extended.

WHISTLE SIGNAL

In diving, whistles are used only in emergency situations. Five or more short blasts on a whistle is an international distress signal for immediate assistance.

UNDERWATER RECALL
(SIREN, SPEAKER)

Surface and look to vessel for instructions.

Basic line-pull signals.

8
Night Diving

Diving at night adds a new dimension of fun and excitement to the sport. Many species of marine life that you might never see during the day mysteriously appear in abundance at night. Other species that you might be accustomed to seeing during daylight dives seem to vanish, but might be found sleeping peacefully in some weird location that you would never suspect. Many species that are shy and wary during daylight hours seem to be mesmerized by the diver's light. You can actually pick them up and gently fondle them. In short, darkness imbues the already enchanting world beneath the sea with an extra element of dreamlike beauty and intrigue that can make each night dive an unforgettable experience.

PREPARATION

You should be certified as an Open Water Diver or be a Basic Scuba Diver with at least ten open water dives to your credit before embarking on a night dive. Even then, you should have the direct supervision of a certified instructor who is experienced in night diving. It is highly recommended that students do a couple of practice night dives in a pool or in protected waters before they venture into the sea at night.

All divers in the group—and there should be no more than ten—should be familiar with the dive area before embarking on a dive at night. If possible, they should have all dived the same site in daylight within the previous two days.

The site selected should have easy access and exit and be located away from heavy boat traffic. Generally, it is better to start a night dive from a boat rather than from a beach. The boat must be legally equipped for night operations and preferably have plenty of auxiliary light power and an extra anchor.

Clear, calm water under the light of a full moon offers the best conditions for night diving. A natural or artificial reef offers the most abundant marine life. Regarding marine life, the later the dive the better, but anytime after dark will reveal striking behavioral changes in local sea life.

EQUIPMENT

In addition to the normal diving gear, every diver should be equipped with at least one underwater light and preferably two. The second light can be a chemical tube light or glowlight that can be worn around the diver's head, tank valve, or shoulder area. The tank valve is a good place for it, as this facilitates head counting by the group leader. The main light should be freshly serviced with at least three new D cells or one 6-volt battery pack. Surface lights from the boat or beach are very useful as they provide a kind of homing beacon for the divers below. The divers should limit their sorties to the vicinity of the boat and stay in a group. Buddies should be familiar with each other and if possible have dived with each other before. It is very easy to confuse your buddy with someone else at night. A divemaster or monitor should remain topside and be in constant attendance, perhaps on a float where he can lend immediate assistance.

NIGHT DIVE BRIEFING

After the predive check, the instructor or divemaster should brief all divers regarding the dive area and any local hazards that might be encountered—sea urchins, barnacles, rocks, surge, kelp, caves, etc. He should also brief them on special night diving problems such as disorientation, buddy separation, light failure, ascent rates and procedures. Any local rules or regulations regarding night diving should also

be covered. The same goes for special nighttime communications. When the group is over the dive site, he should have them turn around in the water so he can point out the distinguishing features of any landmarks and ask the divers to take a compass bearing on them. This will aid reorientation at the end of the dive.

NIGHT DIVE COMMUNICATIONS AND PROCEDURES

1. The "OK" signal at night is a slow movement of the underwater light in a circle to form a large "O".

2. The signal to request assistance is to rapidly move the light up and down with the arm extended. (On the surface, these signals should be made above the water.)

3. To gain attention, rapidly wave the light back and forth horizontally or bang on your tank with your light or your knife.

4. Your light can momentarily blind a diver if you shine it in his or her eyes. Shine it on the diver's chest or body instead.

5. Keep track of your buddy's light. If it is not visible, the light may be defective. If you lose your buddy, surface and look for your buddy with a 360-degree sweep. If your buddy is not on the surface, point your light downward so it may be seen.

6. When buddy lines are used (as they should be in murky waters) the line-pull signals should be reviewed during the predive briefing.

7. Remember that any hand signals must be made in front of your light or they can not be seen.

8. Review the distinguishing features of your dive buddy's attire before descent to avoid confusion in the water.

9. Whistles are excellent to gain attention on the surface in case of light difficulties.

BEACH OR BOAT RECOVERY

All night dives should end where they begin—either on the beach or aboard the boat. If the dive is launched from a beach, the point of entry and exit should be well protected from heavy surf and offer a flat, gently sloping and unobstructed bottom. Before the dive begins the dive site should be marked with a buoy—preferably one with a light. At least two lights should be placed on the beach in line with the dive site, one above the other and at least 100 feet apart. These lights will serve as range lights that will guide the divers back to their point of departure. Upon surfacing, the divers need only to line the two lights up, one above the other, and follow them back to the beach. They can be bonfires, battery-driven flashers, road beacons, or electrical lights, but whatever they are, they must be tended by someone who remains ashore during the dive and not be easily confused with other lights in the background.

If the dive is launched from a boat, the divers' hand lights should be lit when they enter the water. This is to avoid collisions. The boat can remain at anchor or follow the divers' lights while they are below. In either case, the deck should be well lit. Lights should be kept shining over each side of the boat so it can be easily seen by the divers from below. The boat operator should be familiar with night diving procedures and stop the engine as soon as the divers approach for reboarding. The divemaster should conduct a head count before the boat departs the dive area to make sure all divers are safely aboard.

POSTDIVE CHECK

The postdive check is the same as for daytime dives with the following exceptions. In the cool darkness of night things dry slowly and are easily lost or misplaced. It is useless to attempt to dry your gear at night before packing it. Rinse and pack it in a plastic bag (if you can) and leave the drying process until you get back to home base. Be sure you go back with everything you brought however.

A hot drink or soup goes down mighty well after a night dive. It also gives the divers a chance to compare notes and perhaps plan their next night dive adventure.

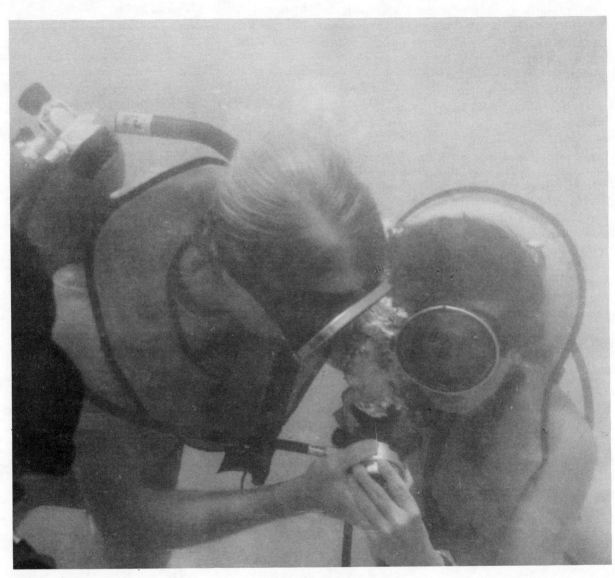

Buddy breathing.

9
Emergency Procedures

An old axiom states that "An ounce of prevention is worth a pound of cure." This is especially appropriate to diving. There are few emergency situations in diving that cannot be avoided or successfully handled if you carefully prepare and plan. Your preparation includes a thorough understanding of the theory of diving physics and physiology, of your own physique and psyche and how they work, of your equipment and how it works, and of the marine environment and how it works. This entails study, practice, and experience. Given these elements and a common measure of common sense, you should be able to avoid or cope with most emergency situations. Underwater accidents do occasionally happen, however, so if you care about life it is best that you be prepared for the eventuality. The most important thing you can do in this respect is to *plan your dive for safety and dive your plan safely*.

BUDDY SELECTION

Self-reliance is the most important element in diving safety, but after that comes the buddy system. Buddies are a team of divers that operate as one, each being responsible for the other's safety. It is nice to go diving with a friend, but in choosing a buddy, your buddy's experience, qualifications, and interests should be commensurate with your own. If one buddy is interested in photography and the other is interested in stalking fish, there is likely to be a conflict of interests that will tend to separate the buddies or at least distract them from their chosen interest. One should maintain constant awareness of one's buddy at all times. Murky waters may require the use of a buddy line in order to do this. This is a length of line that is looped (not tied) around the wrists of the two divers. Otherwise, the buddies should maintain visual contact. If your buddy becomes lost, bang on your tank with your knife and stay where you are until your buddy finds you. If your buddy does not answer or show up after a predetermined amount of time (say five minutes), you should both meet on the surface and then dive again. This amounts to lost diving time, however, and it can be avoided by maintaining buddy contact while below.

You and your chosen buddy should run through your predive check together. This includes not only your plans and equipment but also precisely what signals and emergency procedures you plan to use. It should also include any special desires or apprehensions that one might have. You should also determine who will lead and who will follow.

Through planning you can prevent a surprise or problem from developing into an emergency situation. Should one arise however, DON'T PANIC. Stop and think before you act and then act as you have been trained. In an emergency, panic is the diver's worst enemy, for it robs you of both your breath and your logic when you need them most.

EQUIPMENT FAILURE

Since all scuba equipment is made to rigid standards, the chances of diver failure are much greater than the chances of equipment failure. All scuba regulators are made so that if they should fail, they will fail safe. That is, the airflow will never abruptly stop. Rather a continuous flow of air will issue from the regulator, and thus give you time to reach the surface. A sudden rupture in the rubber diaphragm of the regulator will allow water to enter on inhalation, but by manually depressing the purge button on the second stage, you will induce a constant flow and thus be able to reach the surface. Should you otherwise be suddenly deprived of your air supply, you have three alternatives that are stated here in order of preference: (1) Make an emergency swimming ascent. (2) Breathe from an octopus regulator, if any. (3) Buddy breathe. We will consider these alternatives below in reverse order of their preference. All of them should be practiced, but only under the supervision of your instructor.

Buddy Breathing

Buddy breathing is the act of two or more divers sharing one breathing regulator. Once you get the hang of it, the most difficult part of buddy breathing is making known your urgent need to do it. In time of a real emergency, the actual method might vary according to circumstances, but here is the accepted procedure.

1. Attract your buddy's attention. Indicate that you are out of air and need to buddy breathe by wiping your finger across your throat in the traditional cutthroat gesture and removing your regulator with one hand while pointing to your buddy's regulator with the other.

2. Indicate your desire to buddy breathe by pointing to your buddy's mouthpiece and then to your own as you take it from your mouth.

3. As you reach for your buddy's regulator with your right hand, grasp his right shoulder strap or even his tank valve with your left hand. Your buddy should follow suit, placing his right hand on top of yours as he or she offers the regulator to you.

4. As you start breathing from your buddy's regulator, both of you start kicking for the surface. After a couple of breaths, pass the regulator back to your buddy. When not breathing constantly emit a stream of bubbles through pursed lips as you ascend. It is the donor (your buddy in this case) who controls both the passing of the regulator and the ascent rate.

5. Keep repeating the last two steps, remembering to continuously exhale, when not breathing, until you have reached the surface and can inflate your B.C.

In practice sessions, you can swim back and forth along the bottom of the pool or beach by grasping each other's tank valve and swimming side by side. *Caution: Never hold your breath.*

Octopus Breathing

All instructors and many novice divers now carry a second octopus regulator which taps into the high-pressure outlet on the first stage of their scuba. Octopus regulators greatly facilitate emergency ascents as they permit two people to breathe off the same tank of air simultaneously without the necessity of passing a single regulator. Should you ever need it, all you need do is communicate your intentions, grasp the octopus regulator, clear it of water and breathe normally as you both head for safety. If you are equipped with an octopus rig and your main regulator fails, chances are that you can breathe from your own octopus rig. Whenever you share air on ascent, you should continue to do so until you both reach the surface.

Emergency Swimming Ascents

Because of the risk of embolism, all practice emergency swimming ascents are conducted with a weighted descent/ascent line under the personal supervision of your instructor. After you have adjusted to being underwater, the instructor grasps you by your harness strap or tank valve and signals that your air supply has suddenly stopped. Looking and reaching for the surface, you kick off the bottom and begin exhaling continuously through your regulator. You can sing "oh" or "ah" through it if you like. As you rise toward the surface, your B.C. will expand and provide more buoyancy. (In an actual emergency you would drop your weight belt as you left the bottom.) Expansion of the residual air in your tank would give you one or two additional breaths while you ascend. The ascent rate should be the normal 60 feet per minute, although this might be exceeded in a true emergency. Throughout the ascent the instructor should remain slightly above you with one hand on the ascent line. If he thinks you might be going too fast, he should signal you to slow down or to increase your exhalation. If for any reason he wants to abort the ascent, he can simply wrap a leg around the ascent line and stop you. On other occasions he may ask you to practice emergency ascents while buddy breathing or octopus breathing. In an actual emergency, the swimming ascent is your best bet if you are within 30 feet of the surface and have free access to it. If you are deeper than 30 feet and have a buddy nearby, an octopus breathing ascent or a buddy breathing ascent is recommended in that order.

Use a "free ascent" only as the last resort—if your gear is hopelessly entangled in something like fish netting, for example. If there is no buddy nearby and you seriously doubt that you can reach the surface by swimming, you can do a buoyant ascent by "popping" the CO_2 cartridge on your B.C. and exhaling continuously as you ascend to the surface. Your B.C. will tend to balloon as you approach the surface. If your speed should accelerate beyond your ability to control it by flaring your body out horizontally, then pull the dump valve on your B.C. to purge it of air as you continue your ascent by swimming. Free and buoyant ascents are so dangerous that they are no longer permitted in training sessions.

RESCUE PROCEDURES

It is the duty of every diver to go to the rescue whenever one sees that another diver is in distress. Since this is basic, you must learn the techniques of rescue and resuscitation in your basic training. There are five basic skills needed to meet rescue emergencies in the water: (1) providing a victim with air if needed, (2) getting the victim to the surface, (3) getting the victim to a point of safety, (4) administering artificial respiration in the water if it is required, and (5) giving cardiopulmonary resuscitation (CPR).

Providing emergency air beneath the surface was covered in the section on emergency ascents.

Getting a victim to the surface involves considerable risk to both the rescuer and the rescued. Semiconscious and even unconscious victims sometimes grasp onto anything that touches them with a death grip that is difficult to break. Sometimes victims instinctively lock their throats shut. This is called the "trapdoor effect." It leaves the victim liable to air embolism. If you encounter a victim on the bottom, unfasten his weight belt and inflate his B.C. (pop the CO_2 cartridge, if any) and get the victim to the surface as quickly as possible. En route, keep his head and chin extended to allow the free passage of air. Note if any air bubbles come out of his mouth or regulator. This would indicate that there is still air in his lungs and that you can start mouth-to-mouth resuscitation immediately upon surfacing. If there are no bubbles, you might try inserting his regulator into his mouth and then alternately squeezing his abdomen and hitting the purge button on his regulator to stimulate respiration. As you ascend, any residual air in the lungs will expand and help purge the lungs of water. Once you hit the surface, immediately call for help and start mouth-to-mouth resuscitation. The procedure for this is described in Chapter 14 on Diving First Aid. Once you reach land or a boat, or if help arrives, check the pulse at the jugular vein in the neck. If no pulse, have someone else administer cardiopulmonary resuscitation (CPR), also described in the diving first aid chapter. Continue mouth-to-mouth resuscitation until a doctor arrives with further instructions.

10

U.S. Navy Decompression Tables and Practices

This chapter should never be needed by the sport diver. Dives requiring decompression as a precaution against the bends are for pros only. They should never be undertaken for the mere sake of pleasure; the added risks far outproportion any added pleasure. However, there is always the chance that a no decompression dive might become one that does require decompression because you have neglected to stay within the no-decompression depth-time limits—or an unforeseen emergency has arisen. In all events, it is essential that you learn how to plan and execute a decompression dive and how to decompress a diver who needs it in an emergency.

PLANNING

Sports divers should never plan a decompression dive, but every minute of a decompression dive must be thoroughly planned. The predive planning is basically the same as that described for an open water dive, but is more intensive.

Weather and Water Conditions

Weather and water conditions become doubly important, for a decompression dive that must be interrupted by storm conditions can lead to serious complications and perhaps the bends.

Air Supply

During your predive check, your air supply deserves special consideration. You will need enough air to see you through your bottom time and through your decompression stages as well. This might involve a double air tank block or yoking two single tanks together. (Decompression dives are the only dives on which I recommend the use of double 3,000 p.s.i., 80-cubic-foot tanks.) It might also involve taking a spare tank of air or a hookah diving rig along with you to see you through your decompression stages. Air tanks should be charged to their maximum working pressures, including the 10 percent overcharge allowed by the Department of Transportation (DOT).

Decompression Stage Marker

You must know how much time at what depth you will have to decompress before beginning your dive. After sounding the depth, calculate your depth-time ratio and make certain that it is precisely accurate. Then refer to the proper table in the U.S. Navy Standard Air Decompression Tables for the correct information. Slide a heavy shackle or weight to the proper depth over your descent line and make it fast. If need be, an extra regulator and tank or hookah rig can be attached to the weight for use during decompression. The weight will not only mark the proper decompression depth but will provide extra weight needed to stabilize you while you decompress.

Light

The deeper you dive the less light you have to see by. It might be wise to carry a pressure-proof underwater light with you during deep dives. If visibility is poor you might use a buddy line.

SPECIAL CONSIDERATIONS

Timekeeper and Log

In case of a mishap, adequate recompression and other treatment cannot be prescribed unless all pertinent information is available. Therefore one man on the surface should have the responsibility for keeping a log of your dive. The log should include the time you left the surface, the time you reached bottom, bottom time, type of work done, time you left bottom, decompression time, and time you returned to surface, as well as any special remarks. It is the timekeeper's job to inform your tender when you should next move. Because this responsibility is easily neglected, the timekeeper should have no other duties if possible.

Surface Tender

One man on the surface should tend your lifeline (if you have one), maintain signal contact with you, and see that you have adequate air to complete your decompression. He receives instructions from the timekeeper to signal you when to ascend and when to change your decompression stage. If no other solution is available, one man can act as timekeeper and surface tender, but he should not handle more than one buddy pair at a time.

Recompression Chamber

Before attempting a decompression dive, you should verify the location of the nearest recompression chamber and the quickest way to get there in case of a mishap. The local U.S. Coast Guard office or the nearest retail dive store will give you instructions for handling emergency decompression cases in your area and the address and phone number of the nearest chamber.

U.S. Navy Decompression Tables

A copy of the U.S. Navy Decompression Tables must be taken on all dive trips requiring decompression. Only in this way can you determine the correct amount of decompression time in accordance with your depth-time ratio. Waterproof tables printed on plastic are available at all dive retail stores.

Standby Divers

One or more standby divers must be fully dressed and ready to go to the aid of a diver in distress at an instant's notice. Ideally, one man should be stationed on the descent line at the no-decompression limit, ready to go at a signal from either the diver or the tender, while a second man is standing by on the surface fully prepared to assist. If divers intend to enter a sunken wreck or other submarine structure, they must wear a buddy line, and the first standby diver must station himself outside the wreck and tend the lifeline, which is mandatory on such dives. The standby diver should carry a spare tank of air with regulator.

THE DIVE

Descent and Overexertion

It is vital that you expend as little energy as possible throughout a deep dive. At great depths the pressures are so great and the air so dense that the mere physical act of breathing can be very taxing. Once you lose your breath you are not likely to get it back until you ascend. Therefore, physical action should be kept to a minimum. Once on the bottom, swim as little as possible and move as if in very slow motion. Do not lose track of your descent line if possible. Think! Do not let the excitement of the dive run away with your control. Keep your lungs well ventilated and—think some more! Rationalize every move. If you are deep enough to decompress, you are probably deep enough to suffer nitrogen narcosis. Concentrate on what you have to do and how to do it. Keep an eye on your watch and depth gauge, and do not hesitate to begin your ascent when your bottom time is up. If you go deeper than you had planned during your bottom time, do not fail to consider this in doing your decompression stages. If possible, always allow yourself a safety factor of several minutes when doing decompression.

Ascent and Decompression Techniques

Ascend via the descent line at a rate not exceeding 60 feet per minute to the first decompression-stage marker. Do not exceed this rate, as it is also part of your decompression process. To repeat an earlier exhortation, ascend

no faster than your smallest bubbles. At that point, there are four ways to execute your decompression time in relation to air supply:

1. If decompression requirements are small, your original tank may provide all the air you need for decompression. In any case you should stick with your original tank until you have opened your reserve. Then you can switch to one of the other three methods, which follow.

2. Surface Supply: an air hose can supply air to a hookah rig from a small compressor on the surface. The hookah rig is weighted and lowered down the descent line to the appropriate depth. You can shift to the hookah rig at the first decompression stop and use it throughout the entire decompression procedure.

3. Second scuba tank: a second scuba tank can be lowered down the descent line to the first decompression stage to supply the air needed for decompression.

4. Surface Decompression (Recompression): if you are fortunate enough to have a working decompression chamber and crew standing by on the surface, they can replace all the water decompression provided the diver loses no time in entering the chamber and returning to simulated decompression depth, as prescribed in the U.S. Navy Recompression Tables. Sport divers are not likely to have such equipment available, however.

Throughout your decompression, you should keep contact with your tender on the surface. Line-pull signals or a slate on the end of a line are satisfactory. If possible, the last decompression stop should be given a few extra minutes as a safety precaution. If, for any reason, your decompression time is interrupted and cannot be resumed quickly, you should assume that you will need recompression (surface decompression) and head for the nearest recompression chamber immediately, without waiting for symptoms of the bends (decompression sickness, or compressed air illness). If no recompression chamber is within reasonable distance, or no transportation facilities are readily available, telephone the U.S. Navy Diving Unit at (904) 234-4353 or the Divers Alert Network (DAN) at Duke University—telephone (919) 684-8111—for the location of the nearest decompression chamber and how to get there.

In emergencies, the U.S. Coast Guard can provide air transportation to a victim, but it must be paid for.

U.S. NAVY AIR DECOMPRESSION TABLES

Decompression is the gradual elimination of inert gases—mostly nitrogen—which have dissolved into the bloodstream under pressure. Since, according to Henry's Law, the solution and dissolution of gases in a liquid occur at a rate almost directly proportional to the pressure of the gases, and since, according to Boyle's Law, the pressure a diver is exposed to varies in direct proportion to his depth, it is possible to calculate the exact amount of time required to saturate or desaturate the diver's bloodstream. Calculations governing the amount of time required to desaturate the bloodstream after exposure to all practical diving depths are given in the U.S. Navy Air Decompression Tables. Since these tables are based on physical laws of nature, there is no changing, interpolating, or modifying them. They must be followed strictly; any failure to do so could result in permanent injury, paralysis, or even death.

Unfortunately, there are other factors influencing the saturation and desaturation of the bloodstream which vary with the individual and his environment. Obesity and temperature are two examples. The U.S. Navy found that a decompression table safely covering all such extraordinary ramifications would be impractical, so it has published a standard to go by. This means though that following the U.S. Navy Decompression Tables to the letter will not always assure adequate decompression. Thus any dive requiring decompression or recompression is a calculated risk and should not be attempted unless unavoidable.

In the following pages, you'll find the U.S. Navy Standard Air Decompression Table, Repetitive Dive Tables, and explanations just as they appear in the official *U.S. Navy Diving Manual,* which is available from the United States Government Printing Office, Washington, D.C. When in doubt, always act in your own favor by adding to the decompression time required. Never shorten decompression time for mere convenience. Record the details of depth and time in case recompression treatment is required. Always know the location and telephone number of the nearest recompression chamber and the quickest route to it. Symptoms and treatment of the bends appear in Chapter 14, "Diving First Aid."

Definition of Terms

Those terms which are frequently used in discussions of the decompression tables are defined as follows:

Depth—when used to indicate the depth of a dive, means the maximum depth attained during the dive, measured in feet of seawater.

Bottom Time—the total elapsed time from when the diver leaves the surface in descent to the time (next whole minute) that he begins his ascent, measured in minutes.

Decompression Stop—specific depth at which a diver must remain for a specified length of time to eliminate inert gases from his body.

Decompression Schedule—specific decompression procedure for a given combination of depth and bottom time as listed in a decompression table; it is normally indicated as feet/minutes.

Single Dive—any dive conducted at least 12 hours after a previous dive.

Residual Nitrogen—nitrogen gas that is still dissolved in a diver's tissues after he has surfaced.

Surface Interval—the time which a diver has spent on the surface following a dive; beginning as soon as the diver surfaces and ending as soon as he starts his next descent.

Repetitive Dive—any dive conducted within a 12-hour period of a previous dive.

Repetitive Group Designation—a letter which relates directly to the amount of residual nitrogen in a diver's body for a 12-hour period following a dive.

Residual Nitrogen Time—an amount of time, in minutes, which must be added to the bottom time of a repetitive dive to compensate for the nitrogen still in solution in a diver's tissues from a previous dive.

Single Repetitive Dive—a dive for which the bottom time used to select the decompression schedule is the sum of the residual nitrogen time and the actual bottom time of the dive.

Table Selection

The following tables are actual decompression tables:

Standard Air Decompression Table
No-Decompression Limits and Repetitive Group Designation Table

They present a series of decompression schedules which must be rigidly followed during an ascent following an air dive. Each decompression table has specific conditions which justify its selection. These conditions are basically depth and duration of the dive to be conducted, availability of a recompression chamber, availability of an oxygen breathing system within the chamber, and specific environmental conditions such as sea state, water temperature, etc.

The Residual Nitrogen Timetable for Repetitive Air Dives provides information relating to the planning of repetitive dives.

General Use of Decompression Tables

Variations in Rate of Ascent   The rate of ascent for all dives is 60 feet per minute (fpm).

. . . Since conditions sometimes prevent this ascent rate from being maintained, a general set of instructions has been established to compensate for any variations in rate of ascent. These instructions, along with examples of their application, are listed below:

Example No. 1

Condition—Rate of ascent less than 60 fpm, delay occurs greater than 50 fsw (feet of seawater).

Procedure—Increase BOTTOM TIME by the difference between the actual ascent time and the time if 60 fpm were used.

A dive was conducted to 120 feet with a bottom time of 60 minutes. According to the 120/60 decompression schedule of the Standard Air Decompression Table, the first decompression stop is at 30 feet. During the ascent the diver was delayed at 100 feet and it actually took 5 minutes for him to reach his 30 foot decompression stop. If an ascent rate of 60 fpm were used, it

would have taken him 1 minute 30 seconds to ascend from 120 feet to 30 feet. The difference between the actual and 60 fpm ascent times is 3 minutes 30 seconds. Increase the bottom time of the dive from 60 minutes to 63 minutes 30 seconds and continue decompression according to the schedule which represents this new bottom time . . . the 120/70 schedule. (Note from the Standard Air Decompression Table that this 3 minute 30 second delay increased the diver's total decompression time from 71 minutes to 92 minutes 30 seconds—an increase of 21 minutes 30 seconds).

Example No. 2

Condition—Rate of ascent less than 60 fpm, delay occurs less than 50 fsw.

Procedure—Increase TIME OF FIRST DECOMPRESSION STOP by difference between the actual ascent time and the time if 60 fpm were used.

A dive was conducted to 120 feet with a bottom time of 60 minutes. From the Standard Air Decompression Table the first decompression stop is at 30 fsw. During the ascent, the diver was delayed at 40 feet and it actually took 5 minutes for him to reach his 30-foot stop. As in the preceding example, the correct ascent time should have been 1 minute 30 seconds causing a delay of 3 minutes 30 seconds. Increase the length of the 30 foot decompression stop by 3 minutes 30 seconds. Instead of 2 minutes, the diver must spend 5 minutes 30 seconds at 30 feet. (Note that in this example, the diver's total decompression time is increased by only 7 minutes; the 3 minute 30 second delay in ascent plus the additional 3 minutes 30 seconds he had to spend at 30 feet).

Example No. 3

Condition—Rate of ascent greater than 60 fpm, no decompression required, bottom time places the diver within 10 minutes of decompression schedule requiring decompression.

Procedure—Stop at 10 feet for the time that it would have taken to ascend at a rate of 60 fpm.

A dive was conducted to 100 feet with a bottom time of 22 minutes. During ascent, the diver momentarily lost control of his buoyancy and increased his ascent rate to 75 fpm. Normally, the 100/25 decompression schedule of the Standard Air Decompression Table would be used, which is a no-decompression schedule. However, the actual bottom time of 22 minutes is within 10 minutes of the 100/30 dive schedule which does require decompression. The diver must stop at 10 feet and remain there for 1 minute and 40 seconds, the time that it would have taken him to ascend at 60 fpm.

Example No. 4

Condition—Rate of ascent greater than 60 fpm, decompression required.

Procedure—Stop 10 feet below the first decompression stop for the remaining time that it would have taken if a rate of 60 fpm were used.

A diver ascending from a 120/50 scheduled dive takes only 30 seconds to reach his 20-foot decompression stop. At a rate of 60 fpm his ascent time should have been 1 minute 40 seconds. He must return to 30 feet and remain there for the difference between 1 minute 40 seconds and 30 seconds, or 1 minute 10 seconds.

The rate of ascent between stops is not critical, and variations from the specified rate require no compensation.

Selection of Decompression Schedule The decompression schedules of all the tables are given in 10- or 20-foot depth increments and, usually, 10-minute bottom time increments. Depth and bottom time combinations from actual dives, however, rarely exactly match one of the decompression schedules listed in the table being used. As assurance that the selected decompression schedule is always conservative: (a) always select the schedule depth to be equal to or the next depth greater than the actual depth to which the dive was conducted, and (b) always select the schedule bottom time to be equal to or the next longer bottom time than the actual bottom time of the dive.

If the Standard Air Decompression Table, for example, was being used to select the correct schedule for a dive to 97 feet for 31 minutes, decompression would be carried out in accordance with the 100/40 schedule.

NEVER ATTEMPT TO INTERPOLATE BETWEEN DECOMPRESSION SCHEDULES

If the diver was exceptionally cold during the dive, or if his work load was relatively strenuous, the next longer decompression schedule than the one he would normally follow should be selected. For example, the normal schedule for a dive to 90 feet for 34 minutes would be the 90/40 schedule. If the diver were exceptionally cold or fatigued, he should decompress according to the 90/50 schedule.

No-Decompression Limits and Repetitive Group Designation Table for No-Decompression Air Dives The No-Decompression Table serves two purposes. First it summarizes all the depth and bottom time combinations for which no decompression is required. Secondly, it provides the repetitive group designation for each no-decompression dive. Even though decompression is not required, an amount of nitrogen remains in the diver's tissues after every dive. If he dives again within a 12-hour period, the diver must consider this residual nitrogen when calculating his decompression.

Each depth listed in the No-Decompression Table has a corresponding no-decompression limit given in minutes. This limit is the maximum bottom time that a diver may spend at that depth without requiring decompression. The columns to the right of the no-decompression limits column are used to determine the repetitive group designation which must be assigned to a diver subsequent to every dive. To find the repetitive group designation enter the table at the depth equal to or next greater than the actual depth of the dive. Follow that row to the right to the bottom time equal to or next greater than the actual bottom time of the dive. Follow that column upward to the repetitive group designation.

Depths above 35 feet do not have a specific no-decompression limit. They are, however, restricted in that they only provide repetitive group designations for bottom times up to between 5 and 6 hours. These bottom times are considered the limitations of the No-Decom-

U.S. NAVY AIR DECOMPRESSION TABLE

NO-DECOMPRESSION LIMITS AND REPETITIVE GROUP DESIGNATION TABLE FOR NO-DECOMPRESSION AIR DIVES

Depth (feet)	No-decompression limits (min)	A	B	C	D	E	F	G	H	I	J	K	L	M	N	O
10		60	120	210	300											
15		35	70	110	160	225	350									
20		25	50	75	100	135	180	240	325							
25		20	35	55	75	100	125	160	195	245	315					
30		15	30	45	60	75	95	120	145	170	205	250	310			
35	310	5	15	25	40	50	60	80	100	120	140	160	190	220	270	310
40	200	5	15	25	30	40	50	70	80	100	110	130	150	170	200	
50	100		10	15	25	30	40	50	60	70	80	90	100			
60	60		10	15	20	25	30	40	50	55	60					
70	50		5	10	15	20	30	35	40	45	50					
80	40		5	10	15	20	25	30	35	40						
90	30		5	10	12	15	20	25	30							
100	25		5	7	10	15	20	22	25							
110	20			5	10	13	15	20								
120	15			5	10	12	15									
130	10			5	8	10										
140	10			5	7	10										
150	5			5												
160	5				5											
170	5				5											
180	5				5											
190	5				5											

Repetitive group at the beginning of the surface interval

```
A   0:10
    12:00*
B   0:10   2:11
    2:10   12:00*
C   0:10   1:40   2:50
    1:39   2:49   12:00*
D   0:10   1:10   2:39   5:49
    1:09   2:38   5:48   12:00*
E   0:10   0:55   1:58   3:23   6:33
    0:54   1:57   3:22   6:32   12:00*
F   0:10   0:46   1:30   2:29   3:58   7:06
    0:45   1:29   2:28   3:57   7:05   12:00*
G   0:10   0:41   1:16   2:00   2:59   4:26   7:36
    0:40   1:15   1:59   2:58   4:25   7:35   12:00*
H   0:10   0:37   1:07   1:42   2:24   3:21   4:50   8:00
    0:36   1:06   1:41   2:23   3:20   4:49   7:59   12:00*
I   0:10   0:34   1:00   1:30   2:03   2:45   3:44   5:13   8:22
    0:33   0:59   1:29   2:02   2:44   3:43   5:12   8:21   12:00*
J   0:10   0:32   0:55   1:20   1:48   2:21   3:05   4:03   5:41   8:41
    0:31   0:54   1:19   1:47   2:20   3:04   4:02   5:40   8:40   12:00*
K   0:10   0:29   0:50   1:12   1:36   2:04   2:39   3:22   4:20   5:49   8:59
    0:28   0:49   1:11   1:35   2:03   2:38   3:21   4:19   5:48   8:58   12:00*
L   0:10   0:27   0:46   1:05   1:26   1:50   2:20   2:54   3:37   4:36   6:03   9:13
    0:26   0:45   1:04   1:25   1:49   2:19   2:53   3:36   4:35   6:02   9:12   12:00*
M   0:10   0:26   0:43   1:00   1:19   1:40   2:06   2:35   3:09   3:53   4:50   6:19   9:29
    0:25   0:42   0:59   1:18   1:39   2:05   2:34   3:08   3:52   4:49   6:18   9:28   12:00*
N   0:10   0:25   0:40   0:55   1:12   1:31   1:54   2:19   2:48   3:23   4:05   5:04   6:33   9:44
    0:24   0:39   0:54   1:11   1:30   1:53   2:18   2:47   3:22   4:04   5:03   6:32   9:43   12:00*
O   0:10   0:24   0:37   0:52   1:08   1:25   1:44   2:05   2:30   3:00   3:34   4:18   5:17   6:45   9:55
    0:23   0:36   0:51   1:07   1:24   1:43   2:04   2:29   2:59   3:33   4:17   5:16   6:44   9:54   12:00*
    0:10   0:23   0:35   0:49   1:03   1:19   1:37   1:56   2:18   2:43   3:11   3:46   4:30   5:28   6:57   10:06
    0:22   0:34   0:48   1:02   1:18   1:36   1:55   2:17   2:42   3:10   3:45   4:29   5:27   6:56   10:05   12:00*
```

REPETITIVE DIVE DEPTH	Z	O	N	M	L	K	J	I	H	G	F	E	D	C	B	A
40	257	241	213	187	161	138	116	101	87	73	61	49	37	25	17	7
50	169	160	142	124	111	99	87	76	66	56	47	38	29	21	13	6
60	122	117	107	97	88	79	70	61	52	44	36	30	24	17	11	5
70	100	96	87	80	72	64	57	50	43	37	31	26	20	15	9	4
80	84	80	73	68	61	54	48	43	38	32	28	23	18	13	8	4
90	73	70	64	58	53	47	43	38	33	29	24	20	16	11	7	3
100	64	62	57	52	48	43	38	34	30	26	22	18	14	10	7	3
110	57	55	51	47	42	38	34	31	27	24	20	16	13	10	6	3
120	52	50	46	43	39	35	32	28	25	21	18	15	12	9	6	3
130	46	44	40	38	35	31	28	25	22	19	16	13	11	8	6	3
140	42	40	38	35	32	29	26	23	20	18	15	12	10	7	5	2
150	40	38	35	32	30	27	24	22	19	17	14	12	9	7	5	2
160	37	36	33	31	28	26	23	20	18	16	13	11	8	6	4	2
170	35	34	31	29	26	24	22	19	17	15	13	10	8	6	4	2
180	32	31	29	27	25	22	20	18	16	14	12	10	8	6	4	2
190	31	30	28	26	24	21	19	17	15	13	11	10	8	6	4	2

RESIDUAL NITROGEN TIMES (MINUTES)

U.S. NAVY AIR DECOMPRESSION TABLE

Depth (feet)	Bottom time (min)	Time first stop (min:sec)	50	40	30	20	10	Total ascent (min:sec)	Repetitive group
40	200						0	0:40	*
	210	0:30					2	2:40	N
	230	0:30					7	7:40	N
	250	0:30					11	11:40	O
	270	0:30					15	15:40	O
	300	0:30					19	19:40	Z
50	100						0	0:50	*
	110	0:40					3	3:50	L
	120	0:40					5	5:50	M
	140	0:40					10	10:50	M
	160	0:40					21	21:50	N
	180	0:40					29	29:50	O
	200	0:40					35	35:50	O
	220	0:40					40	40:50	Z
	240	0:40					47	47:50	Z
60	60						0	1:00	*
	70	0:50					2	3:00	K
	80	0:50					7	8:00	K
	100	0:50					14	15:00	L
	120	0:50					26	27:00	M
	140	0:50					39	40:00	N
	160	0:50					48	49:00	O
	180	0:50					56	57:00	Z
	200	0:40				1	69	71:00	Z
70	50						0	1:10	*
	60	1:00					8	9:10	K
	70	1:00					14	15:10	L
	80	1:00					18	19:10	M
	90	1:00					23	24:10	N
	100	1:00					33	34:10	N
	110	0:50				2	41	44:10	O
	120	0:50				4	47	52:10	O
	130	0:50				6	52	59:10	O
	140	0:50				8	56	65:10	Z
	150	0:50				9	61	71:10	Z
	160	0:50				13	72	86:10	Z
	170	0:50				19	79	99:10	Z
80	40						0	1:20	*
	50	1:10					10	11:20	K
	60	1:10					17	18:20	L
	70	1:10					23	24:20	M
	80	1:00				2	31	34:20	N
	90	1:00				7	39	47:20	N
	100	1:00				11	46	58:20	O
	110	1:00				13	53	67:20	O
	120	1:00				17	56	74:20	Z
	130	1:00				19	63	83:20	Z
	140	1:00				26	69	96:20	Z
	150	1:00				32	77	110:20	Z
90	30						0	1:30	*
	40	1:20					7	8:30	J
	50	1:20					18	19:30	L
	60	1:20					25	26:30	M
	70	1:10				7	30	38:30	N
	80	1:10				13	40	54:30	N
	90	1:10				18	48	67:30	O
	100	1:10				21	54	76:30	Z
	110	1:10				24	61	86:30	Z
	120	1:10				32	68	101:30	Z
	130	1:00			5	36	74	116:30	Z

* See No Decompression Table for repetitive groups

U.S. NAVY AIR DECOMPRESSION TABLE

Depth (feet)	Bottom time (min)	Time first stop (min:sec)	Decompression stops (feet)					Total ascent (min:sec)	Repetitive group
			50	40	30	20	10		
100	25						0	1:40	•
	30	1:30					3	4:40	I
	40	1:30					15	16:40	K
	50	1:20				2	24	27:40	L
	60	1:20				9	28	38:40	N
	70	1:20				17	39	57:40	O
	80	1:20				23	48	72:40	O
	90	1:10			3	23	57	84:40	Z
	100	1:10			7	23	66	97:40	Z
	110	1:10			10	34	72	117:40	Z
	120	1:10			12	41	78	132:40	Z
110	20						0	1:50	•
	25	1:40					3	4:50	H
	30	1:40					7	8:50	J
	40	1:30				2	21	24:50	L
	50	1:30				8	26	35:50	M
	60	1:30				18	36	55:50	N
	70	1:20			1	23	48	73:50	O
	80	1:20			7	23	57	88:50	Z
	90	1:20			12	30	64	107:50	Z
	100	1:20			15	37	72	125:50	Z
120	15						0	2:00	•
	20	1:50					2	4:00	H
	25	1:50					6	8:00	I
	30	1:50					14	16:00	J
	40	1:40				5	25	32:00	L
	50	1:40				15	31	48:00	N
	60	1:30			2	22	45	71:00	O
	70	1:30			9	23	55	89:00	O
	80	1:30			15	27	63	107:00	Z
	90	1:30			19	37	74	132:00	Z
	100	1:30			23	45	80	150:00	Z
130	10						0	2:10	•
	15	2:00					1	3:10	F
	20	2:00					4	6:10	H
	25	2:00					10	12:10	J
	30	1:50				3	18	23:10	M
	40	1:50				10	25	37:10	N
	50	1:40			3	21	37	63:10	O
	60	1:40			9	23	52	86:10	Z
	70	1:40			16	24	61	103:10	Z
	80	1:30		3	19	35	72	131:10	Z
	90	1:30		8	19	45	80	154:10	Z
140	10						0	2:20	•
	15	2:10					2	4:20	G
	20	2:10					6	8:20	I
	25	2:00				2	14	18:20	J
	30	2:00				5	21	28:20	K
	40	1:50			2	16	26	46:20	N
	50	1:50			6	24	44	76:20	O
	60	1:50			16	23	56	97:20	Z
	70	1:40		4	19	32	68	125:20	Z
	80	1:40		10	23	41	79	155:20	Z

* See No Decompression Table for repetitive groups

(Courtesy PADI International)

PADI® DIVE TABLES

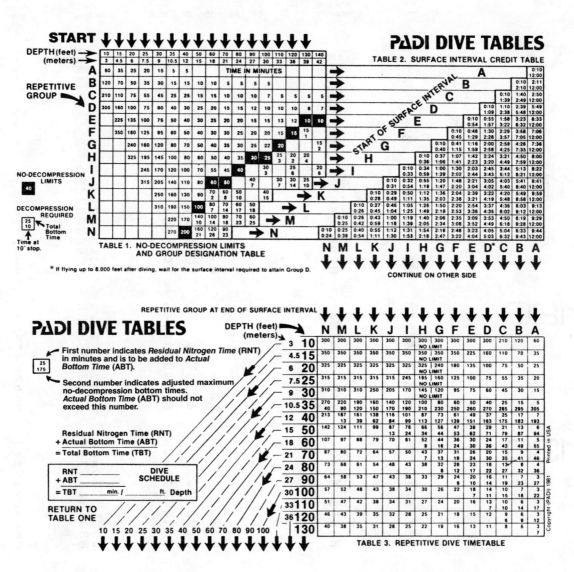

(Courtesy PADI International)

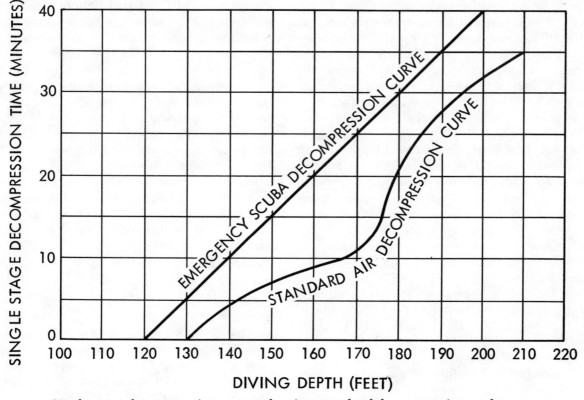

Single-stage decompression curves showing standard decompression and emergency decompression for fifteen minutes of bottom time. Standard curve concurs exactly with U.S. Navy Decompression Tables, whereas the emergency curve is a straight-line approximation (well on the safe side) for the sake of convenience and rapidity.

pression Table and no field requirement for diving should extend beyond them.

Any dive below 35 feet which has a bottom time greater than the no-decompression limit given in this table is a decompression dive and should be conducted in accordance with the Standard Air Table.

Example

Problem—In planning a dive, the Master Diver wants to conduct a brief inspection of the work site, located 160 feet below the surface. What is the maximum bottom time which he may use without requiring decompression? What is his repetitive group designation after the dive?

Solution—The no-decompression limit corresponding to the 160-foot depth in the No-Decompression Table is 5 minutes. Therefore, the Master Diver must descend to 160 feet, make his inspection and begin his ascent within 5

minutes without having to undergo decompression.

Following the 160-foot-depth row to the 5-minute column, the repetitive group designation at the top of this column is D.

Residual Nitrogen Timetable for Repetitive Air Dives   The quantity of residual nitrogen in a diver's body immediately after a dive is expressed by the repetitive group designation assigned to him by either the Standard Air Table or the No-Decompression Table. The upper portion of the Residual Nitrogen Table is composed of various intervals between 10 minutes and 12 hours, expressed in minutes:hours (2:21 = 2 hours 21 minutes). Each interval has two limits; a minimum time (top limit) and a maximum time (bottom limit).

Residual nitrogen times, corresponding to the depth of the repetitive dive, are given in the body of the lower portion of the table. To determine the residual nitrogen time for a repetitive dive, locate the diver's repetitive group designation from his previous dive along the diagonal line above the table. Read horizontally to the interval in which the diver's surface interval lies. The time spent on the surface must be between or equal to the limits of the selected interval.

Next, read vertically downwards to the new repetitive group designation. This designation corresponds to the present quantity of residual nitrogen in the diver's body. Continue downward in this same column to the row which represents the depth of the repetitive dive. The time given at the intersection is the residual nitrogen time, in minutes, to be applied to the repetitive dive.

If the surface interval is less than 10 minutes, the residual nitrogen time is the bottom time of the previous dive. All of the residual nitrogen will be passed out of the diver's body after 12 hours, so a dive conducted after a 12-hour surface interval is not a repetitive dive.

There is one exception to this table. In some instances, when the repetitive dive is to the same or greater depth than the previous dive, the residual nitrogen time may be longer than the actual bottom time of the previous dive. In this event, add the actual bottom time of the previous dive to the actual bottom time of the repetitive dive to obtain the equivalent single dive time.

If the bottom time of a dive is less than the first bottom time listed for its depth, decompression is not required. The diver may ascend directly to the surface at a rate of 60 feet per minute. The repetitive group designation for no-decompression dives is given in the No-Decompression Table.

As will be noted in the Standard Air Decompression Table, there are no repetitive group designations for exceptional exposure dives. Repetitive dives following an exceptional exposure dive are not permitted by the U.S. Navy and have no place in sport diving.

Example

Problem—Diver Bowman has just completed a salvage dive to a depth of 143 feet for 37 minutes. He was not exceptionally cold or fatigued during the dive. What is his decompression schedule and his repetitive group designation at the end of the decompression?

Solution—Select the equal or next deeper depth and the equal or next longer decompression schedule.

Action	Action Time	Total Elapsed Ascent Time
	(min:sec)	(min:sec)
Ascend to 30 feet at 60 fpm	1:53	1:53
Remain at 30 feet	5:00	6:53
Ascend to 20 feet	0:10	7:03
Remain at 20 feet	19:00	26:03
Ascend to 10 feet	0:10	26:13
Remain at 10 feet	33:00	59:13
Ascend to surface	0:10	59:23
Repetitive Group Designation "N"		

REPETITIVE DIVE WORKSHEET
PREVIOUS DIVE:

minutes   ☐ Standard Air Table
feet   ☐ No-Decompression Table
repetitive group designation

II. SURFACE INTERVAL:

hours   minutes on surface.
Repetitive group from I
New repetitive group from surface
Residual Nitrogen Timetable

III. RESIDUAL NITROGEN TIME:

feet (depth of repetitive dive)
New repetitive group from II
Residual nitrogen time from
Residual Nitrogen Timetable

IV. EQUIVALENT SINGLE DIVE TIME:

minutes, residual nitrogen time from III.
minutes, actual bottom time of repetitive dive.
minutes, equivalent single dive time.

V. DECOMPRESSION FOR REPETITIVE DIVE:

minutes, equivalent single dive time from IV.
feet, depth of repetitive dive
Decompression from (check one):
☐ Standard Air Table ☐ No-Decompression Table
☐ Surface Table Using Oxygen ☐ Surface Table Using Air
☐ No decompression required

Decompression Stops:	feet	minutes
	feet	minutes
	feet	minutes
Schedule used	feet	minutes
Repetitive group	feet	minutes

THE TEA METHOD FOR REPETITIVE DIVES

The TEA method is a simplified approach to planning, calculating, and recording repetitive dives. When used in conjunction with either the U.S. Navy or the dive tables of the Professional Association of Diving Instructors (PADI), the TEA method insures quicker learning, faster and more accurate calculations, and greater retention than other methods. It is probably the most efficient aid for the new diver in understanding and retaining one of the hardest subjects to be learned in diving. Commander James B. Williams (U.S.N., retired), president of the PADI International College in Santa Ana, California, was responsible for improving and updating this time-tested method of planning and recording repetitive dives. He is the foremost expert in teaching the TEA method and he has generously given me permission to publish herewith the following material from his lectures at PADI International College.

When using the TEA method, as presented here, refer to Figures I and II throughout for ready reference. Now, draw a straight line horizontally across a piece of paper or a blackboard. This line represents sea level and is called the "surface" or planning line. All planning is done on the surface before each dive. Each dive is represented by a vertical line which intersects the surface line. On the top of each vertical line, as shown in Figure I, we record the various *times* related to diving and at the bottom of each vertical line the *depth* of each dive is recorded.

Notice here that we are actually looking at the "side view" of the dive (ocean, lake, quarry, or river). Visualize yourself on a boat or, at the beach, on the surface, preparing to plan your first dive. After the dive is planned you enter the water and descend to the bottom. This is depicted for the sake of this presentation in Figure I by the little "buddy pair" shown in dive number 1. "Visualizing" the dive as you plan helps make learning the tables fun. The classroom instructor, by visualization, simulates taking his students to the ocean. Each student can visualize the instructor as his or her dive buddy and can visualize or simulate all the dive evolutions, including planning, suiting up, water entries, descent, hand signals, who is to *lead* the dive, in which direction, and what will be done, collected, or looked for on the dive. A little imagination can put a lot of interest in an otherwise dry, tedious, and boring subject.

In Figure I, please note that dive number 1 is a *single dive*. (The first dive after twelve hours or more of surface interval.) Now, let's plan our first dive using the TEA method and the PADI Dive Tables.

Our dive is to 40 feet. From Table 1 of the PADI Dive Tables we find that the no-decompression limit (NDL) is 200 minutes. This is recorded on the top of the left-hand side of the vertical line under the "P" for planning. Lines labeled "E" (for equivalent residual nitrogen time) and "A" (for actual bottom time) are not used in planning this single dive as they are not needed since no residual nitrogen time exists. This completes planning for the first dive. The maximum dive time of 200 minutes could be

taken. However, the five-minute safety rule must be applied. *Never make a dive to the no-decompression limit. Always cut bottom time on each dive five minutes short of the no-decompression limit.* We can now make the dive and record it. In this case a bottom time of 38 minutes is simulated. This is recorded on the right-hand top line labeled "T" (which indicates total nitrogen uptake time). Note that on this single dive the actual bottom time is the same as the total nitrogen uptake time. For this reason, there is no purpose in also logging the actual bottom time on the "A" line. Thus, the "A" and "E" lines are not utilized for the single dive.

Upon completion of dive number 1, Table 1 of the PADI Dive Tables indicates a repetitive group designator of "E." This is placed in the repetitive group box on the right-hand side of the vertical line, as shown in Figure I. This completes the planning and the diving for the single dive. Note throughout the TEA method that all planning information is recorded and considered *before actually making the dive*. Once the planning information has been recorded, the dive can then be made. Upon surfacing, the actual bottom time (ABT) and repetitive group designator is recorded on the right-hand, or diving side, of the vertical line. The surface interval (S.I.) is recorded between dives on a separate line as indicated in Figure I. Be sure it's labeled S.I. and that you always so label it and enter the surface interval on the line. There is a specific reason for this. Deviation from this particular procedure will soon find students putting the surface interval *almost anyplace*.

The number 2 dive is a repetitive dive (less than a twelve-hour surface interval). In this case a surface interval of one hour and 14 minutes is simulated. PADI Dive Table Number 2, the Surface Interval Credit Table, is used to find the "adjusted repetitive group designator" (ARG). Place this designator in the "ARG" box on the planning side of dive number 2. In this case the ARG is "D."

Note in Figure I that the letters "P," "D," "RG," and "ARG" are dropped in dives 3

FIGURE I

THE COMPLETED FORMAT FOR PLANNING AND RECORDING DIVES USING THE TEA METHOD

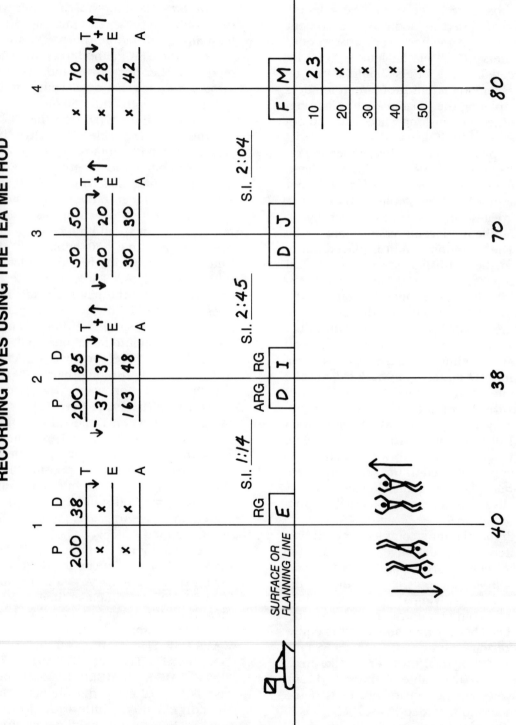

and 4. When initially introducing the TEA method, these letters are used to help students remember how each side of the line is utilized and how each of the two designator boxes are to be used. These letters can be dropped as soon as the student learns the TEA method. In no case should the letters "TEA" or the letters "S.I." be eliminated. These letters should always be used as important indicators and reminders in completing the "roadmap" to planning, recording, and making successful no-decompression limit dives.

Next, plan the second dive, which is a repetitive dive. In this case the simulated dive is to 38 feet. (Since 38 feet does not appear on PADI Dive TAble 1, go to 40, the next greatest depth.) Start the plan by recording the no-decompression limit for 40 feet. The 200-minute limit is placed under "P" on the left-hand side of the vertical line opposite "T." PADI Dive Table Number 3, the Repetitive Dive Timetable, indicates that a diver with an adjusted repetitive group of "D" has the equivalent residual nitrogen time of 37 minutes at 40 feet. At this point record the residual nitrogen time, 37 minutes, on *both sides* of the "E" line. Plan the dive for 200 minutes minus the 37 minutes of equivalent residual nitrogen time which will permit a total actual bottom time of 163 minutes. (Note here that PADI Dive Table Number 3 does the simple subtraction for us.) With these important planning figures in hand, we may now dive 163 minutes of actual bottom time.

With the planning complete and all data recorded, make the dive, simulating 48 minutes of bottom time and record it as actual bottom time on the "A" line on the right-hand, or diving side, of the vertical line. Add going up on the right-hand side. The actual bottom time added to the equivalent residual nitrogen time totals 85 minutes of "T" or total nitrogen uptake time. From PADI Dive Table Number 1, the repetitive group designator of "I" is determined and so recorded in the "RG" box.

In dive number 3 the flexibility of the TEA method is illustrated. Assume a requirement to determine a minimum sur-

face interval in order to calculate a maximum bottom time at a particular depth. Assume also that dive number 3 in Figure I is to a depth of 70 feet. Now determine the *minimum* surface interval to do this within the no-decompression limit and have at least an actual bottom time of 30 minutes. In using the TEA method to do this, go directly to the next dive and record *all known data* for that dive. Thus, log in 70 feet for the depth and a 50-minute no-decompression limit (NDL) on the "T" line on the planning side. The dive being planned is for 30 minutes. Go to PADI Dive Table Number 3, the Repetitive Dive Timetable, and enter that table at 70 feet. Go across from 70 feet to the right, to find the dive time desired, which in this case is 30 minutes, or if it should not be present, the next greatest time—30 minutes is there. Enter 20 and 30 in the appropriate box under "E" and "A." Thus, 30 minutes goes opposite "A" on the planning side and 20 goes opposite "E" on BOTH the planning side and diving side. The double entry on the "E" line should be emphasized.

On Table Three, proceed directly up from the 20/30 position opposite 70 feet to the letter "D" or, using the phonetic, Delta. Using **the PADI Dive Tables,** keep a finger on Delta on Table 2, locate the letter "I" or India on Table 1, which represents the repetitive group from the previous dive of 38 feet. Opposite "I" and above "D" find that the minimum surface interval of two hours and 45 minutes is required in order to make the dive that is being planned.

After making the 30-minute dive, record the actual bottom time on the right-hand or diving side opposite "A." Add this to "E" for a total nitrogen uptake time of 50 minutes. The little arrow pointing down on the "T" line is a reminder to the diver to ALWAYS USE THE TIME ON THE "T" LINE TO OBTAIN THE REPETITIVE GROUP FROM TABLE NUMBER 1, which in this case is "J" or, using the phonetic, Juliet. Mentally extend the little arrow down from the "T" line to the repetitive group box. Without it the student will occasionally use the figure on the "A" line (in this case, 30 minutes) to find the total nitrogen uptake time from Table Number 1. *This particular dive provided no safety factor and would have been a violation of the safety rule.* Since we know that the U.S. Navy Air Decompression Tables (from whence the PADI Dive Tables are derived) have *no safety factor,* we should not have made this dive for 30 minutes. Following the five-minute safety rule we should have dived no more than 25 minutes actual bottom time. This is all that is involved in using the TEA method for planning and recording no-decompression dives.

Although developed specifically for sport divers in planning no-decompression dives, the TEA method easily and conveniently adapts to recording decompression dives. The TEA method can be used for decompression diving by simply ignoring the no-decompression planning side. See dive number 4 in Figure I. Here the diver remains on the bottom for whatever time is indicated by the job he is doing. Consider that this is a decompression dive. The diving supervisor records the diver's actual bottom time on the "A" line *as the diver leaves the bottom.* For example, let us assume 42 minutes at 80 feet after a surface

interval of two hours and four minutes from the previous dive. Equivalent residual nitrogen time is then added. In this case, add 28 minutes of equivalent residual nitrogen time, assuming that this decompression dive was made following the three previous dives in Figure I. With a total nitrogen uptake time of 70 minutes we find, by going to PADI Dive Table Number 1, that the stage of decompression required is 23 minutes at 10 feet. (PADI Dive Table Number 1 only shows 10-minute stops. If deeper decompression stops become necessary, Table 1–10 of the U.S. Navy Repetitive Dive Tables should be used.) Decompression stops are recorded as shown.

Figure II is an annotated format of the TEA method for planning and recording dives. This format may be duplicated by the instructor and provided to students as a handout to assist them in learning the TEA method. Most students can assimilate the TEA method rapidly. Once you learn the format thoroughly, "P," "D," "RG," and "ARG," can be eliminated as in Figure III. The experienced diver using the TEA method finally has a very simple planning and diving record which can be recorded wherever he likes.

FIGURE II
ANNOTATED FORMAT FOR THE TEA METHOD

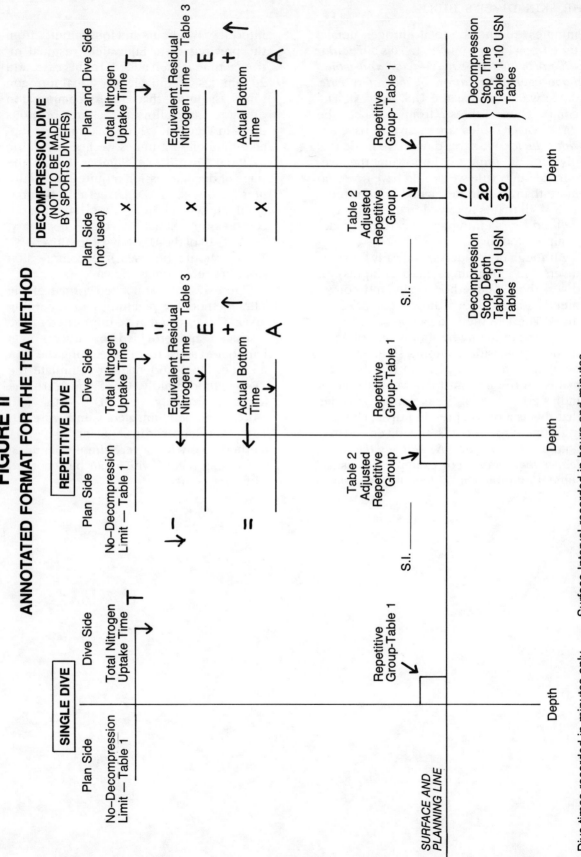

Dive times recorded in minutes only.   Surface Interval recorded in hours and minutes.

FIGURE III

TEA METHOD FORMAT WITH "TEACHING AIDS" REMOVED

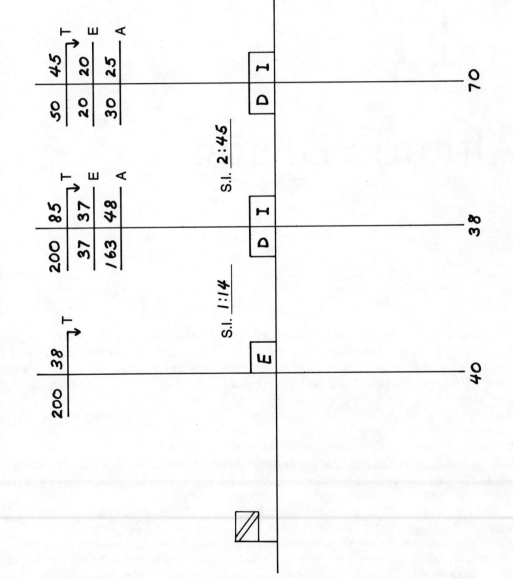

11

Altitude Diving

Although this book is oriented toward the ocean diver, there are many fine lakes and rivers at altitudes above sea level that offer excellent diving. However, diving at altitudes above sea level confronts divers with certain geophysical changes that affect the safe planning and execution of every dive. These are based on the fact that atmospheric pressure diminishes as altitude increases, and the fact that fresh water is less dense and therefore less buoyant than salt water. Both of these factors affect the readings of all depth gauges. The lower atmospheric pressure also increases the diver's susceptibility to decompression sickness, oxygen hunger, and nitrogen narcosis. Consequently every altitude dive requires the diver to: (1) Readjust the weight belt for neutral buoyancy in fresh water. (2) Use special decompression procedures and/or special altitude dive tables. (3) Adjust depth gauge readings (either mechanically or

mathematically) to determine true diving depth and rate of ascent. (4) Treat the first altitude dive as a repetitive dive if you arrive from sea level or fly on the same day. (Please see Table 1 on page 122).

Now let us consider these points in greater detail.

CHANGES REQUIRED

Because fresh water weighs only 62.4 lbs. per cubic foot (as opposed to 64 lbs. per cubic foot for sea water), and because a diver is buoyed up by a force equal to the amount of water he and all his equipment displace, he will be heavy and sink like a stone if he uses the same amount of weight in fresh water as he normally uses in salt water. Although he will displace the same amount of water in both cases, the fresh water he and his gear displace will weigh 2.5 percent less than the equivalent amount of sea water. Therefore he should remove 2.5 percent of his total weight in order to maintain the same neutral buoyancy in fresh water that he would have in sea water. If you want to be a stickler for detail the actual difference in buoyancy can be worked out mathematically by the following formula:

Where: BC is the change in buoyancy
TW is the total weight of the diver
and his gear
FW is the density of fresh water, and
SW is the density of sea water

Then: $BC = TW \left(1 - \dfrac{FW}{SW}\right)$

In actual practice, however, certain chance factors make it easier to actually get into the fresh water with your gear on and add or subtract weights until you are neutrally buoyant (floating eye level with the surface with your B.C. deflated). For example:

Wet Suits

If you are wearing a wet suit, and you probably would be, the tiny air bubbles inside the neoprene rubber will tend to expand as the atmospheric pressure decreases. This would tend to make you more buoyant, especially near the surface. But when you dive, the increasing water pressure will compress the bubbles and tend to make you less buoyant. There is a mathematical formula for this also, but because of other chance factors that affect buoyancy (a leaking camera housing, for example) it is usually easier and more accurate to try it out rather than to figure it out.

ALTITUDE DECOMPRESSION PROCEDURES

When diving at altitude, guessing at the need for decompression, as many old-timers do on ocean dives, is especially risky. For example, the no-decompression limits of a dive in the ocean to 60 feet is 60 minutes. But at 3,000 feet of altitude, it is only 40 minutes—a full 20 minutes less. Furthermore, at that altitude the div-

er's depth gauge reads only 50 feet. And the recommended ascent rate is reduced from 60 to 46 feet per minute. To add yet more confusion, if a diver dives at altitude on the same day he arrives from sea level, he must consider himself as a repetitive diver and figure his repetitive dive group classification with the utmost care. In this case, he would be in repetitive dive group "F." Thus, if the diver were to arrive at 8,000 feet of altitude from sea level and wanted to make a no-decompression dive to 60 feet, his no-decompression bottom time—now only 40 minutes instead of the normal 60 minutes due to reduced atmospheric pressure—would be further reduced by 36 minutes. This leaves only 4 minutes of no-decompression bottom time. If he had made an ocean dive within the past 12 hours a no-decompression dive would be impossible.

The accepted procedure is to treat any dive made at altitude within 12 hours of arrival from sea level as a repetitive dive according to the ambient pressure at the dive site. Last, but not least, the diver must interpolate the U.S. Navy Standard Decompression Tables according to the altitude in order to arrive at his safe bottom time and ascent rate.

Please see the repetitive dive group classifications, according to altitude.

REPETITIVE DIVE GROUP ON ARRIVAL AT ELEVATION FROM SEA LEVEL

Elevation, Feet	Group Letter on Arrival
1,000	B
2,000	B
3,000	C
4,000	D
5,000	D
6,000	E
7,000	E
8,000	F
9,000	F
10,000	G
11,000	G
12,000	G
13,000	H
14,000	H
15,000	I

As an example of the use of this table, consider the person who drives from sea level to a mountain lake at 7,000 feet and wishes to dive at once to a true depth of 60 feet. He arrives in group E and, applying this letter to the U.S. Navy Standard Decompression Table on page 119, a corresponding residual nitrogen time of 30 minutes is found. The total allowable bottom time at that depth and altitude is only 40 minutes (80 feet equivalent ocean depth). Thus, by diving immediately, the available bottom time is only ten minutes, a quarter of what it would have been had the diver waited until the next day.

HIGHEST REPETITIVE GROUP LETTER ADVISABLE WHEN ASCENDING TO ALTITUDE FOLLOWING AN OCEAN DIVE

Altitude or Elevation Feet	Highest Advisable Group Letter
1,000	M
2,000	L
3,000	K
4,000	J
5,000	I
6,000	H
7,000	G
8,000	F
9,000	E
10,000	D
11,000	C
12,000	C
13,000	B
14,000	A
15,000	A

USING DIVE TABLES AT ALTITUDE

The U.S. Navy Standard Decompression Tables from which all "short form" dive tables are derived (PADI, NU-WAY, NAUI, NASDS, YMCA, CMAS, FMAS) are based on diving at sea level in salt water. Therefore, they are useless until they have been interpolated to conform to the conditions prevailing at the altitude at which

you are diving. To fail to do so might result in serious overexposure and decompression sickness in a locale where qualified help and recompression chambers are not likely to exist.

The simplest solution is to use a capillary depth gauge. This is an open-end tube exposed to and activated by the ambient atmospheric pressure according to Boyle's Law, regardless of altitude. It is the only gauge that can give direct, reliable readings of depth at altitude that can be applied directly to the Standard Decompression Tables without interpolation, although they tend to be less reliable at depths beyond 100 feet. Furthermore, when a capillary depth gauge is used, an ascent rate of 60 feet per minute is acceptable at any altitude in any density of water. Needless to say, the use of a capillary depth gauge is highly recommended for altitude diving.

If you use other than a capillary depth gauge (oil-filled, diaphragm, bellows, or Bourdon tube), you must interpolate your depth gauge readings according to the altitude to arrive at the "equivalent ocean depth" of the dive so that you can determine the safe bottom time, ascent rate, and need for decompression stops by consulting the Standard Decompression Tables. These "ocean depth equivalencies" are given in the table "Theoretical Depth at Altitude for Given Actual Diving Depth in Fresh Water."

In most cases the true depth is of little importance since the primary concern is to avoid decompression sickness. However, should true depth be needed and a lead line or fathometer is unavailable, the true depth can be determined for a given altitude simply by multiplying it by a factor corresponding to that altitude as given in the table.

If you know the true depth simply divide it by the factor corresponding to the altitude to get the "equivalent ocean depth."

To find the safe rate of ascent at a given altitude multiply the corresponding factor by 60 feet per minute.

To know the true atmospheric pressure at a given altitude multiply 14.7 p.s.i. or 760 millimeters of mercury by the corresponding factor in the table.

THEORETICAL DEPTH AT ALTITUDE FOR GIVEN ACTUAL DIVING DEPTH IN FRESH WATER

Theoretical Depth at Various Altitudes (in feet)

Actual Depth	1,000	2,000	3,000	4,000	5,000	6,000	7,000	8,000	9,000	10,000
0	0	0	0	0	0	0	0	0	0	0
10	10	11	11	12	12	12	13	13	14	15
20	21	21	22	23	24	25	26	27	28	29
30	31	32	33	35	36	37	39	40	42	44
40	41	43	45	46	48	50	52	54	56	58
50	52	54	56	58	60	62	65	67	70	73
60	62	64	67	69	72	75	78	81	84	87
70	72	75	78	81	84	87	91	94	98	102
80	83	86	89	92	96	100	103	108	112	116
90	93	97	100	104	108	112	116	121	126	131
100	103	107	111	116	120	124	129	134	140	145
110	114	118	122	127	132	137	142	148	153	160
120	124	129	134	139	144	149	155	161	167	174
130	135	140	145	150	156	162	168	175	181	189
140	145	150	156	162	168	174	181	188	195	203
150	155	161	167	173	180	187	194	202	209	218
160	166	172	178	185	192	199	207	215	223	232
170	176	182	189	196	204	212	220	228	237	247
180	186	193	200	208	216	224	233	242	251	261
190	197	204	212	220	228	237	246	255	265	276
200	207	215	223	231	240	249	259	269	279	290
210	217	225	234	243	252	261	272	282	293	305
220	228	236	245	254	264	274	284	296	307	319
230	238	247	256	266	276	286	297	309	321	334
240	248	258	267	277	288	299	310	323	335	348
250	259	268	278	289	300	311	323	336	349	363

(Courtesy of E.R. Cross)

If the altitude of your dive does not correspond exactly with that given in the table, take the next highest reading.

MULTIPLICATION FACTORS TO INTERPOLATE ALTITUDE DIVING DATA TO SEA LEVEL EQUIVALENTS

Altitude in meters	Altitude in feet	Multiplication Factor
914	3,000	.91
1,220	4,000	.88
1,524	5,000	.85
1,829	6,000	.82
2,134	7,000	.79
2,438	8,000	.76
2,743	9,000	.73
3,048	10,000	.70
3,353	11,000	.67
3,658	12,000	.65
3,962	13,000	.62
4,267	14,000	.60
5,486	18,000	.50

Here is an example of how to use the table "Multiplication Factors":

We dive to 80 feet in a lake that is 10,000 feet above sea level for a total bottom time of 50 minutes.

Q. What is the multiplication factor for 10,000 feet?

A. Consulting the above table we see it is .70.

Q. What is the atmospheric pressure at 10,000 feet?

A. 14.7 (1 atms) × .70 = 10.29 p.s.i.

Q. What is the true depth of our dive?

A. 80 feet × .70 = 56 feet.

Q. What is the proper ascent rate according to our capillary depth gauge and our watch?

A. 60 feet per minute.

Q. What is our true ascent rate?

A. 60 feet per minute × .70 = 42 feet per minute.

Q. Need we make any decompression stops?

A. Yes. According to the standard decompression tables, we need to stop 10 minutes at 10 feet as marked on our capillary depth gauge.

Q. What is the true depth of our decompression stop?

A. 10 feet × .70 = 7 feet.

Q. What would be the maximum bottom time at 80 feet for a no-decompression dive?

A. 40 minutes.

Q. Suppose that our depth gauge was broken and we measured the depth with a lead line that marked 56 feet. What would be the equivalent ocean depth so that we could apply it correctly to the standard decompression tables?

A. Divide the true depth of 56 feet by the multiplication factor of .70. This gives 80 feet—the same as the capillary depth gauge would mark it (if only it weren't broken).

In summary, a dive to a true depth of 56 feet at 10,000 feet of altitude would be the equivalent of a dive to 80 feet at sea level.

Please see the tables "Modified Fresh Water Decompression Stops" and "Theoretical Depth" for more detailed information.

MODIFIED FRESH WATER DECOMPRESSION STOPS CORRESPONDING TO STANDARD OCEAN STOP DEPTHS

Altitude, Feet	Proper Actual Depth of Indicated Ocean Stop (in feet)		
	Standard 10-Ft. Stop	20-Ft. Stop	30-Ft. Stop
0	10.3	20.6	30.8
2,000	9.6	19.1	28.7
4,000	8.9	17.7	26.6
6,000	8.2	16.5	24.7
8,000	7.6	15.3	22.9
10,000	7.1	14.1	21.2
12,000	6.5	13.1	19.6
14,000	6.0	12.1	18.1

THEORETICAL DEPTH OF DECOMPRESSION STOP AT ALTITUDE

Prescribed Depth	Theoretical Depth of Decompression Stop (in feet)									
	1,000	2,000	3,000	4,000	5,000	6,000	7,000	8,000	9,000	10,000
0	0	0	0	0	0	0	0	0	0	0
10	10	9	9	9	8	8	8	7	7	7
20	19	19	18	17	17	16	15	15	14	14
30	29	28	27	26	25	24	23	22	22	21
40	39	37	36	35	33	32	31	30	29	28

(Courtesy of E.R. Cross)

12

Underwater Photography

When skin diving first became popular, the greatest attraction seemed to be spearfishing. The number of poor helpless fish you could skewer in one dive session became the measure of how good a diver you were. Consequently, any living thing that had the misfortune to cross a diver's path usually wound up on his spear. Underwater life soon became scarce around the more popular diving areas. Heaps of fish were left to rot on the beach, incurring the wrath of bathers and conservationists alike. The predictable result was that divers acquired a bad reputation and skin diving soon became outlawed in many areas.

Today the situation has changed. Most divers who once got their kicks from the wanton killing of fish have discovered that it is much more gratifying and challenging to shoot fish with a camera instead of a spear gun. Consequently the underwater camera has replaced the spear gun as the diver's primary tool and the popular attitude toward skin divers has vastly improved. In fact, many conservationists and water sportsmen use the findings of underwater photographers to their advantage. Thus skin diving for underwater photography has come to be accepted as a constructive and interesting use of the privilege of exploring the last frontier left on earth. With the new breed of marine scientists, the diver must share the responsibility of preserving the wonders of the underwater world as best he can. Underwater photography reveals the wonders of the deep for others to enjoy vicariously as well. It's a game everybody wins—even the fish!

SPECIAL REQUIREMENTS

If you are already a competent diver, all you need in order to take good underwater pictures

is a basic knowledge of photography, some film, and a watertight camera or camera housing.

If you do not already have it, a basic knowledge of photography can be acquired by reading a good book on the subject and then practicing what you learned by shooting a few rolls of film on land. Once you discover what you must and must not do to get good pictures on land, it is an easy matter to get reasonably good pictures in clear water. Of all the special requirements of underwater photography, clear clean water is by far the most important. The camera is not so adaptable as your eye. If the water in which you plan to shoot is so dirty or full of suspended matter that everything seems blurred, that's the way it will look on film, and there is nothing you can do about it!

UNDERWATER CAMERAS AND HOUSINGS

If you already own a camera, the chances are that it will work just as well underwater as it does on land. All you need is an absolutely watertight housing to protect it against highly corrosive salt water. It's easy to construct a makeshift underwater housing for your camera by enclosing it in a heavy plastic bag sealed around an ordinary faceplate. However, flexible plastic is easily torn or punctured, and if you value your camera at all, I do not recommend this procedure. There are available a number of so-called "universal camera housings" made of rigid quarter-inch plastic or cast aluminum that accept a variety of cameras. Most of them can be rented at nominal fees from your local dive retail store, and you should rent before you actually invest in a housing of any kind. When you are ready to buy a housing for your camera, I recommend the cast-aluminum variety over the plastic models simply because of their sturdier construction. You will probably be able to find a housing that is custom-made for your particular camera. (Ikelite Inc. makes a plastic housing or kit for almost all popular cameras on the market.)

If you do not already own a camera and you want to buy one with underwater photography in mind, I strongly suggest that you consider the new amphibious cameras. There are several cameras on the market today made to operate underwater as well as on land without special housings.

For the serious amateur or professional, however, the best bet is the Nikonos V amphibious camera made by the Nikon Camera Company of Japan. I watched the prototype of this revolutionary camera being developed by Captain Jacques-Yves Cousteau and Jean DeWouters aboard the M/V Calypso and can vouch for its remarkable versatility. Small enough to fit into your hand, the lens and mechanism of this 35mm camera are hermetically sealed with O-rings within an aluminum body that can withstand pressures of depths to three hundred feet. A single lever triggers the shutter and advances the film, then locks in place to prevent accidental firing. Focus problems are minimal because the wide-angle lens gives great depth of field. Unlike the earlier models, the new Nikonos V has an automatic exposure control with manual override, a swing-open back that makes for easy loading and unloading of the 35mm film, and a new companion SB-102 strobe unit especially made for underwater shooting. I shot most of the underwater photos in this book with a Nikonos and I highly recommend it for the serious photographer.

For the beginner and novice, there are cheaper, smaller amphibious cameras on the market that are almost as good, though not so versatile. Foremost among them are the 110 pocket-type cameras such as the Minolta Weathermatic and the Hanimex 110MF. Both are O-ring-sealed with a built-in strobe unit that is somewhat weak for underwater work. The latter is good for depths to 150 feet, but the former is good only to depths of 15 feet. All amphibious cameras, including the Nikonos, require the use of a sportsfinder, which makes for difficult framing. We all await the invention of a truly amphibious single-lens reflex camera that does not require a special underwater housing.

Underwater Movie and Television Cameras

If you prefer motion picture to still photography, you can find plastic or cast-aluminum housings to fit most 8mm or 16mm movie cameras and some TV cameras as well. Whether you shoot in super-8mm (recommended for all amateurs), 16mm, or 35mm (recommended for all professionals), I suggest that you use a camera with a battery-driven motor so that you can avoid having to stop and rewind the spring right in the middle of that once-in-a-lifetime shot. Although motor-driven cameras are readily available in the 8mm field, they are hard to come by in the 16mm category. Beautiful cast-aluminum housings are custom-made especially for the 16mm Bolex, Bell & Howell, and Kodak K-100 cameras. Beautiful battery-driven motors are also made for them. But none of the housings will accept the motors! All of them must be spring wound. The K-100 has the longest wind (forty feet) of these three most popular 16mm cameras. The ultimate underwater movie cameras are those made by those who use them. Al Giddings, for example, makes cameras for a select group of underwater pros like Jack McKenney, Stan Waterman, and Chuck Nicklin, and is himself an expert underwater cameraman.

Though still in its infancy, I believe that underwater television is destined to replace motion picture film as the most effective medium of underwater photography. For most amateurs, the cost of underwater motion picture equipment, film, and processing is prohibitively high. The use of television permits one to bypass the expensive intermediary steps involved in working with film. One can record, screen, and edit directly from the original TV tape without processing and printing, then use the same tape to shoot some more. The biggest problem at this writing is that most TV electronics are highly susceptible to the marine environment, and only a few reliable underwater TV housings are as yet available. These are manufactured by Hypertech Underwater Video Systems Inc. of Fort Lauderdale, Florida, Aqua Video Underwater Systems Inc. of Minneapolis, Minnesota, and Ikelite Inc. of Indianapolis, Indiana.

Nikonos V underwater camera system.

UNDERWATER EXPOSURE METERS

An underwater exposure meter is indispensable to good underwater photography. The human eye is so adaptable to adverse light conditions that it can see many things that the camera cannot. Besides, different kinds of film require different exposures under given lighting conditions, and underwater lighting conditions are never the same from place to place, from depth to depth, or even from day to day. It is practically impossible to guess the proper exposure underwater, regardless of how experienced you may be. Never trust your own judgment in determining underwater exposure settings.

If you already own an exposure meter, you can rig a makeshift underwater housing for it by placing it inside a strong glass jar. However, the lid must be sturdy enough to withstand the pressure of the depths you expect to be working in or it will buckle and leak water. Round glass jars also cause slight errors in exposure readings due to the optical surface they create with the water. So, if you plan to shoot more than a

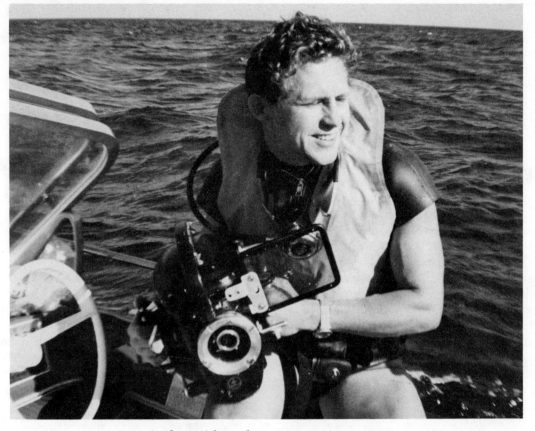

Author with underwater movie camera.

few rolls of film underwater, it is best if you rent, purchase, or build a rigid plastic housing for your meter or purchase an amphibious meter that works equally well on land or underwater without a special housing. I recommend the Sekonic marine meter.

Even if you have no exposure meter or no underwater housing for it, you can still get fairly good exposures by making a qualified guess as recommended later and then bracketing your shots—that is, taking one shot at the exposure you think best, then taking two more, one at one stop under that exposure and one at one stop over that exposure. This may seem to be unnecessary extravagance to some, but the chances are that the film you expose will be the cheapest and most rewarding expenditure on your entire trip. You can make a fairly well-qualified guess at the proper exposure in the following manner.

Before you dive, look down into the water you are about to enter from several feet above it, and judge its clarity. If you can distinguish objects clearly on the bottom in fifteen or more feet of water, the clarity can be considered excellent. If you can distinguish form but no detail, the clarity is good. If you can see only shadow, the clarity is only fair. If you can see nothing at all, don't bother to take your camera with you.

Having once evaluated the clarity, take a light meter exposure reading or use the film-data sheet provided in the package to determine what the proper exposure would be if you were shooting on the surface but in shadow. Then determine your underwater exposure by opening up one f-stop or the equivalent at the following depths according to the clarity of the water. Then open one f-stop for every ten feet of distance from camera to subject:

If the clarity is:	Open one f-stop at:						
	Feet						
Excellent	7 to 10	25	50	100	150		
Good	1 to 10	20	35	60	85	110	
Fair	1 to 8	15	25	50	60	80	100
Bad	Results dubious; try opening one f-stop every eight feet ·						

For example, if your surface exposure were 1/100 second at f/11, and you were 10 feet down in water of excellent clarity, shooting your buddy who was 10 feet away, you would open your aperture one f-stop for the depth and one more f-stop for the camera-to-subject distance. This would give you an exposure of 1/100 second at f/5.6.

Passing clouds and a windy, choppy surface will also affect exposures. A troubled surface will affect your judgment of the water conditions, and you must also stay alert for any light changes due to passing clouds obscuring the sun when you are submerged.

For crisp, clear pictures it is best not to at-tempt shooting when your subject is near the limits of your visibility. Remember, the closer the better. Make it a rule to keep your main subject within a third of the distance of your visibility limit.

LENS, FILM, AND PROCESSING

The type of lens you use plays a very important role in the results of your underwater photography. Because of the suspended matter in water, it is best to stay as close as possible to your subject when shooting. Thus, the wider the angle lens you use, the closer you can get

Underwater photographer using a superwide angle lens.

Wide-angle lens lends depth of field and perspective.

to your subject without sacrificing picture content or quality. The wide-angle lens also gives you greater depth of field for better focus, perspective, and finer definition.

Film Stock

The type of film stock you use is another important consideration. Generally speaking, the faster the film speed the wider the leeway, but also the heavier the grain of the emulsion and the fuzzier the resulting picture. Conversely, the slower the film speed, the finer the grain and the better the definition. This holds true for both color and black and white film. Thus, it is best to use the slowest, least grainy film that the light and clarity of the water will permit. Thus if you were shooting black and white, in order of preference I would suggest Panatomic-X or its equivalent at ASA 32 to 100. Otherwise, I would use the equivalent of Plus-X Pan at ASA 160 to 320 or Tri-X Pan at ASA 200 to 1200, in

that order. If I were shooting color, I would suggest using the equivalent of Kodachrome II at ASA 25, Ansochrome or Ektachrome at ASA 32, or Ektachrome-X at ASA 64. Otherwise, I would use the equivalent of High Speed Ektachrome at ASA 160 to 400.

If I were shooting 16mm movies instead of stills, I would use Kodachrome II or its equivalent at ASA 25 to 64 if I intended to project the original. If I intended to pull copies for projection and keep the original intact, I would use the equivalent of Commercial Ektachrome 7252 at ASA 16 to 25 (with conversion filter in), or better yet the new Eastmancolor Negative (#7294) at ASA 400 tungsten, the new Video News Film (VNF #7239) at ASA 160, or the remarkable Video News Film Reversal (VNX #7250) which is rated at ASA 250 using a Wratten 85B conversion filter and at a superfast ASA 400 using tungsten lights at 3,200 degrees Kelvin. Most of these films can be "pushed" one or two stops without great loss of quality. The latter film is a revolutionary exception to the high-speed/high-grain problem. I happily relied upon it in shooting my recent color films and the results were great. In spite of its high speed, it provides practically grain-free pictures with total color saturation and high definition even when pushed beyond its normal speed. Besides, its color is rather on the warm side, and this compensates somewhat for the bluishness caused by the filtering effect water has on the color spectrum of light.

CAUTION: If you shoot a film at an ASA rated speed that is any higher than that recommended by the manufacturer, you must develop it accordingly or else notify your laboratory to do so.

RECOMMENDED 16mm COLOR FILM STOCKS FOR UNDERWATER WORK

Name	Stock No.	Day	Tungsten	Can Be Pushed
Ektachrome Commercial	7252	16*	25	1 stop
Ektachrome VNF (VNF = Video News Film)	7239	160	125	1–2 stops
Ektachrome VNF	7240	80*	40**	1–2 stops
Eastmancolor Negative	7247	64*	100	1–2 stops
VNX (Video News Film Reversal)	7250	250**	400	1–2 stops

*   = Wratten 85 conversion filter for tungsten to daylight.
** = Wratten 85B conversion filter for daylight to tungsten.

Color versus Depth

The color spectrum of daylight is comprised of red, orange, yellow, green, blue, indigo, and violet. (Just remember: "Roy G. Biv.") But water acts as a filter on the color spectrum of light. Consequently the color composition of light changes progressively with the depth. Just two inches beneath the surface, all the infrared rays of the color spectrum are absorbed and scattered by the water. Within twenty to thirty feet, all the reds have been filtered out. Orange is the next color to go. Then yellow vanishes and then, one by one, the other colors until from about one hundred feet only indigo and violet remain. This creates the blue-green cast characteristic of most waters. Blue and green are simply the only two colors that exist in deeper water depths, so everything appears to be blue-green. Even the surface of the sea appears to be blue-green (unless the water is so dirty that it transmits no light at all) for they are the only two colors that are reflected back into the sky.

Although color corrective filters may help in depths of less than twenty feet, the only sure way to reveal the true colors that exist underwater (but that are invisible to the human eye) is to restore the entire color spectrum of light with artificial illumination. This can be done by using flashbulbs, strobe lights, or underwater photoflood lights of at least 3,200 degrees Kelvin.

Shooting the remains of a Roman galley with an underwater television camera.

13

Advanced Diving and Specialty Training

Once your instructor has shepherded you through the required open water checkout dives and you have passed your final written examination, your basic scuba diving course is completed and you are awarded your coveted certification card ("C" card). Your "C" card is truly your passport to the underwater world and you should be duly proud to have won it. It proves that you have learned all the basic knowledge and skills of the open water scuba diver according to the strict standards of the organization that certified you. You are now qualified to buy, rent, and use compressed-air diving gear in any country of the world. Yes, congratulations are certainly in order. However, a glance at the "Summary of PADI Key Course Standards" offered by the Professional Association of Diving Instructors (and most other cer-

tifying organizations) will reveal that your "C" card is not the end of your underwater training. It is only the beginning!

Inevitably, just like driving a car or flying a plane, the excitement of diving for the mere sake of diving alone is not enough. It becomes merely a tool. In order to sustain the initial gratification of diving, it must transport you across new horizons to some new objective that is equally rewarding. These new objectives may lead you in the direction of a new profession, such as marine science professional diving, or becoming an underwater instructor yourself. Or they may open the doors to any number of special interests for which scuba diving is only an entrée. Most of these are included in the following list; any five of them qualify you as a Master Scuba Diver.

Summary of PADI Key Course Standards

Level	Min. Age	Recommended Hours	Minimum Open Water Training	Ratio	Minimum Instructor Rating	Prerequisite
Skin Diver	8	12	None required	10:1 *16:1	Assistant Instructor	
Introductory Scuba	12	3	None required	4:1	Instructor	
Basic Scuba Diver	15	27	2 dives (optional skin dive recommended)	10:1	Instructor	
Junior Basic Scuba Diver		27	2 dives (optional skin dive recommended)	10:1	Instructor	
Open Water Diver	15	31	4 dives (optional skin dive recommended)	10:1	Instructor	
Junior Open Water Diver		31	4 dives (optional skin dive recommended)	10:1	Instructor	
Advanced Open Water Diver	15	15	5 dives	10:1	Instructor	Open Water Diver
Rescue Diver	15	25	5 dives	8:1		Advanced Open Water Diver
Divemaster	18	30	10 dives	6:1	Instructor	Advanced Open Water Diver
Assistant Instructor	18	66	10 dives	10:1 (dry) 1:1 (water)	Open Water Scuba Instructor	Divemaster
Open Water Scuba Instructor	18	80		6:1	Course Director	Divemaster
Specialties:						
Cavern Diver	18	**	**	2:1	Instructor certified as a Specialty Instructor for the particular specialty area	Advanced Diver
Deep Diver	15	24		8:1		Advanced Diver
Equipment Specialist	15	6	None required			Open Water Diver Junior Open Water Diver
Ice Diver	18	24	3 dives on 2 days	2:1		Advanced Diver
Night Diver	15	12	3 dives on 2 nights	8:1		Open Water Diver Junior Open Water Diver
Research Diver	15	12	2 dives	8:1		Open Water Diver Junior Open Water Diver

*From PADI STANDARDS AND PROCEDURES, © PADI, 1983, 1984

Summary of PADI Key Course Standards* *(continued)*

Level	Min. Age	Recom- mended Hours	Minimum Open Water Training	Ratio	Minimum Instructor Rating	Prerequisite
Search and Recovery Diver	15	12	4 dives on 2 days	8:1		Advanced Diver
U/W Hunter	15	12	2 dives	8:1		Open Water Diver Junior Open Water Diver
U/W Photographer	15	12	2 dives	8:1		Open Water Diver Junior Open Water Diver
Wreck Diver	15	24	4 dives on 2 days	†8:1		Advanced Diver
Master Scuba Diver	15				Headquarters	Advanced Open Water Diver
Master Instructor	20				Headquarters	Open Water Scuba Instructor

*Pool or confined open water only
** See PADI Cavern Diving Standards available from Headquarters
† 2:1 for wreck penetrations

ADVANCED COURSE STANDARDS AND PROCEDURES

Open Water Training Outline

After you receive your scuba diver certification, Open Water Diver is the level of study for which you are qualified. The following are the skills which you will practice in open water for each training dive. After satisfactory performance of the required skills for a dive under the direct observation of a qualified Instructor, you will be allowed the opportunity to use remaining air for experience and pleasure under supervision.

Open Water Training Dive Number One

Equipment Inspection
Buoyancy Check
Controlled Descent
Use of B.C. Underwater
Mask Clearing—partial
Regulator Recovery, Clearing
Alternate Air Source Use
Normal Ascent

Open Water Training Dive Number Two

Equipment Inspection
Free Descent with Reference
Use of B.C. Underwater
Mask Clearing—complete
Alternate Air Source Ascent

Open Water Training Dive Number Three

Equipment Inspection
Buoyancy Check
Surface Swim
Surface Dives
Breath-hold Diving

Open Water Training Dive Number Four

Equipment Inspection
50-yard Surface Compass Swim
Free Descent without Reference
Buddy Breathing Underwater
Mask Clearing—complete
Buddy Breathing Ascent
Removal/Replacement of Scuba
Underwater Navigation to Exit

Open Water Training Dive Number Five

Equipment Inspection
Free Descent without Reference
Underwater Navigation with Compass
Mask Removal and Replacement
Midwater Buoyancy Control—hovering
Emergency Swimming Ascent
Underwater Navigation to Exit

All dives should be recorded in your log book.

The dive tables should be used for all scuba dives for familiarization with their use in actual diving situations.

Advanced Open Water Diver

Purpose: To enhance the experience, skill, and knowledge of the diver for practical application in the diving environment. To provide additional skills beyond the beginning training levels. To introduce special interest areas in diving.

Prerequisites: Age 15 and certified as Open Water Scuba Diver or certified as a Basic Scuba Diver with at least 10 logged dives.

Training: Underwater navigation without a compass, underwater distance measuring, compass navigation, knot tying underwater, search and recovery techniques, night or limited visibility diving, and deep diving techniques. Five open water training dives are required in the advanced course.

Divemaster

Purpose: To develop divers who are qualified to serve as underwater guides, safety officers for organized diving activities, or safety guides for open water instruction.

Prerequisites: Age 15 and certified as an Advanced Diver.

Training: Diving emergency procedures; boat diving procedures; mapping of underwater terrain; planning, organizing, and directing dives; safety assisting; rescue techniques; guiding divers underwater. Ten open water training dives are required in the Divemaster course.

Master Scuba Diver

The Master Scuba Diver rating is the highest noninstructional rating in the PADI diver program. It is an expert diver classification and denotes superior achievement.

Achieving the rating requires certification as a PADI Divemaster and *certification* in any five PADI specialty ratings.

CERTIFICATION PERFORMANCE REQUIREMENTS FOR DIVEMASTERS

In order to be certified as a PADI Divemaster, a person is required to:

1. Satisfactorily complete the PADI Divemaster Watermanship and Skill Assessment.

2. Satisfactorily complete a diver rescue evaluation.

3. Score satisfactorily on the PADI Divemaster Exams.

4. Prepare an Emergency Assistance Plan for diving emergencies in the local area and include the appropriate contact information.

5. Prepare an outline of boat-diving procedures useful for an area likely to be visited by the Divemaster.

6. Prepare a map of the shoreline and underwater terrain of a local Open Water training site selected by the Instructor.

7. Satisfactorily serve as an instructional assistant for no less than 10 PADI Open Water Training Sessions and 5 PADI Pool Training Sessions.

GENERAL STANDARDS FOR SPECIALTY COURSES

The purpose of the PADI Specialty diving courses is to familiarize divers with the skills, knowledge, planning, organization, procedures, techniques, problems, and hazards for various special interest areas in diving. A Specialty course provides limited experience in the Specialty and serves more as a safe and supervised introduction to the special interest area than to develop proficiency in the Specialty.

General Standards for Specialty Courses

1. The instructor conducting the Specialty course is to be certified as a PADI Specialty Instructor for the particular Specialty being taught. (See Specialty Instructor Ratings, page 51.)

2. The minimum age for certification is 15 years of age except for Cavern Diving and Ice Diving with a minimum age requirement of 18 years of age.

3. The minimum certification level required for enrollment in all Specialty courses is Open Water or Junior Open Water Diver, except for Cavern, Deep, Ice, Wreck, Rescue, and Search and Recovery diving, which have a minimum certification level requirement of Advanced Open Water Diver.

4. The student-to-instructor ratio for Cavern and Ice Diving courses are two students per certified Specialty Instructor. The student-to-instructor ratio for all other Specialty courses is eight students per certified Specialty Instructor. An exception is Wreck Diving where a two to one ratio is not to be exceeded during any training dives involving penetration of a wreck.

5. The maximum depth for the training of Specialty divers (any Specialty) is 130 feet.

6. The combining of two or more Specialty courses so that credit is received for more than one rating during any training session of a course is *not* acceptable. In order to ensure meaningful learning experiences, all Specialty course training, including open water dives, is to restrict training to a single Specialty topic. For example, when photos are taken on a wreck dive, the dive may *not* be credited toward both the Underwater Photographer and Wreck Diver ratings. Also, a deep dive (60'-130') on a wreck may *not* be counted for both Deep Diver and Wreck Diver Specialty ratings. If the wreck is located in deep water, the Deep Diver rating should be a prerequisite for the Wreck Diving course.

7. The following dives, conducted during the Advanced Open Water Diver course, may (but are not required to be) credited toward the respective Specialty Diver rating: Night dive, Search and Light Salvage dive, and Deep dive. No other dives may be credited. All dives credited are done so at the discretion of the instructor conducting the Specialty course.

The minimum requirements for each Specialty course sanctioned by PADI are as follows:

Wreck Diving

This course develops the necessary skills and knowledge for safe wreck diving. The planning, organization procedures, techniques, problems, and hazards of wreck diving should be covered, including, but not limited to, the following subjects: lights, air supplies, special equipment, limited visibility diving, life lines and reels, and emergency procedures.

The minimum number of course hours for certification is 24. The minimum open water training for certification is four dives on two days (two per day).

Underwater Photography

This course covers basic underwater photography with special emphasis on practical photographic techniques, covering such subjects as: available light, flash photography, film types, camera handling, composition, photographic principles, and care and maintenance of equipment.

The minimum number of course hours for certification is 12. The minimum open water training for certification is two dives on two days (two days recommended).

Underwater Hunting and Collecting

This course covers the use of equipment for taking game, preparation of fish and game, spearfishing techniques, equipment modifications for hunting, spearfishing safety, conservation, and fish and game regulations plus related knowledge and skills for underwater hunting and/or collecting. The course may also be used to develop the required knowledge and skills for underwater collecting of items such as shells, bottles, or fish.

The minimum number of course hours for certification is 12. The minimum open water training for certification is two dives on two days (two days recommended).

Search and Recovery Diving

This course covers the techniques and application of all search and recovery methods, including the planning, organization, procedures, techniques, problems, and hazards of search and recovery diving. Coverage includes, but is not limited to, the following subjects: navigation, limited visibility diving, object locating, and salvage methods.

The minimum number of course hours for certification is 12. The minimum open water training for certification is four dives on two days (two per day).

Research Diving

This course covers areas such as oceanography (practical), biology (marine life and plant identification and preservation), and oceanology (men and equipment under water). Research projects and ecology projects may meet the requirements for certification.

The minimum number of course hours for certification is 12. The minimum open water training for certification is two dives on two days (two days recommended).

Ice Diving

Ice Diver training involves the planning, organization, procedures, techniques, problems, and hazards for ice diving, including but not limited to, the following topics: safety lines, signals and communications, special equipment, hole cutting procedures and line securing, line tending, safety diver procedures, effects of cold, and emergency procedures.

The minimum number of course hours for certification is 24. The minimum open water training for certification is three dives on two days.

Equipment Specialist

This course is intended to familiarize divers with the operation and maintenance of equipment. It is *not* an equipment repair course, and training on the repairing and overhauling of equipment, except for very minor servicing, is *not* to be part of the curriculum. The course is to cover the theory and principles of operation of diving equipment, maintenance procedures (which may include an *orientation* to repair procedures), and simple suggestions for comfortable equipment configurations. Common problems with equipment, recommendations for maintenance and storage of equipment, and an introduction to new equipment should also be included.

The minimum number of hours for certification is six. Open water training is *not* required. *Note: To qualify for an* instructor rating *in*

this Specialty, a person is required to be trained in equipment repair by a major diving manufacturer. Proof of this training is to be submitted along with the Specialty application.

Deep Diving

This course provides the diver with the necessary skills and knowledge for deeper diving. Deep diving is defined as dives made between 60 and 130 feet. All dives are to be no-decompression dives, and no dives are to be conducted beyond a depth of 130 feet. Topics covered are to include, but not be limited to, the following: planning, organization, procedures, techniques, problems, hazards and decompression, special equipment, buoyancy control, descending lines, and emergency procedures. Altitude diving, flying after diving, and decompression chamber orientation should be included.

The minimum number of course hours for certification is 24. The minimum open water training for certification is four dives on two days (two per day).

Cavern Diving

Cavern Diving is defined as any dive conducted *within* the light zone of a cave. Cave diving is any dive conducted *beyond* the light zone of a cave. The light zone of a cave is defined as that part of the cave from which natural light illuminating the entrance is visible at all times.

This course develops the necessary skills and knowledge for Cavern Diving and describes the dangers involved with cave diving. The planning, organization, procedures, techniques, and problems of cavern diving should be covered, including but not limited to: lighting, body positioning and buoyancy control, guidelines, reel handling, air consumption management, and emergency procedures. Information describing the specific hazards of cave diving should include, but not be limited to: silting, line entanglement and breakage, disorientation from permanent lines, and emergency situations unique to cave diving. Cavern diving is in no way intended to provide instruction for cave diving.

The minimum requirements for Cavern Diving certification are detailed in separate standards available from PADI Headquarters.

Night Diving

This course is to prepare the diver to dive safely at night and is to include the planning and preparation, procedures, techniques, problems, and hazards of night diving. The following topics should also be covered in the course: dive lights, navigation, buddy system techniques, buoyancy control, communications, disorientation, and nocturnal aquatic life.

PADI Open Water Diver certification, its equivalent, or a higher level of certification is required for participation.

Open water training should be conducted at dive sites at which the participants have dived during daylight hours so the divers will be familiar with the area to be dived at night.

The minimum number of course hours for certification is 12. The minimum open water training for certification is three dives on at least two different nights. For the purposes of this Specialty, nighttime is defined as one hour after sunset until one hour before sunrise.

Night Diving training conducted as part of Advanced Open Water Diver training may be counted toward the certification requirements for this Specialty.

14

Diving First Aid

(See alphabetical listing beginning on page 162 of signs, symptoms, and first aid treatments.)

In diving an ounce of prevention is worth many pounds of cure. Diving safely is largely a frame of mind and it works from the inside out. The bottom line is that in order to dive safely you must take responsibility for being a safe diver and then act on that premise. Your instructor can teach you how to dive safely but only you can actually do it. Nevertheless, even under the best and safest conditions accidents do happen, so it behooves you to prepare yourself for that eventuality. Every diver should be familiar with diver rescue procedures, decompression needs, cardiopulmonary resuscitation (CPR) techniques, and basic first aid, and be able to use this knowledge quickly and efficiently. In addition, a good diving first aid kit and the location and phone number of your nearest recompression chamber should be as much a part of your standard diving equipment as your mask, snorkel, and fins.

DIVING EMERGENCY ACTION CENTERS

> IN CASE OF DIVING EMERGENCIES . . .
> Anyone needing EMERGENCY help in a diving accident may call (919) 684-8111 and ask for Divers Alert Network (DAN).
>
> This number reaches the telecommunications unit at DUKE MEDICAL CENTER which will then connect the caller with an experienced Duke physician, trained in hyperbaric medicine, available 24 hours a day. The physician will either advise the caller direct or put them in touch with the nearest regional coordinator. (The network offers a membership program that includes a comprehensive emergency treatment manual describing acute U/W accident signs, symptoms and immediate first aid procedures for $10 per year. Proceeds help fund DAN. Send check, made out to Duke University, to Administrative Coordinator, Duke University Medical Center, DAN, Box 3823, Durham, N.C. 27710.)
>
> TO LOCATE YOUR NEAREST RECOMPRESSION CHAMBER and get an expert consultation, you can telephone either Brooks Air Force Base, Leo-Fast Command Post (512) 536-3278 or U.S. Navy Experimental Diving Unit, EDU duty phone (904) 234-4353. Officers on duty twenty-four hours a day, seven days a week.

DIVING FIRST AID KIT

Your diving first aid kit should be based upon the "Standard American Red Cross First Aid Kit" (which follows) but should also contain these special items for divers:

1. Plastic tubes for mouth-to-mouth artificial resuscitation—both adult and child sizes or plastic adapter tube.

2. A written copy of instructions regarding both mouth-to-mouth resuscitation and cardiopulmonary resuscitation (CPR) (see on pages 155–158).

3. A copy of the PADI or Nu-Way no-decompression and repetitive dive tables on waterproof plastic.

4. A small container of the following items for use in the treatment of jellyfish stings and coral cuts: household ammonia, baking soda, meat tenderizer, and rubbing alcohol.

5. A mild ear-wash solution. If none is available use a 50/50 percent solution of boric acid and alcohol or a mixture of 30 percent alcohol and 70 percent water.

6. Optional: Sea Sting Kit Model SSK (Dacor Corp.).

Standard American Red Cross First Aid Kit

First Aid Book
Two dimes taped to emergency phone number card
Band-Aids
Aspirin and/or Midol
Triangle Bandages (3 or more)
Gauze Roller Bandages
Tourniquet
Soap (Antibacterial)
Razor Blades or Exacto Knife
Tweezers or Forceps (fine tipped)
Needles
Safety Pins
Mild Antiseptic (Hydrogen Peroxide, Listerine)
Snake Bite Kit
Waterproof Matches
Water Heating Device (Sterno)

If room is available:
  Scissors
  Side Cutting Pliers
  Adhesive Tape
  Q-tips
  Tongue Depressors
  Paper Cups
  Salt
  Gauze Scrub Pads
  Chapstick

Also have available:
  Blanket of some type
  Drinking water

All items can be carried in a small plastic tackle box.

U.S. COAST GUARD FIRST AID PROCEDURES FOR BOATMEN AND DIVERS

First aid, in any situation, consists of the emergency treatment of the sick and injured before trained medical attention can be obtained. The purposes of first aid are:

1. To save life.
2. To prevent further injury or unfavorable progression.
3. To preserve resistance and vitality.

A real knowledge of first aid and its purposes, when properly applied, may mean the difference between life and death, between rapid recovery and long hospitalization, between temporary disability and permanent injury.

Proper knowledge and skill in first aid are musts for every boatman. Boats frequently operate at a considerable distance from sources of medical care and certain injuries or illnesses may be fatal unless intelligent care is given immediately.

The following material provides the boatman with information pertinent to life threatening injuries. The first aid advice is based on the American National Red Cross Standard First Aid and Personal Safety Textbook, Cardiopulmonary Resuscitation Manual (CG-139), and Handbook of the Hospital Corps (NAVMED-P-5004).

Before discussing care of the wounded and injured, a word or two is directed to the boatman or diver who will have the responsibility of providing first aid. You should:

1. Keep calm, never permitting yourself to become excited or confused.
2. Act quickly, with efficiency and confidence, making a decision on priorities as soon as possible.

You should practice the first aid skills described in this brochure before you are involved in an emergency situation. An even better idea is to enroll in the Standard First Aid Course conducted by the American Red Cross. You will gain additional first aid knowledge and skills that could save a life or prevent unnecessary suffering.

THE FOUR PRINCIPLES OF FIRST AID

The following four principles of first aid present a topical outline for learning and retaining the essential knowledge and skills in first aid. Memorizing these principles will also assist you in knowing how to act and in what order to act if you encounter a situation requiring first aid:

1. Check and clear the airway.
2. Stop the bleeding.
3. Protect the wounds.
4. Treat for shock.

Check and Clear the Airway

Resuscitation is a general term which covers all of the measures taken to restore life or consciousness to an individual who is apparently dead. These measures include artificial respiration to restore normal respiratory function, and closed chest heart massage to restore normal heartbeat. Time is of prime importance. **SECONDS COUNT.** If a person stops breathing, he can die within 4–6 minutes. Mouth-to-mouth or mouth-to-nose artificial respiration should be started at once in any case where breathing has ceased.

Only after artificial respiration has been initiated and after it has been determined that the heart has stopped, should CPR external heart massage be started and combined with artificial respiration to give cardiopulmonary resuscitation.

The following techniques should govern cardiopulmonary resuscitation (CPR) procedures:

Mouth-to-Mouth Breathing (Resuscitation)
Note: See Chapter 9 for in-water resuscitation techniques.

1. This is **ALWAYS** started first, and then the necessity for external heart massage is determined.
2. Place victim on his back.
3. Kneel beside the victim's shoulder.
4. Clear the victim's mouth and air passages of foreign objects, i.e., chewing gum, dentures, seaweed (drowning victim), etc.
5. Place one hand under victim's neck.
6. Place other hand on victim's forehead so that thumb and forefinger can close the nose.
7. Lift gently with hand under neck while

pushing down with hand on forehead. This will extend the neck and open the air passages in the vast majority of cases.

8. Initially, give the victim four (4) quick breaths without interruption, then take a deep breath (about twice the normal), open your mouth wide, place your mouth over the victim's mouth and blow.

9. Watch for victim's chest to rise. As soon as this happens, remove your mouth from the victim's and allow the air to expire from the victim's chest.

10. Repeat 12–14 times a minute for adults and 18–20 for children.

11. If the chest does not rise, one or more of the following conditions exists and must be corrected:

   a. Airleak.
   Make sure that there is an airtight seal between your mouth and the victim's and that the seal on the victim's nose is secure.
   b. Airway obstruction (more likely).
   Insert your finger in the victim's mouth and remove any foreign objects (false teeth, etc.), vomit and/or blood clots.
   For children—roll the child over your forearm and give a sharp blow between the shoulder blades.

12. If the chest still fails to rise, remove hand from neck, insert your thumb into the victim's mouth and grab lower jawbone (mandible) between the thumb and finger, lift jawbone upward, holding it in this position while you continue to perform mouth-to-mouth breathing.

13. Mouth-to-nose breathing may be carried out using much the same technique as for mouth-to-mouth, except, of course, the victim's mouth is held closed while your mouth is placed over the victim's nose.

14. If you are hesitant to place your mouth over the victim's, satisfactory mouth-to-mouth breathing may be carried out through a handkerchief.

CARDIOPULMONARY RESUSCITATION (CPR)
External Heart Massage

NOTE: CPR should not be attempted in the water; use float, boat, or beach.

1. After artificial respiration has been insti-tuted with four quick breaths, and only then, check to see if external heart massage should be started.

   a. It is needed only if the heart has stopped.
   b. In many cases, the initiation of artificial respiration will be sufficient to cause resumption of the heartbeat.

2. Check for pulse.
   a. The best pulse to check is the carotid in the neck. This is a large artery lying close to the surface on either side of the Adam's apple. Practice feeling your own carotid pulse.

3. Check the pupils.
   a. If the pupils are dilated and do not constrict (get smaller) when light hits them, the blood flow to the brain is insufficient.

4. If there is no pulse and/or the pupils are dilated and do not constrict, start external heart massage.

5. For external heart massage to be effective, the victim must be on a firm surface, i.e., ground, spineboard, or floor.

6. Locate notch at top of breastbone.

7. Locate the lower end of the breastbone. Great care must be exercised *not* to place your hand over the tip of the breastbone (xiphoid process).

8. Measure two fingerwidths up from the xiphoid process, and place the heel of one hand over lower one-third of breastbone, and the other hand on top of first.

9. Bring shoulders directly over the victim's breastbone. Keep your arms straight and rock back and forth slightly from the hip joints exerting pressure vertically downward to depress the lower breastbone.

10. Then release pressure immediately. Compression and relaxation must be of equal duration. Do not remove the heel of your hand from the victim's chest when the pressure is released. Be sure that the pressure is completely released so that the breastbone returns to its normal resting position between compressions.

11. The breastbone should be compressed 1 1/2 to 2 inches for adults. For small children only the heel of one hand is used to compress the sternum. In small children, the heart lies higher in the chest and external compression should be applied over the mid-sternum.

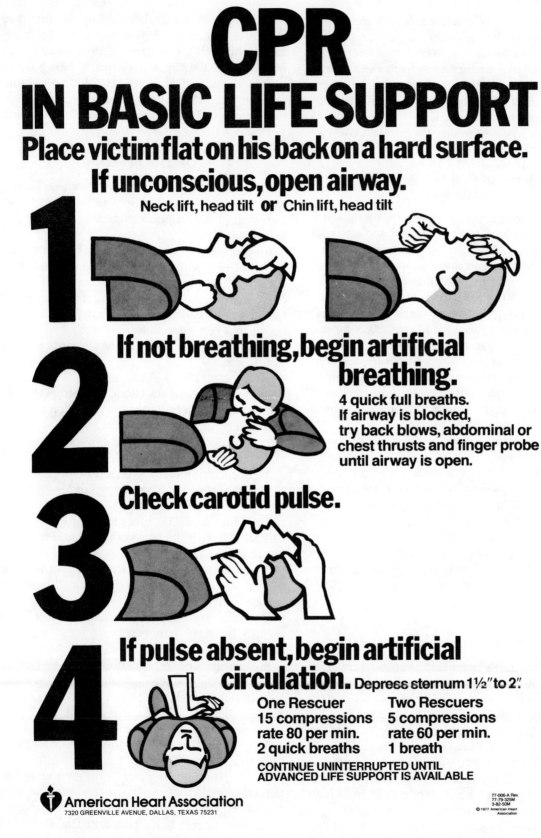

CPR
IN BASIC LIFE SUPPORT

Place victim flat on his back on a hard surface. If unconscious, open airway.

Neck lift, head tilt **or** Chin lift, head tilt

1

If not breathing, begin artificial breathing.

2

4 quick full breaths.
If airway is blocked,
try back blows, abdominal or
chest thrusts and finger probe
until airway is open.

Check carotid pulse.

3

If pulse absent, begin artificial circulation. Depress sternum 1½" to 2".

4

One Rescuer	Two Rescuers
15 compressions	5 compressions
rate 80 per min.	rate 60 per min.
2 quick breaths	1 breath

**CONTINUE UNINTERRUPTED UNTIL
ADVANCED LIFE SUPPORT IS AVAILABLE**

♥ American Heart Association
7320 GREENVILLE AVENUE, DALLAS, TEXAS 75231

77-006-A Rev.
77-79-325M
3-82-50M
© 1977 American Heart
Association

12. This cycle is repeated 60–80 times per minute in adults, 80–100 in children, and *should be in a smooth, rhythmic fashion.*

13. Keep your fingers away from the victim's ribs to avoid fractures. Fingers may be interlocked during this procedure to assist in keeping them off the chest wall.

14. Check pulse frequently to see if the victim's heart has restarted.

Techniques of CPR For One and Two Rescuers

1. If only one rescuer is present, he must administer both artificial respiration and external heart massage. This can be managed by interrupting external heart massage every 15 beats to give 2 deep lung inflations. Because of the interruptions for the lung inflation, the single rescuer must administer each series of 15 chest compressions at a more rapid rate, 80 compressions per minute, in order to achieve an actual compression rate of 60 compressions per minute. The two deep inflations must be administered in quick succession, within a period of 5 seconds. **DO NOT** allow full, long exhalation between breaths.

2. If two rescuers are present, they should work as follows:
   a. One, positioned at the victim's head
      (1) Administers artificial respiration
      (2) Monitors pulse at carotid artery (neck) without interrupting artificial respiration.
   b. One positions himself on the *opposite side* of the victim's body at shoulder level and begins external heart massage.

Some Additional Factors in Cardiopulmonary Resuscitation

1. The victim's stomach may become distended with air. This is especially true in children and if the airway is not clear. It is not dangerous, but may interfere with lung inflation. It can be remedied by applying pressure over the stomach with the palm of your hand. This expels the air, but may also lead to regurgitation of the stomach contents, so you must be ready to turn the victim's head to one side and clean out the mouth with your fingers or a cloth.

2. Cardiopulmonary resuscitation, once started, must be continued until spontaneous breathing and a heartbeat occur or until the victim is turned over to a physician. In many cases, this will mean that the procedures must be continued while the victim is being transported to a medical facility. Under no circumstances should cardiopulmonary resuscitation be interrupted for more than a five (5) second period.

STOP THE BLEEDING

After checking the victim's airway, or having reestablished his breathing and/or heartbeat, the next most important step is to stop the bleeding.

Bleeding is the escape of blood from arteries, veins, or even capillaries because of a break in their walls. Control of severe bleeding is an urgent matter. Arterial bleeding from a major blood vessel can cause a casualty to bleed to death in a very short time.

Identification of the types of bleeding may be as follows:

1. *Arterial bleeding:* Blood escaping is bright red, gushes forth in jets or spurts which are synchronized with the pulse.
2. *Venous bleeding:* Blood is dark red and escapes in a steady flow.
3. *Capillary bleeding:* Blood is intermediate in color, and oozes from the wound.

To control severe bleeding apply DIRECT PRESSURE with the palm of your hand over the entire area of the wound. Also, raise the affected part to a level higher than the heart, if there are no fractures, or if additional pain or harm will not be inflicted.

If immediately available, a thick pad of cloth should be held between your hand and the wound, or add the cloth as soon as possible.

Preferably, the cloth should be sterile or clean. However, unclean material can be used. Do not remove this dressing if it becomes blood soaked. Rather, add more layers of cloth and continue direct pressure and elevation.

A pressure bandage can replace direct hand pressure on most parts of the body. Apply the pressure bandage by placing the center of the bandage or strip of cloth directly over the pad; hold the pad in place by circling the bandage ends around the body part and tie off with a knot directly over the pad.

If direct pressure does not control the bleeding, apply pressure at the appropriate PRESSURE POINT *maintaining pressure over the wound and elevation*. Pressure on the PRESSURE POINT will control arterial bleeding in the region supplied by that artery.

If the bleeding is from a wound in the lower arm, apply pressure to the *brachial artery*. This pressure point is located on the inside of the arm in the groove between the biceps and triceps, about midway between the armpit and the elbow.

Pressure should be applied by grasping the middle of the victim's upper arm, with the thumb on the outside of his arm and your fingers on the inside. Press or pull your fingers toward your thumb, using the flat inside surface of your finger, not your finger tips.

If the bleeding is from a wound in the leg, apply pressure to the *femoral artery*. This pressure point is located on the front center part of the diagonally slanted "hinge" of the leg, in the crease of the groin area, and over the pelvic bone.

Apply pressure by placing the heel of your hand directly over the spot described above. Lean forward with the arm straightened to apply pressure.

It is IMPORTANT when using the pressure points (brachial and femoral arteries) that you maintain pressure over the wound as well as elevation.

It is also important to remember, especially in situations involving mass casualties, that a conscious victim may apply pressure to his own wound to restrict or stop the bleeding allowing you to assist others.

If the above methods do not control severe bleeding and the victim is in danger of bleeding to death, a tourniquet may be used as a last resort to save a life.

The TOURNIQUET should be used ONLY for the severe, life-threatening bleeding that cannot be controlled by other means. This method is used only on the arm or leg. To apply a tourniquet:

1. Place the tourniquet just above the wound edges. If the wound is in a joint area or just below, place the tourniquet directly above the joint.

2. Wrap the tourniquet band tightly twice around the limb and tie a half knot.

3. Place a short, strong stick, screwdriver or any similar object that you can find on the half knot and tie a full knot.

4. Twist the stick until bleeding stops.

5. Secure the stick in place.

6. Attach a note to the victim giving the location of the tourniquet and the time it was applied.

7. Once the serious decision to apply a tourniquet has been made it should not be loosened (except on the advice of a physician).

8. Treat for shock and get medical attention IMMEDIATELY.

NOTE: A TOURNIQUET SHOULD ONLY BE TIGHT ENOUGH TO STOP THE BLEEDING.

PROTECT THE WOUNDS

When the airway has been checked or breathing/heartbeat reestablished and the bleeding has been stopped, the next step is to protect the wounds. Wounds may be classed as open flesh wounds, fractured bones and burns. Regardless of the class of wound, all must be protected from further aggravation or injury while transporting the victim to a hospital to help relieve his pain and discomfort. Burn wounds will be considered in detail at this point since they are most critical and are common in boating accidents.

TREAT FOR SHOCK

Shock is a state of circulatory deficiency associated with depression of the vital processes of the body. It must be considered and followed for each victim, regardless of the nature or extent of his injuries. Always remember that a victim may go into shock hours after he is rescued and given first aid.

Injury related shock, commonly referred to as traumatic shock, is decidedly different from electric shock, insulin shock, and other special forms of shock. This section relates to traumatic shock which is a condition resulting in a depressed state of many vital body functions that could threaten life, even though the injuries would not otherwise be fatal.

Evaluation of the situation, according to the extent and severity of the injuries, is more important than any particular sign or symptom. The shock syndrome (set of symptoms which occur together) is variable and the symptoms listed below do not appear in every casualty, nor are they equally noticeable. The following findings are, however, representative of the varied picture which may be presented by the casualty in shock:

1. Eyes may be glassy, lackluster, pupils are dilated or suggest fear and apprehension.

2. Breathing may be normal, rapid, or labored.

3. The lips may be pale or cyanotic (bluish-gray).

4. The skin may be very pale or a peculiar ashen-gray (if dark complexion).

5. The skin temperature may be lowered and the body covered with a clammy sweat.

6. The pulse may be nearly normal or it may be rapid, weak, thready, and of poor volume.

7. There may be retching (trying to vomit; heave), nausea, vomiting, hiccups and dryness of the mouth, lips and tongue.

8. Restlessness, apprehension, are usual signs.

9. Veins in the skin are collapsed. Veins normally visible at the front of the elbow or forearm, and back of hands, may become invisible.

10. Frequent complaints of thirst. Shock victims may complain of thirst rather than pain, even when they are severely wounded. It's easy to recognize the fully developed picture of shock, but it is not so easy to recognize the victim about to go into shock.

First aid for SHOCK should be given to any seriously injured person.

To prevent or give first aid for shock, the following steps should be taken: (1) Keep the victim lying down; (2) Maintain the victim's normal body temperature; and, (3) Get medical care as soon as possible.

Depending on the injury, the victim's body should be positioned to minimize the danger of shock. The most desirable position is lying down with the feet raised 6 to 8 inches. If you are uncertain as to the type of injury, keep the victim flat on his back. The following chart gives variations in this position based on the injuries the victim has sustained:

Injury or Condition   Position

Injury or Condition	Position
1. Back or neck	1. Do not move the victim
2. Wounds of face and jaw	2. Sitting and leaning forward
3. Unconscious	3. On side
4. Head injury	4. Flat or propped up (head never lower than body)
5. Breathing difficulty	5. Head and shoulders raised

Maintain normal BODY TEMPERATURE (98.6 degrees F.). If environmental conditions are cold or damp, protect the victim by placing blankets or additional clothing over and under the victim. If conditions are hot, provide protection from the heat or sun (shade) and do not add heat.

Obtain MEDICAL CARE as soon as possible. If this care will be delayed for an hour or more, water, preferably containing salt and baking soda (1/2 level teaspoon of salt and 1/2 level teaspoon of baking soda to each quart of water) is recommended. An adult should be given about 4 ounces every 15 minutes, a child approximately 2 ounces, and an infant about one ounce. DO NOT give fluids if the victim is unconscious, having convulsions, vomiting, becoming nauseated, or if surgery is likely.

MISCELLANEOUS INJURIES AND ILLNESSES

Injuries and sudden illnesses other than those mentioned previously may occur. If a medical emergency occurs on the water and your boat is equipped with a two-way radio, do not hesitate to call the Coast Guard to obtain medical advice and possible evacuation.

TRANSPORTING A DIVER VICTIM

If medical assistance is on the way, do not move an accident victim. However, if you must transport a victim to special treatment facilities such as a recompression chamber or expert medical help, then follow these rules:

1. If the victim requires artificial respiration alone, do not move him any farther than necessary before normal breathing resumes, unless you continue artificial respiration en route.

Once you begin artificial respiration, you must continue it, even during transportation. Keep the victim horizontal at all times, or in slightly head-up position if more comfortable, even if he regains consciousness, for sitting or standing too soon may produce fainting, heart failure, or shock.

2. If the victim requires recompression alone, and recompression in the water is not possible because of unconsciousness, lack of air, shallow water, and so forth, call the local U.S. Coast Guard search and rescue squad or the nearest Port Captain immediately by telephone or radio. They will provide transportation to the nearest recompression chamber—probably by helicopter. Try to make certain of your diagnosis, however, for they are permitted to charge you for rescue expenses and may do so if it is a false alarm.

If the victim needs both artificial respiration and recompression, start artificial respiration first and keep it up by some means while transporting him to a recompression chamber. If no recompression chamber is available, phone the Divers Alert Network.

3. If a recompression chamber happens to be *immediately* available and air embolism appears to have caused cessation of breathing, recompress the victim at once and begin artificial respiration as soon as he is in the chamber. If more than a couple of minutes is involved, do not delay artificial respiration.

4. When transporting a decompression or embolism victim by air, request that the aircraft fly at low altitudes to avoid aggravating the victim's condition due to bubble expansion in the lesser pressure at high altitudes.

5. Administer oxygen to the victim whenever possible.

6. Keep the victim flat and look out for tongue swallowing or air-passage obstruction if he is unconscious.

DAN'S DIVING ACCIDENT MANAGEMENT FLOWCHART

In a suspected diving accident, the first question is "Did the victim take a breath underwater?" from a scuba tank, hose, bucket, submerged car, or any compressed air source, regardless of depth.

If the answer is no, give CPR and oxygen if needed and evaluate as a medical problem not related to diving.

If the injured diver did breathe underwater and only mild symptoms are present (fatigue and itching only), place the patient in a left-side-down-head-low position and administer two aspirin, oxygen, and oral fluids while maintaining close observation.

If these mild symptoms clear totally within thirty minutes, have the person contact a diving physician at his or her earliest convenience.

If the symptoms do not clear, seek medical advice and treat as serious injury.

If the injured diver did breathe underwater and has serious symptoms, do the following:

1. Administer CPR if required.

2. Keep airway open and prevent aspiration of vomitus. Intubate unconscious injured diver if possible.

3. Keep injured diver in left-side-down-head-low (Trendelenberg) position.

4. Administer oxygen by tight-fitting double-seal mask at the highest possible oxygen concentration. Do not remove oxygen except to reopen the airway or if the victim shows signs of oxygen convulsions.

5. Protect the injured diver from excessive heat or cold.

6. Give conscious patients nonalcoholic liquids such as fruit juices or oral balanced salt solutions, e.g., Gatorade.

7. Intravenous fluid replacement with electrolyte solutions is preferred for unconscious or seriously injured victims. Ringer's lactate, normal saline, or 5 percent dextrose in saline may be used. Do not use 5 percent dextrose in water.

8. Give two aspirin, as an antiplatelet agent, as a onetime dose to a conscious diver only.

9. If there is evidence of involvement of the central nervous system, give steroids, hydrocortisone hemisuccinate, 1 gm IV or dexamethasone, 20–30 mgm IV.

10. Evaluate and stabilize patient at the nearest hospital emergency room prior to transfer to recompression chamber if needed.

11. Contact a physician experienced in diving medicine.

12. If air evacuation is used, it is critical that

the patient not be exposed to decreased baro-metric pressure at altitude. Flight crews must maintain cabin pressure at sea level.

13. Contact Hyperbaric Trauma Center be-fore transporting the injured diver.

14. Send these pages and recorded history with the patient.

15. Send all diving equipment with the pa-tient for examination. If that is not possible, ar-range for local examination and gas analysis.

16. When in doubt, telephone:

DIVERS ALERT NETWORK
(919) 684-8111
(Call collect if necessary in an
emergency.)
Ask for diving physician.

DIAGNOSIS AND TREATMENT OF DIVING ACCIDENTS (ALPHABETICAL LISTING)

Since I am no physician, I have relied almost entirely upon the medical personnel of the U.S. Navy Experimental Diving Unit, the Medi-cal Research Laboratory at the Submarine Es-cape Training School, the *U.S. Navy Diving Manual,* DAN—the Divers Alert Network, and the *U.S. Navy Manual for Submarine Medicine Practice.* The following pages contain a list, gathered from these sources, of all diving acci-dents and diseases in alphabetical order, to-gether with their causes, symptoms (indications experienced by the victim), signs (indications visible to an observer), and treatment. This in-formation has been read, corrected, and up-dated by the late Charles V. Brown, M.D. who was a renowned specialist in emergency and hy-perbaric medicine from Riverside, California and the contributing medical editor of *Skin Diver Magazine.*

Air Embolism and Related Accidents

Air embolism and its related conditions—subcutaneous emphysema, mediastinal emphy-sema, and pneumothorax—are caused by over-expansion of the lungs by excessive air pressure during a diving ascent, with the resultant tear-ing of lung tissue and leakage of air. The most common cause of these conditions is voluntary breath holding during ascent from depths of three feet or more.

Air embolism refers to the leakage of air bub-bles directly from the lungs into the blood-stream. It is the most serious of the embolic dis-eases, because air bubbles are likely to lodge in the brain and cause rapid and permanent dam-age there.

Subcutaneous emphysema refers to escaped lung air that has lodged in tissue just beneath the skin, causing a swelling. This usually occurs around the neck and collarbone areas.

Mediastinal emphysema refers to the pres-ence of pockets of air that have escaped from the lungs into the area surrounding the heart, great vessels, trachea, larynx, etc.

Though not very serious in themselves, the presence of either kind of emphysema may in-dicate the presence of air embolism.

Pneumothorax refers to the presence of air pockets between the lungs and the walls of the chest cavity, which can cause collapse of a lung and extreme difficulty in breathing.

Air embolism. Symptoms and signs are likely to occur *within seconds* of surfacing and to be dramatic in impact. The effects may begin long before the surface is reached, but sometimes a diver will not reveal any symptoms and signs before he loses consciousness.

Symptoms:
    weakness
    dizziness
    paralysis or weakness of limbs
    visual disturbance such as blurring
    unconsciousness
    (all the above indicate brain involve-
        ment)
    possible chest pain
Signs:
    staggering
    confusion or difficulty in seeing
        (bumping into objects or moving in
        wrong direction)
    favoring affected side of chest
    rapid, shallow breathing
TREATMENT:
Air embolism. If a recompression chamber is immediately available, send him down as quickly as possible without observing standard rate of descent and seek the assistance of a qual-ified chamber operator.

If no recompression chamber is immediately available, you may be able to save the victim, if you do not lose a second, after the first sign or symptom of air embolism, in getting him to a pressure chamber while he is still able to act rationally. Then follow DAN's Diving Accident Management Flowchart on page 161.

Make sure that he has a tender diver by his side at all times. Send immediately for medical help and more air if required, or radio the U. S. Coast Guard or the nearest Port Captain.

Emphysema. In cases of mediastinal or subcutaneous emphysema that are not complicated by the presence of air embolism, recompression may not be desirable. Seek medical help immediately and administer oxygen when possible.

Pneumothorax. If uncomplicated by the presence of air embolism, do not recompress. Seek medical help immediately and administer oxygen when possible. Keep the victim resting.

Note: If breathing should stop during treatment, artificial respiration (possibly with recompression) should be given to help all other treatment until breathing returns to normal. In case of air embolism, artificial respiration can be administered while the victim is in or being transported to a recompression chamber. Shock must also be treated where it exists, but it does not take precedence over other treatments.

Anoxia (Oxygen Deficiency), Hypoxia, Asphyxia, and Carbon Dioxide Poisoning

For all practical purposes, anoxia, hypoxia, asphyxia, and carbon dioxide CO_2 (excess) poisoning are closely similar in cause, prevention, symptoms, and treatment. All can be caused by the loss or inadequacy of an air supply, but CO_2 poisoning can be caused by a buildup of an excessive partial pressure of CO_2 within an air supply as well. Excess of CO_2 is known to complicate cases of the bends and nitrogen narcosis. For example, breathing from a tank that has been mistakenly filled with a gas other than pure air can cause all three. So can overexertion, excessive breath holding, shallow-water blackout during snorkel diving, excessive pace or skip breathing, or obstructed air passage.

All three conditions can be prevented by avoiding the causes: by resting when breathing becomes labored, by not hyperventilating or overtaxing your breath-holding limits, and by seeking fresh air if you can't catch your breath.

Note: Never breathe air from an unventilated underwater air pocket, as might exist inside a sunken wreck, for example. Oxidation (rusting) and organic metabolism usually consume all the oxygen, leaving only carbon dioxide, which causes instant blackout without warning and often results in drowning. Red Raisch, one of the best known scuba instructors on the East Coast, died in this way and so can you.

Symptoms:
- sometimes no warning, as in sudden blackout
- usually acute air hunger
- panting
- fogging of mask
- feeling of intoxication, mental confusion
- headache, dizziness, weakness, sweating, or nausea
- spots before the eyes

Signs:
- cyanosis (blueness of skin, nail beds, and lips)
- slowing of responses, confusion like drunkenness
- unconsciousness, if severe
- possible violent increase in breathing, followed by cessation of breathing
- if unconscious, possible muscular twitching

TREATMENT:

Be moderate in breath holding and skip breathing. When you feel air hunger or the need to pant, then stop and rest, breathing regularly and deeply, until breathing returns to normal. When doing heavy work with scuba gear, anticipate the need to pant and start breathing deeply. Surface if you cannot catch your breath. If you are treating a victim, remove any obstructions from air passages (including tongue if the diver is unconscious). Usually the exposure to fresh air quickly remedies all three maladies.

Artificial Respiration

See *Drowning.*

Asphyxia

See *Anoxia.*

Barnacle and Mussel Cuts

Much of our coastline is thickly populated by sharp-edged shellfish, such as barnacles and mussels, which can cause severe cuts and abrasions to divers who are thrown in contact with them by wave action while entering and leaving the water. Such areas should be avoided if possible. Cleanse the cuts with soap and fresh water or hydrogen peroxide, apply antiseptic bandage, and treat generally as a physical injury.

Barracuda Bite

Barracuda are known to instinctively bite at bright, flashing objects, so avoid wearing such objects wherever barracuda abound. Though not aggressive, barracuda have been known to attack divers. Their bite is similar to a dog's. It should be cleansed thoroughly, disinfected, and treated as a physical injury.

The Bends

See *Decompression sickness.*

Blackout

See *Anoxia.*

Bleeding

Bleeding, whether internal or external, indicates the presence of some other malady. External bleeding from cuts, etc., should be stopped immediately by using bandages, pressure points or, if necessary, a tourniquet. Internal bleeding after diving may indicate the presence of air embolism and related maladies.

Body Squeeze

See *Squeeze.*

Caisson Disease

See *Decompression sickness.*

Carbon Dioxide Poisoning

See *Anoxia.*

Carbon Monoxide Poisoning

Carbon monoxide poisoning is usually caused by contamination of a diver's air supply by carbon monoxide fumes. The presence of carbon monoxide in breathing air prevents the blood from carrying sufficient amounts of oxygen by saturating the hemoglobin. The result is that the body tissues are starved for oxygen (tissue anoxia).

Carbon monoxide poisoning can be prevented by seeing to it that your air supply is always certified pure. Air sources should be tested periodically for traces of carbon monoxide, and compressors should be maintained in tip-top working order. Be certain that the compressor air intakes are as far removed from engine exhausts as possible and upwind. A long extension tube fitted onto the engine exhaust will facilitate this.

    Symptoms:
        sometimes none before unconsciousness sets in
        headache, nausea, dizziness, weakness, tightness in head
        confusion and clumsiness similar to drunkenness or anoxia
    Signs:
        slow response, clumsiness, bad judgment
        unconsciousness
        breathing stops in severe cases
        abnormally red lips and pale skin
        blood is extremely red

TREATMENT:

Get victim into fresh air as soon as possible and give him oxygen if available. If unconscious, treat accordingly. Victim will usually recover rapidly with exposure to fresh air, but may suffer lingering aftereffects, such as headache and nausea.

Cardiac Arrest

See *Heart failure.*

Compressed-Air Illness

See *Decompression sickness.*

Cone Shell Poisoning

There are more than four hundred species of cone shells in the sea, and all contain a highly developed venom apparatus, some of which can cause death. If disturbed, the tiny, sluglike animal within can thrust out a cluster of microscopic venom-filled teeth that can easily puncture the skin. Although they are beautiful to look at and are prized collector's items, divers should avoid contact, or at least wear heavy gloves when handling them. Never carry cone shells in your pocket.

Symptoms:
  sharp stinging or burning sensation
  local shut-off of blood supply
  numbness and abnormal sensations may spread from the sting throughout the entire body, particularly the lips and mouth.

Signs:
  paralysis may follow in severe cases
  local cyanosis (blueness)
  coma and heart failure in severe cases

TREATMENT:
There is no specific treatment for cone shell stings. Cone shell poisoning should be treated as poisonous fish stings. Phone, if possible, a local poison center.

Coral Cuts

Almost all divers in tropical waters encounter coral formations, which can cause severe cuts and abrasions upon contact. Although usually not serious, coral wounds are extremely bothersome, itchy, slow to heal, and inducive to infection. A few corals produce a slow-healing, oozing type of wound by means of stinging cells similar to those of jellyfish, though not so violent. A few corals, such as brown mustard coral, produce a burning sting that soon disappears.

Coral wounds can easily be prevented by wearing gloves, shirts, and other protective clothing when diving amid coral formations.

Signs and Symptoms:
  burning pain
  inflammation of local area
  lingering itching
  red welt formation
  lingering, oozing wound

TREATMENT:
1. Wash area with alcohol, meat tenderizer, papaya juice, baking soda, or weak ammonia and water solution if available; follow with soap and fresh water.
2. Use cortisone ointment and antihistamine cream on the wound and give antihistamine by mouth to reduce initial pain.
3. As soon as pain begins to subside, cleanse wound thoroughly with soap and water to remove all foreign matter. Apply an antiseptic and dressing.
4. In severe cases (as when washed against coral head by surf) give patient bed rest and elevate affected limbs. Apply kaolin poultices or dressings wet with magnesium sulfate and glycerine solution.

Cramps

Overexertion of untrained muscles, extreme heat or cold, and diving too soon after meals sometimes causes a muscle or group of muscles to contract involuntarily and cause great pain. If cramps occur in the water, the pain can be relieved by firmly pressing the affected muscle and then working it out with gentle massage. Or, if you can return to boat or shore, the application of heat to the affected area will provide quick relief.

Cuts

See *Stop the Bleeding,* page 158.

Decompression Sickness

Decompression sickness (also known as the bends, caisson disease, compressed-air illness, and diver's disease) is caused by the formation of gas bubbles in the bloodstream due to inadequate decompression or desaturation of gases following a dive. A man cannot have decompression sickness unless he has been exposed to a sudden decrease in ambient pressure, as in caisson work or diving; if signs and symptoms appear, but not before twelve to fifteen hours after exposure, the chances are that the signs and symptoms are not those of decompression sickness. Generally speaking, the likelihood of decompression sickness increases in proportion to the depth-time ratio and the amount of work involved in a dive; it increases drastically when a diver does not receive stage decompression in accordance with the U.S. Navy Standard Air Decompression Tables.

The fact that decompression (the act of decompressing) was carried out in exact accordance with those tables does not rule out the possibility of decompression sickness, however, for a casualty factor of about 5 percent is considered normal in decompression cases, even when the decompression tables are followed to the letter.

The proper diagnosis of decompression sickness must depend upon an evaluation of the factors involved in the dive—depth, time, recommended decompression time, and workload—and the signs and symptoms manifest in the diver. Signs and symptoms of decompression sickness are usually apparent shortly after surfacing and almost always before twelve hours have elapsed. A review of U.S. Navy data concerning the onset of signs and symptoms of decompression sickness following a dive reveals:

50 percent occurred within 30 minutes
85 percent occurred within 1 hour
95 percent occurred within 3 hours
1 percent occurred after 6 hours

Symptoms of decompression sickness have been found to occur with the following frequency:

local pain	89 percent
leg	70 percent
arm	30 percent
dizziness (the "staggers")	5.3 percent
paralysis	2.3 percent
shortness of breath (the chokes)	1.6 percent
extreme fatigue and pain	1.3 percent
collapse with unconsciousness	0.5 percent

Signs:
evidences of local pain
the staggers—clumsiness and lack of response as if drunk
paralysis or partial paralysis
blotchy and mottled rash on skin
shortness of breath
collapse with unconsciousness
visual disturbance; extreme fatigue

A typical case of decompression sickness may begin with localized itching or burning or a tingling, numb sensation, and sometimes with the feeling that ants are crawling over the victim; the most frequent and dominating symptom is a deep piercing pain in the bones or joints which becomes progressively worse. A muscle strain or joint sprain suffered during a dive is sometimes confused with decompression sickness. However, sprains and strains are usually painful to touch and accompanied by swelling and discoloration, whereas, areas affected by the bends are not. The dizziness and ringing in the ears that accompany middle-ear damage, usually caused by squeeze, can also be confused with that experienced in decompression sickness. When in doubt, however, treat the diver as if he had the bends, for failure to treat doubtful cases is the most frequent cause of lasting injury.

The most serious signs and symptoms of decompression sickness are those resulting from bubbles in the brain, spinal cord, or lungs. Paralysis, the "chokes," unconsciousness, loss of speech or hearing, convulsions, or dizziness must be treated accordingly.

Examination. One fairly safe way to diagnose the presence of decompression sickness is to run through the following U.S. Navy checklist while examining the victim. If need be, ask the victim to walk or do light exercises to provoke manifestation of any of the more serious symptoms.

How does he feel? Any pain? Where and how severe? Changed by motion? Sore to touch or pressure? Bruise marks in the area? Mentally clear? Weakness, numbness, or peculiar sensations anywhere? Can he see and hear clearly? Can he walk, talk, and use his hands normally? Any dizziness?

Does he look and act normal? (Don't just take his word for it if he says he is all right.) Can he walk normally? Any limping or staggering? Is his speech clear and sensible? Is he clumsy or does he seem to be having difficulty with any movement? Can he keep his balance when standing with his eyes closed?

Does he have normal strength? (Check his strength against your own and compare his right side with his left.) Normal hand grip? Able to push and pull strongly with both arms and legs? Able to do deep-knee bends and other exercises?

Are his sensations normal? Can he hear clearly? Can he see clearly both close (reading) and distant objects? Normal vision in all directions? Can he feel pin pricks and light touches with a wisp of cotton all over his body? (Note that some areas are normally less sensitive than others—compare with yourself if in doubt.)

Look at his eyes. Are the pupils of normal size and equal? Do the pupils constrict when you shine a light in his eyes? Can he follow an object around normally with his eyes?

Check his reflexes if you know how. Note that it should not take a great deal of time to examine a man reasonably well.

If the victim is not suffering more than local pain, examine him on the surface, but do not waste time if decompression sickness is obvious.

TREATMENT:

If the above symptoms indicate any serious possibility of decompression sickness, get the victim on the way to the nearest recompression chamber immediately. If you do not know its location, contact the local port captain, the local U.S. Coast Guard office (they can provide air rescue at cost), or any one of the diving emergency action centers listed on page 154 in this book. Follow DAN's Diving Accident Management Flowchart on page 161.

Dermatitis

Frequent and continued exposure to water, especially tropical salt waters and contaminated waters, encourages skin disorders such as fungus infections, eczema, and allergies. While not very serious in themselves, they can incapacitate a man if neglected and ruin an otherwise perfect diving excursion.

    Symptoms:
        red rashes
        welts and local infection
        severe itching without obvious cause
        burning sensation when sweating
    Signs:
        inflammation of affected areas, blotchy
            complexion, welts or infection
        affected skin splitting or peeling
        rashes
        exudation of fluid

TREATMENT:

Dermatitis is best attacked by preventive treatment. Wash and dry thoroughly after each exposure to water. Remove rubber suits, swimsuits, wet clothing, supporters, and so forth as soon as possible and keep clean. Pay particular attention to your toes, ears, armpits, and crotch. Clean and dry them thoroughly and, if affected, sprinkle with medicinal powder. Avoid contamination by scratching, and treat evidence of skin infections with antibiotic or steroid ointments and bandage. Avoid contaminated waters, and if you are allergic to certain aquatic plants avoid them or wear protective clothing. Do not aggravate infections by continuing to dive before they heal. Seek a cool, dry climate. See a doctor if trouble persists.

Drowning

Drowning is the cause of over 85 percent of all deaths that occur in diving. It is usually the direct result of some other condition or mishap, but the result is still the same. Failure of breathing regulator or air supply, loss or flooding of mask or mouthpiece, surface exposure to rough water, overexertion or exhaustion, unconsciousness, electrocution, heart failure, or almost any mishap in water followed by failure of an emergency procedure or by panic can cause the victim to drown.

Adequate training and proper equipment (including flotation gear) and the heeding of all safety precautions are your best assurance against drowning. Your second-best assurance is to ascertain that everyone in your diving party is prepared to aid a diver in distress and is thoroughly schooled in the various methods of administering artificial respiration, both in and out of the water.

    Signs:
        unconsciousness
        cyanosis (blueness)
        cessation of breathing

TREATMENT:

There is only one treatment for drowning or cessation of breathing, and that is immediate application of artificial respiration and/or CPR.

Artificial respiration methods. In expert hands, a mechanical resuscitator is by far the most effective way of applying artificial respiration, but if one is not available there are other ways to administer artificial respiration. Of these, the mouth-to-mouth method is the most effective (see page 155) and also the most immediately available because it can be applied by a buddy diver even while the victim is still in the water. Every serious diver should familiarize himself with this procedure. Better yet, you should enroll in a formal course of instruction through your local chapter of the American Red Cross, the YMCA, or your certifying organization. See page 110 for techniques of administering mouth-to-mouth artificial respiration in the water.

Eardrum Rupture

Ear squeeze and eardrum rupture result from failure to equalize air pressure in the inner ear with water pressure on the outer ear while ascending or descending in the water. There are two kinds of squeeze: (1) Inner-ear squeeze, in which the inner ear is distended and may rupture inwardly (generally caused by failure to equalize during descent or by a blocked Eustachian tube), or by an overly anxious diver who insists on continuing his descent in spite of the telltale pain in his ears and (2) External-ear squeeze, in which the eardrum is distended and may rupture outwardly. The latter is generally caused from a partial vacuum in the outer ear—usually caused by the use of earplugs or from a seal inadvertently made by a dry suit blocking the outer ear passage. It can also occur due to failure of the eustachian tubes to ventilate during ascent because of congestion. Eardrum rupture can be prevented by perfecting your ear-clearing techniques and by not diving when you suffer from colds.

Symptoms:

    severe pain on descent as rupture occurs

    dizziness and nausea as cold water enters middle ear

    temporary disorientation

    loss of hearing in affected ear

Signs (depending on extent of damage):

    redness and swelling of eardrum

    bleeding into middle ear or outer ear canal

    spitting up blood

    blood blisters around drum

TREATMENT:

Hands off! If eardrum rupture is suspected, do not allow anything, whether water, instruments, or medications, to enter the ear. Close the outer passage with a bit of cotton and get the victim to a doctor as soon as possible to avoid possible infection. If rupture does not heal in from two weeks to a month, victim will require surgery.

Ear Infections

Divers who frequent tropical waters are peculiarly susceptible to external ear infections, especially by gram-negative bacteria. While not especially dangerous if treated properly, infections can be very uncomfortable and sometimes incapacitating.

Symptoms:

    crusting of ear canal

    itching or pain in ears

    exudation of fluid from ear canal

Signs:

    pain when ear is tugged

    heavy accumulations of "fungus growth"

    dry flakes of same at external ear opening

    redness and swelling around ear canal

TREATMENT:

Preventive treatment is the best. Keep the ears always clean, dry, and clear of *excess* ear wax. Use drops of alcohol diluted with boric acid and water to dry ears after each dive. Do not dive until healed. Look out for recurrences and see doctor if it persists.

Electrocution

Electrocution can result from careless handling of underwater electrical apparatus, such as electric cutting and welding torches and photographic lighting equipment. All electrical apparatus used in diving should be perfectly insulated and in perfect condition. To be on the safe side, in handling such equipment you must insulate yourself as well as the equipment.

Signs:

    unconsciousness

    cessation of breathing

    heart failure

    victim may have been unable to pull away from source of shock

TREATMENT:

Cut the electric current immediately and do not touch victim before doing so. Bring victim to surface and treat for heart failure (pages 155–158). Give CPR until victim is revived or pronounced dead. Get medical assistance at once if possible. Keep victim at bed rest for at least twenty-four hours after he revives.

Embolism

See *Air embolism.*

Emphysema

See *Air embolism.*

Face Mask Squeeze

See *Squeeze.*

Fainting

Fainting (syncope) is caused by a temporary failure in the body's automatic blood-pressure control system, which provides oxygen to the brain tissue. This failure, in turn, is caused by some acute stress, pain, or emotion. Unless it is accompanied by shock due to injury or loss of blood, it is not serious and the victim usually recovers in a minute or two.

Symptoms:
dizziness
weakness
nausea
pallid or green color
staggering
collapse and unconsciousness

TREATMENT:

Fainting can often be avoided if, at the first symptoms, the victim either lies down with his head back and legs elevated, or sits down and leans over, placing his head between his knees. This allows oxygen-carrying blood to reach the vital brain tissue more readily. A fainting victim should be stretched out with legs elevated and head back until revived and rested. If he fails to revive within a few minutes, seek medical help immediately, for that indicates the presence of a more serious ailment. If the victim stops breathing, artificial respiration should be applied at once.

Fish Poisoning

Internal fish poisoning. Certain species of fish are poisonous to eat and should be avoided as food at all times. These include porcupine fish and sunfish. Fish meat that has become old, rotten, or rancid can also induce internal poisoning.

In addition, certain fish around some tropical coral reefs become poisonous to eat during brief periods of the year because of a mysterious disease called ciguatera. This disease is undoubtedly caused by some seasonal environmental food—probably a blue-green alga—which has not yet been isolated, and it can affect even prized table fish such as grouper and snapper, as well as other reef fish like barracuda, squirrel fish, parrot fish, jacks. Although there are as many methods of detecting fish infected with ciguatera as there are areas where it occurs, most are products of folklore rather than medical science and should not be relied upon. Consequently, you will have to take your chances when spearfishing in areas known to be affected by ciguatera, or test suspected fish by feeding samples to an animal and observing its reaction. The disease usually is not serious, but it can cause great discomfort.

Symptoms (one to ten hours after eating fish):
stomach cramps
nausea and weakness
vomiting
diarrhea
prolonged numbness and tingling sensations
lack of coordination
difficulty in breathing
confused senses
relapses on eating fish
temperature reversal (hot feels cold and cold feels hot)

TREATMENT:
purge stomach as soon as symptoms appear
try antihistamine
avoid eating fish

External fish poisoning. Certain fishes are equipped with venomous spines poisonous to touch and should be avoided. These include stonefish, scorpionfish, stingrays, zebrafish, horned sharks, catfish, weaverfish, ratfish, toad-fish, surgeon fish, and rabbit fish.

Although not really fish, almost all species of the jellyfish family are equipped with long, streaming tentacles containing thousands of tiny cells of venom, which cause severe acid stings.

Finally, the bite of some marine creatures, such as the octopus and the sea snake, can be very poisonous.

1. *Fish with poisonous spines* are lethargic and do not tend to scare off easily. Many camouflage themselves against the bottom and are difficult to detect, but a few are very colorful—black and orange being the predominant colors. Almost all favor tropical waters, and local authorities should be consulted for information concerning them before you dive.

Symptoms:
    local pain within a few minutes
    reddening and inflammation of affected area
    hot, burning sensation
    dizziness, possible shock and fainting
    weakness
Signs:
    puncture wound
    local swelling and inflammation
    in stingray wounds, a spiny sheath may be left in wound

TREATMENT:

Get the victim out of the water as quickly as possible and put him at rest. Remove all foreign matter from the wound and wash thoroughly with antiseptic or clean, fresh water. If severe, encourage local bleeding. If need be apply a venous tourniquet—then make small incisions and apply suction. Follow by soaking, preferably in hot or icy fresh water. Very, very hot compresses can neutralize many venoms, but if only mildly hot they simply dilate the blood vessels, increase circulation, and thus speed absorption of the poison into the circulatory system. So make the compresses as hot as the victim can tolerate. When pain has subsided, cover the wound and elevate the affected limb. Watch for signs of shock. If the wound is in the chest or abdomen, seek medical help immediately, for the victim's heart action may be affected.

2. *Jellyfish,* although not fish but coelenterates, are found in all waters of the world. There are 2,500 known species, some dangerous and some not. The two most dangerous types—the Portuguese man-of-war and the sea wasp—favor tropical waters, the latter being found almost exclusively around northern Australia, the Philippines, and the Indian Ocean. Most jellyfish are small, their bodies seldom exceeding six inches in diameter, but their stinging tentacles may reach fifty feet. Avoid contact at all times—even when they are found "dead" on the beach. Wear protective clothing in infested waters.

Symptoms (depending on species and extent and site of sting):
    from a mild prickly or stinging sensation to intense burning, throbbing, or shooting pain, which may render a victim unconscious
    stomach cramps
    numbness
    nausea
    backache
    loss of speech and frothing at the mouth
    constriction of throat
    difficult breathing
    sweating
    paralysis
    delirium
    convulsions
    shock
Signs:
    reddening and inflammation of affected area
    clinging pieces of almost transparent blue-green tentacles
    welts
    blisters
    swelling
    small skin hemorrhages

TREATMENT:

Get the victim out of the water and at rest quickly. Remove as many of the clinging tentacles as possible. Do not touch with hands; use gloves, cloth, seaweed, or even sand. Wash with salt water; fresh water will only cause any still intact stinging cells to trigger and release their acid. Apply weak ammonia, alcohol, or baking soda solution. If available, apply cortisone ointment, antihistamine cream, or anesthetic ointment. Otherwise, try olive oil, sugar, cooling lotions, or ethyl alcohol, followed by cold compresses. Look out for shock (page 175).

3. *Poisonous bites* vary in severity according

to their source. An octopus bite is not likely to occur or to be very serious if it does, although at least one cause of death has been reported as a result of one. Moray eel bites can be considered poisonous only in that they leave particles of slime and rotten matter in the wound that are conducive to infection. Sea snake bites are inflicted by small sets of fangs containing a potent venom, however, and should be treated as lethal snake bites. Octopuses are found in all waters, the moray eels in all tropical waters, and the sea snake in tropical coastal waters, especially in the Pacific and Indian oceans. All should be avoided.

Symptoms:

Octopus bites cause a stinging sensation, with swelling, redness, and fever around the affected area. There is no specific treatment, but severe cases may be treated as a poisonous spine wound.

Moray eel bites can cause severe lacerations, for they have needle-sharp teeth and a tenacious grip. Clean the wound thoroughly and apply antiseptic and dressing. If stitches are needed, see a doctor as soon as possible.

Sea snake bites have a delayed-action effect. There is no pain or reaction at the site of the wound itself, but after a delay of about twenty minutes to one hour, victims are likely to feel a general anxiety or else a general feeling of well-being. This may lead to thickening of the tongue, general muscular stiffness, and pain. Then other symptoms appear as follows:

Symptoms:
- weakness, progressing to possible immobility
- drooping of eyelids
- tightening of jaw muscles as in lockjaw (tetanus)
- partial paralysis of throat area
- parched throat
- shock
- muscular spasms
- convulsions
- paralysis of face and eye muscles
- respiratory difficulty
- unconsciousness
- death (in 25 percent of cases)

Signs:
- local pain and reaction
- absence of pain after initial bite for at least twenty minutes

- two circular dots or two pairs of dots half an inch apart
- possibly a fang left in wound

TREATMENT:

Get victim out of water and at rest as soon as possible. If in the United States, call the Coast Guard, the Port Captain, or send for medical help. Apply venous tourniquet between wound and heart, remembering to loosen it for 90 seconds every ten minutes. Promote local bleeding by making incision around wound and applying suction. Give antivenom treatment if possible. Phone the *Poison Control Center* in Oklahoma City at (405) 271-5454. They can tell you where to find the nearest antivenom for practically every poisonous creature extant in the world. Treat for shock and get the victim to a hospital if at all possible. Try to kill or capture snake for identification.

Gas Pains

See *Stomach pains.*

Gas Poisoning

Unless a diver's air tank is mistakenly filled with some gas other than air, carbon monoxide is the only poisonous gas likely to be encountered in normal scuba diving. In all cases, exposure to fresh air and artificial respiration is the standard treatment. Ventilation with pure oxygen (preferably under pressure) is even better.

Heart Failure (Cardiac Arrest)

Electrocution, shock, and some respiratory accidents sometimes cause the heart to stop beating. When this happens, tissue anoxia (oxygen starvation) sets in rapidly and can cause irreparable brain damage in less than three minutes. Therefore, you cannot lose a second in treating heart-failure victims if permanent brain damage is to be avoided.

Symptoms and Signs:
- shortness of breath
- chest pain
- bluish color of the lips and fingernail area
- chronic cough
- swelling of the ankles

These symptoms may occur in combination, but usually one is outstanding.

TREATMENT:

Administer CPR (pages 155–158). Treat for shock, maintaining normal body temperature and placing in position of greatest comfort for breathing. Call for help.

Heat Exhaustion, Heat Stroke, and Heat Cramps

When a person exerts himself in a hot environment, a considerable part of his circulation must be directed into blood vessels of the skin in order to radiate heat from the surface and to support the activity of the sweat glands. When the nerves that control expansion and contraction of blood vessels and heart output are inadequate to meet the needs of increased skin circulation, in addition to muscle and brain circulation, the individual collapses.

a. *Heat Exhaustion*
Symptoms:
Predominant:
faintness
pounding of the heart
Other:
nausea
vomiting
fainting
headache
restlessness

The victim who has collapsed in the heat and is perspiring freely almost surely has heat exhaustion. Even though his temperature may be somewhat elevated, *sweating rules out the diagnosis of heatstroke.* Under general supportive treatment the victim of heat exhaustion will usually recover consciousness promptly, even though he may not feel well for some time.

TREATMENT:

Move the victim to a cool place. Keep the victim prone and treat him for shock. If the victim is conscious, water to which has been added a half teaspoon of salt to each glass, or stimulants such as coffee or tea may be given freely.

b. *Heatstroke*

Heatstroke has for its distinguishing characteristic an extreme elevation of body temperature. This is due to a failure of the sweating mechanism. Heatstroke may occur whenever heat regulation is dependent upon sweating for a long period of time. Heatstroke calls for heroic measures to reduce body temperature immediately to prevent brain damage and death.

Symptoms and Signs:
headache
dizziness
frequent desire to urinate
irritability
disturbed vision (objects usually have a red or purplish tint)
sudden unconsciousness
hot, dry skin
constricted pupils
pounding pulse
possible convulsions
body temperature from 105 to 109 degrees F.

TREATMENT:

Place the victim in the water, shade, or a cool place. Remove the victim's clothing. Lay him in a supine position with head and shoulders slightly elevated. Try to decrease the victim's body temperature by one of the following methods:

1. Submerge victim in ice bath or pour cold water over the body.

2. Rub the body with ice. Place pieces of ice in armpits and crotch.

3. Cover with sheets soaked in ice water.

Give cool (not iced) drinks after consciousness returns; do NOT give stimulants. The aim of the treatment in heatstroke is to reduce the body temperature to a safe range as rapidly as possible. Brain damage is the product of time as well as temperature. Total immersion in an ice-water bath is probably the most efficient method.

c. *Heat Cramps*

Heat cramps are painful contractions of various skeletal muscles brought about by the depletion of sodium chloride (salt) from the body fluids, via excessive sweating.

Symptoms:
The typical victim has his legs drawn up, is thrashing about, grimacing, and crying out from the excruciating pain.

TREATMENT:

Relieve pain with gentle massage, but the treatment is salt and water. Drinking cool water with a half teaspoon of salt will afford relief and continued protection.

NOTE: THE USE OF HOT PACKS ON CRAMPED MUSCLES WILL ONLY MAKE THEM WORSE.

Injury (Physical)

Divers, especially those on extended expeditions, sustain a variety of cuts, bruises, lacerations, blows, and other physical injuries. These must be anticipated by taking along a good first aid kit (page 154) and a book on first aid practice, such as the American Red Cross First Aid Manual. This chapter pertains only to accidents that result directly from diving.

Jellyfish Stings

See *Fish poisoning, external.*

Lung Squeeze

See *Squeeze.*

Mediastinal Emphysema

See *Air embolism.*

Moray Eel Bites

See *Fish poisoning, external.*

Motion Sickness

See *Sea sickness.*

Mussel Cuts

See *Barnacle and mussel cuts.*

Nitrogen Narcosis

Nitrogen in air breathed under pressure at depths of one hundred feet or more has an intoxicating effect on the body similar to that of alcohol. Susceptibility and reaction vary from person to person and from day to day, but at depths beyond two hundred feet most divers are too "drunk" to operate effectively or safely. Narcosis can be avoided only by avoiding the depths at which it occurs and, to a degree, by mentally combating it with all your powers of concentration.

Symptoms and Signs:
   loss of judgment and skill
   a false feeling of well-being
   lack of concern for job or own safety
   common stupidity
   difficulty in doing even simple tasks
   peals of laughter at slightest provocation
   near unconsciousness at great depths
TREATMENT:
   There is no treatment. The effects of nitrogen narcosis vanish rapidly with ascent into shallower water. No traces remain by the time the diver reaches the surface.

Octopus Bites

See *Fish poisoning, external.*

Oxygen Deficiency

See *Anoxia.*

Pneumothorax

See *Air embolism.*

Rapture of the Depths

See *Nitrogen narcosis.*

Sea Sickness

Sea sickness can be a serious hazard to scuba divers, for it can occur not only on the surface but underwater as well. Never attempt to have a man dive if he feels the possible need to vomit. If the water is extremely rough, postpone diving operations until it calms down. Anyone who feels the need to vomit while participating in a dive should head for the surface immediately. Vomiting beneath the surface can cause strangulation and drowning, but it can be done safely by removing the regulator, letting fly, then returning the regulator to your mouth and clearing it. If the vomit is very liquid, it can be done into the regulator and then expelled by activating the purge button.

Symptoms:
   wooziness
   dizziness
   thick, dry tongue

nausea
vomiting
Signs:
pallid or sickly green complexion
thick speech
lethargy
nausea
vomiting

TREATMENT:

Sea sickness is caused by a motion-induced upset of the balance mechanism in the inner ear. Several brands of motion-sickness tablets are available at most pharmacies without prescription. These will successfully prevent motion sickness in most cases, but they are of little help after motion sickness has set in, and they contain antihistamines, which often render the victim too sleepy and careless to operate effectively during a dive. Unless a diver knows his reaction to motion-sickness tablets, he should avoid taking them before a dive.

Avoiding the thought of sea sickness and staying out on deck and deep-breathing fresh air tend to dampen the nauseous effects of sea sickness. Once the diver gets safely underwater, wave motion generally vanishes by the time he reaches a depth of 20 feet, and so do the adverse effects.

Sea Snake Bites

See *Fish poisoning, external.*

Sea Urchins

Sea urchins of various species are plentiful in all tropical and most temperate waters. Sea urchins are covered with long, needle-sharp spines, which easily penetrate the skin on even slight contact and usually break off. They cling to rocks, coral heads, and beaches. Often they are so numerous that swimmers can hardly avoid contact with them. A few species of the short-spined sea urchin are equipped with small, venom-carrying pincers which can be telescoped out through the spines for added protection.

Since the sharp, brittle spines can easily penetrate clothing, there is little protection against sea urchins except studiously avoiding them. When working at a fixed site, it is best to remove all the urchins from the area with a stick or spear before work begins.

Symptoms:
immediate intense, burning pain
redness and swelling
weakness
Signs:
black dots where spines broke off in skin
redness and swelling of affected area
sometimes white, pallid complexion
possible faintness, numbness, and respiratory distress

TREATMENT:

Remove as many of the broken-off spines as possible with tweezers or forceps, then cleanse, apply antiseptic, and cushion with a large, loose dressing. Leave those which are difficult to get at. Do not "pick around." Spines of most urchins will dissolve and be absorbed into the body within a few days. Others will leave long, lingering blue marks like a faded tattoo unless surgically removed.

The pincers of the venomous short-spined sea urchin remain active for several hours and should be removed immediately. The wound should then be treated as a venomous fish sting. See *Fish poisoning, external.*

Shallow-water Blackout

See *Anoxia.*

Shark Attacks

Shark bites usually appear in a rounded, half-moon shape matching the shape of the shark's jaws. Generally they are very sloppy wounds, with severe lacerations from the shark's many razor-sharp teeth and the sawlike movement of its jaws while feeding. An entire section in the shape of the shark's jaw might be missing from the victim.

TREATMENT:

Get the victim out of the water immediately and stop the bleeding by placing a tourniquet between the wound and the heart. (Remember to loosen it for ninety seconds every ten minutes.) Treat for shock (see *Shock*) and seek medical help immediately by calling the U.S. Coast Guard, the nearest port captain, or DAN— the Divers Alert Network (919) 684-8111.

Shock

Shock results from a traumatic injury with loss of blood, severe burns, or any condition that results in loss of blood or body fluids. When shock occurs, the body cannot keep the blood pressure up, and tissue is starved for oxygen. Unless treated promptly and properly, it can result in death.

Symptoms and Signs:

loss of blood or body fluid
pulse very feeble and very rapid
blue lips and fingernails
weakness
cold sweat, paleness
shallow breathing
dizziness
fainting and unconsciousness

TREATMENT:

Treatment of shock requires prompt medical attention. Stop bleeding by applying a tourniquet between wound and heart, remembering to loosen it for ninety seconds every ten minutes. Lay victim down, with head slightly lower than limbs. Keep victim warm and reassured. Victim urgently needs replacing of fluid loss with blood, plasma, or suitable substitute, and the doctor or paramedic should be notified of this. If conscious and not vomiting, mix one teaspoon of table salt and one-half teaspoon of baking soda in a quart of water and give as much as the victim will take.

Skin Diseases

See *Dermatitis.*

Squeeze

Squeeze (barotrauma) refers to any injury that comes about because of inability to equalize pressure between a closed air space in or on the body and outside water pressure. The scuba diver is subject to a pressure squeeze on the ears, face mask, lungs, sinuses, and suit, and is exposed to the following forms of pressure squeeze.

Ear squeeze. See *Eardrum rupture.*

Face mask squeeze is caused by failure to equalize air pressure inside the standard face mask with water pressure outside the mask during descent, with either snorkel or scuba, by exhaling through nose. (It is impossible to equalize pressure in eye goggles, and they should be avoided.)

Symptoms:

sensation of suction around face and eyes
pain

Signs:

whites of eyes bright red from blood
face swollen and bruised

TREATMENT:

Apply cold packs to bruised or bleeding areas. Give sedatives and pain-relieving drugs if required. Seek medical help for serious cases.

Lung (thoracic) squeeze can theoretically be caused by diving too deeply while holding breath, or by failure of air supply or demand regulator during descent. Usually, discomfort will cause the diver to surface before lung squeeze becomes severe, however.

Symptoms:

sensation of chest being squeezed during descent
pain in chest
difficult breathing after surfacing
bloody, frothy sputum if severe

TREATMENT:

If severe, clear blood from the mouth and place victim on his side so that drainage occurs. Give artificial respiration if breathing stops. Seek medical advice.

Sinus squeeze can be caused by blockage of opening leading from nose to sinuses. This occurs most often when diving while suffering head colds or other respiratory diseases. Avoid diving with head colds. Surface if sinus pain develops during descent.

Symptoms:

increasing pain in sinuses during descent
pain relieved by ascent

Signs:

blood and mucus discharge from nose in mask on ascent
tender or painful sinuses

TREATMENT:

Avoid diving until cause subsides. Use nose drops, spray, or inhalator to open passage and promote drainage and passage of air. Seek medical advice if blood, pus, or other signs of infection appear in sinus discharge.

Suit squeeze is caused by compression of air spaces inside "dry type" exposure suits by the increasing water pressures during descent. If the rubber seals over the outer ear canal, a rigid air space is formed there and can cause external ear squeeze. Unless air is admitted into the dry suit to equalize inside pressures with outside pressures, continued descent will produce a tight, binding sensation that will press the folds into the skin.

> Symptoms:
>> pinching of skin under folds of suit
>> possible symptoms of external ear squeeze
> Signs:
>> red welts where suit folds were squeezed
>> possible blood blisters and bleeding, usually around joints
>> possible signs of external ear squeeze

TREATMENT:

Welts and bruises usually heal in time. Cold compresses will relieve blood blisters and bleeding. When squeeze develops, snort air into hood of suit through mask, or otherwise provide for entry of air into suit during descent. If ears are affected, treat for external ear squeeze.

Stomach Pains

While attempting to clear his ears, sometimes a diver swallows air under pressure into his stomach or intestines during a dive. The air expands on ascent and the excess gas will have to be expelled. This is usually accomplished by Mother Nature, but if the gas is trapped in the middle of the intestine in a pocket it may cause stomach or intestinal pain.

> Symptoms:
>> if mild, abdominal fullness
>> if moderate, abdominal pain and cramps
>> if severe, great pain and fainting

TREATMENT:

Stop ascent when intestinal pain is noted. Redescend until pain is relieved, then attempt to belch or break wind, but be careful not to swallow more air in attempting to belch. Resume ascent slowly and cautiously. Avoid swallowing air during dive, and don't chew gum during dive, or dive with badly upset stomach.

Strangulation

Strangulation is asphyxia caused by obstruction of the body's air passages. Inhalation of foreign material such as chewing gum, false teeth, or vomit might cause strangulation in diving, but it is unlikely. The diver may have spasms of the larynx due to inhalation of water. It may be a cause of drowning, hypoxia, carbon dioxide excess, or other conditions that might require artificial respiration. Remove false teeth before diving and do not chew gum or other things during a dive.

> Symptoms and Signs:
>> extremely difficult breathing
>> noisy breathing, choking, gasping
>> unconsciousness if severe or prolonged
>> struggle to breathe eventually ceases

TREATMENT:

Remove obstruction if possible. Encourage victim to cough; pound him on back, turn him upside down. Try to remove the obstruction with your fingers. If nothing else works, you must perform an emergency tracheotomy, making an opening in the middle of the trachea (windpipe) below the larynx (voice box). The incision is made in the midline of the neck (not across), two fingers' breadth below the point of the Adam's apple. At least one ring of cartilage in the windpipe must be cut through to make a satisfactory opening, and the opening must be held open. The cut can be performed with a penknife. The chance of doing harm in the process is not great when compared to the certainty of death if the strangulation is not relieved.

If breathing has stopped, give artificial respiration by breathing into the hole.

Subcutaneous Emphysema

See *Air embolism.*

Suit Squeeze

See *Squeeze.*

Sunburn

A bad sunburn can be not only an uncomfortable disease but an incapacitating one. It can ruin a diving trip very easily and inspire brilliant hindsight on the part of the victim. The real need is for foresight, however. Gradual exposure to the sun can be accomplished by sensible use of clothing and protective suntan creams, oils, and lotions. The neck and face are especially sensitive in divers who have not built up their tolerance gradually. Remember that reflected sunlight is just as potent as direct sun rays and that it can occur on a hazy, overcast day as well as a sunny day, because ultraviolet rays are not filtered out by clouds. When at sea, always protect your head and eyes from the heat and glare of the sun by wearing a hat and sunglasses.

Symptoms:

fever

pain

dizziness

possible prostration

Signs:

extreme redness

blisters

TREATMENT:

Treat sunburn as any other superficial burn. Use burn ointment or lotions. Bandages soaked with tannic acid (tea), vinegar, and boric acid are also good.

Do not pop blisters or peel skin with fingers, and avoid exposure to sun until skin temperature returns to normal.

Syncope

See *Fainting.*

Lung (Thoracic) Squeeze

See *Squeeze.*

Tracheotomy, Emergency

See *Strangulation.*

Unconsciousness

Here is the U. S. Navy treatment table for unconscious divers:

Loss of Consciousness During or Within 24 Hours After a Dive

1. *If not breathing,* start artificial respiration or CPR at once. (See pages 155–158.)

2. *Recompress promptly* if need is suspected even slightly. Call the Port Captain or U.S. Coast Guard for transportation to nearest recompression chamber or telephone DAN: (919) 684-8111.

3. Examine for injuries and other abnormalities; apply first aid and other measures as required. (Secure the help of a medical doctor as soon as possible.)

Artificial respiration

(a) Shift to a mechanical resuscitator if one is available and working properly, but never wait for it. Always start mouth-to-mouth respiration or (if no pulse) CPR first.

(b) Continue artificial respiration by some method without interruption until normal breathing resumes or victim is pronounced dead. Continue on way to chamber and during recompression. (Do not use oxygen deeper than sixty feet in chamber.)

Recompression

(c) Remember that an unconscious diver may have air embolism or serious decompression sickness even though some other accident *seems* to explain his condition.

(d) Recompress *unless:*

(1) Victim regains consciousness and is free of nervous-system symptoms before recompression can be started.

(2) Possibility of air embolism or decompression sickness can be ruled out without question.

(3) Another life-saving measure is absolutely required and makes recompression impossible.

(e) Try to reach a recompression chamber, no matter how far it is.

Venomous Fish

See *Fish poisoning, external.*

Appendix I

PADI MEDICAL HISTORY/EXAM FOR DIVING

TO THE APPLICANT: Please complete this top section, then sign your name in the appropriate space below.

A. MARK ALL STATEMENTS BELOW which are TRUE of your past or present medical history.

I have a history of:

☐ Respiratory problems   ☐ Dizziness or fainting
☐ Diabetes   ☐ Claustrophobia
☐ Epilepsy   ☐ Emotional problems or nervousness
☐ Heart problems   ☐ Peptic ulcers
☐ Severe or frequent headaches   ☐ Alcoholism
☐ Recent operation or illness   ☐ Drug use
☐ Sinus problems   ☐ Smoking
☐ Asthma   ☐ None of these
☐ Ear infection

B. Indicate ALL serious injuries and/or hospital care in your medical history

_____

_____

_____

C. List ALL medications you are presently taking _____

D. Date of last medical exam _____ Date of chest x-ray _____

I _____ hereby certify that the above is correct to the
          print name

best of my knowledge.

Date _____

                                                       Signature

TO THE PHYSICIAN:

This person is an applicant for training with self-contained underwater breathing apparatus (scuba). This activity takes place under changing environmental pressures, and otherwise subjects the individual to unusual stresses.

Physician's Report of Medical Examination:

Note: Please check items below if considered ABNORMAL. Indicate under "remarks" the pertinent details and your impression of their importance.

A. MEDICAL HISTORY REVIEW (see applicant's report above)
    ☐ Past History
    ☐ Present History

B. STANDARD PHYSICAL EXAMINATION
    ☐ Examination table results
    ☐ Laboratory results

C. "SPECIAL ATTENTION" AREAS
- ☐ Ears and Sinuses (Must permit equalization under pressure differentials).
- ☐ Respiratory System (Lungs must be free from structural weakness and disease).
- ☐ Cardiovascular System (must be free from defects).
- ☐ Physical Fitness (Diving involves physical exertion).
- ☐ Emotional and Psychological Stability (Diving can produce stresses in these areas).

PHYSICIAN'S IMPRESSION

Remarks: _____

_____ Approval (I find no defects which I consider incompatible with diving.)

_____ Conditional Approval (I do not consider diving in this man's best interests but find no defects which present marked risk. I have discussed my impression with the patient and he accepts the responsibility for going ahead with the program.)

_____ Disapproval (This applicant has defects which in my opinion clearly would constitute unacceptable hazards to his health and safety in diving.)

Physician _____
Name (print)

Date _____   _____
Address   City

Phone _____   Signature _____
(Business)

Reprinted from the PADI Study Guide

Appendix II

PADI SCUBA COURSE ENROLLMENT
APPLICATION
(Confidential Information)

Name _____ Home phone _____

Home address _____

_____

Occupation _____ Business phone _____

Certification card info: Date of birth _____
           Month Day Year

Height _____ Weight _____ Color hair _____ Color eyes _____

Why do you want to learn to dive?

Do you have any skin or scuba diving experience? If so, please describe briefly:

How do you rate your current swimming ability?

How do you rate your current health and physical fitness?

Briefly describe your feelings about being underwater:

Are there any activities or interests you intend to pursue as a diver? If so, which ones?

List any diving equipment you presently own:
         Signed _____
         Date _____

Reprinted from the PADI Study Guide

Appendix III

PADI PURE AIR PROGRAM

Air from most scuba tanks would make Mother Nature ashamed of her Rocky Mountain breezes. Before the air is good enough for the diver to use, it has been filtered, heated, dried, and chemically treated until it is pure and safe for use underwater.

Compressors pumping air for human use are severely regulated by a myriad of laws, all of which specify that what goes into a tank must exceed in quality the freshest air in nature. Yet it is possible to get a tank of bad air, whether it be a toxic contaminant or just a plain unpleasant odor. The quality of air supplied and the condition and configuration of the equipment varies greatly from store to store, and boat to boat. While fatalities occurring from contaminated air have been few, there have been many cases of nausea or other illness caused by impure, compressed air.

To assure divers they are getting the best compressed air available, the Professional Association of Diving Instructors conducts a Pure Air Program. The program is essentially one of taking compressed air samples from participating facilities and having the air analyzed by a reliable laboratory. Air samples must meet or exceed the current strictest accepted standards for divers. If the air samples do not meet the standards, then the operator of the compressed air plant must do whatever is necessary to achieve air of suitable quality.

To improve air quality, the operator must have a knowledge of the causes of impure air and its affect on divers, and the steps necessary to obtain pure air. The first consideration in a system that will deliver pure air is to establish a definition of pure air for underwater use. We know that air is a mixture of gases, roughly 78 percent nitrogen, 21 percent oxygen, and 1 percent other atmospheric trace gases. Atmospheric air also contains water vapor, dust, soot, hydrocarbons, and many other impurities in varying degrees. In special situations any one of these may be present in very high concentra-

tions. Air is graded by limiting the concentration of specific trace constituents as shown by the following table.

	U.S. Navy*	Compressed Gas Assoc.**
Oxygen	20–22%	19–23%
Maximum Carbon Dioxide	0.05% (500 ppm)	0.10% (1,000 ppm)
Maximum Carbon Monoxide	0.002% (20 ppm)	0.002% (20 ppm)
Maximum Oil Vapor	5 mg/m³	5 mg/m³
Particles Solid & Liquid	None detectable	
Odor	Not objectionable	

*U.S. Navy Diving Manual, p. 5–18, NAVSHIPS 0994-001-9010
**Compressed Gas Association Pamphlet, G7.1

In urban areas carbon monoxide (CO) may be present in free air at rather high levels, in some cases as high as 50–100 parts per million (ppm). The level of CO in the atmosphere varies from a low of 25 ppb to values as high as 81 ppm in Los Angeles. There are seventeen cities in America that have CO levels in excess of 10 ppm 50 percent of the time over a one year average. The atmosphere is thus a source of concern to diving as this contaminated air may be compressed and supplied to divers. Moreover, the level of CO in air that may be compressed for air diving may exceed proposed standards.

Also, carbon monoxide occurs in high concentration in cigarette smoke and the average concentration inhaled is 400 to 500 ppm. A smoking diver already has his blood polluted with a level that exceeds what he would acquire if he were exposed to air containing 20 ppm CO for twelve hours.

Other impurities such as dust and oxides of sulfur are also present in the atmosphere. These contaminants come from such sources as industrial and automotive exhausts. In addition to the contaminants that may be present in free air, air compressor machinery may also add contaminants. These include oil vapor, hydrocarbons from the compressor motor exhausts, and oil breakdown products from the compressor lubricant. All of these must be avoided or removed before compressed air is suitable for diver use.

The location of the compressor intake with respect to possible sources of contamination is fully as important as any single factor in assuring satisfactory air quality. Compressors should not be operated near the exhausts of internal combustion engines, sewer manholes, sandblasting, painting, electric arcs, or sources of smoke. Intakes must be provided with filters for removing dust and other particles in the respirable size range. Proper orientation to wind direction is also a critical factor in setting up air compressor systems.

FILTERING SYSTEMS

Air leaving a compressor must be cleaned and filtered prior to storage or immediate use. In some compressor systems the compressed gas is passed through an oil and moisture separator to remove entrained oil, mist, and excessive moisture. This is followed by passage through a filter system to remove excess water, oil particulate matter, and odor.

Recently developed systems are on the market that more effectively remove contaminants (National Safety Council 1973). They are designed to remove carbon monoxide, oil vapor, nitrogen dioxide, odor, and taste contaminants. One such system does this by the oxidation of carbon monoxide to carbon dioxide through chemisorption and catalysis with a material called Hopcalite. Hopcalite is a true catalyst in this reaction and is neither consumed nor exhausted in the process until it is deactivated by

water vapor. The amount of carbon dioxide produced by the catalytic action is insignificant.

The amount of oxygen used up is approximately 0.5 part per million of carbon monoxide and has no appreciable effect on the air produced. Nitrogen dioxide is also removed from the air by a combination of adsorption and chemical reaction. Activated carbon is used to absorb odor and taste.

PADI PURE AIR ANALYSIS PROGRAM

PADI provides an air analysis service through a national testing laboratory and strongly recommends all air stations use these facilities. Stores who are presently having their air analyzed locally may participate in this program provided they abide by the standards and pay an annual service charge for filing and handling.

A "Pure Air Station" certificate is issued to stores that participate in the Pure Air Program. The store takes air samples regularly from each compressor and has the air analyzed. Results of the analysis is reported to PADI Headquarters. If the analysis is approved, a gold seal will be issued for that particular analysis to be affixed to the certificate.

Equipment for obtaining meaningful air samples from compressed air supplies has been developed and is in current use on a number of sampling programs. The system employs a method that lowers the pressure of air supplies to less than three atmospheres absolute pressure, which, in turn, reduces the size and weight of the equipment and containers needed to obtain the samples. The equipment is safe and readily transportable by any mode of transportation including U.S. priority mail and United Parcel Service.

Through the PADI Pure Air Program, the diving industry has been provided with its first and only ongoing program of regular air analysis. The analysis is provided by the Texas Research Institute, the leading company in the United States for air analysis. The responsible retailers of the PADI Training Facility program have voluntarily joined together to participate in the Pure Air Program and have set aside a portion of their profits to pay for this service. PADI urges you to support the dealer who displays the Pure Air Station emblem.

PADI DIVE PLANNING CHECKLIST

Advance Planning:

—— Dive buddy(s) _____

—— Date and time (Check tide tables) _____

—— Dive objective _____

—— Location _____

—— Alternate location(s) _____

—— Directions _____
_____

—— Meeting place and time _____

—— Any special or extra gear needed _____

—— Precheck of weather and water conditions

Preparation:

—— Tank(s) filled   —— Equipment packed

—— Equipment inspected   —— Fishing license current

—— Equipment marked (ID)   —— Transportation arranged

—— Spare parts inventoried   —— Obtain info about new location

—— Weights adjusted   —— Get local emergency contact info

Last Minute:

—— Healthy, rested, nourished

—— Good, confident feeling about dive

—— Check weather and water conditions

—— Final inventory of all needed items

—— Leave dive plan info with someone not going (Where going, expected time of return, what to do if you do not notify by agreed time)

—— Pack food, snacks, drinks

—— Be sure you have: —— Ticket   —— Money   —— Medications
          —— Directions   —— Swimsuit   —— Towel   —— Jacket
          —— Sunglasses   —— Other

On-Site:

—— Evaluate conditions, decide whether or not to dive

—— Locate and check nearest communications (telephone, radio)

—— Select entry/exit points, alternates, methods

—— Discuss buddy system techniques

—— Agree on pattern or course for the dive

—— Agree on limits for the dive (depth, time, minimum air)

—— Agree on emergency procedures

Problems?   Call _____ or _____

PADI BOAT DIVING INFORMATION SHEET

Date of trip _____ Name of vessel _____
Landing _____ City _____
Directions _____
Destination _____ Cost _____
Departure time _____ Estimated return time _____

Items needed:

_____ Diving equipment	_____ Suntan lotion
_____ Gear bag	_____ Medication
_____ Extra tank	_____ Ticket
_____ Warm clothes	_____ Money
_____ Jacket	_____ Lunch, snacks
_____ Towel	_____ Drinks

Terminology:

Bow:	Front end of the boat
Stern:	Rear end of the boat
Port:	Left side of the boat when facing bow
Starboard:	Right side of the boat when facing bow
Bridge:	Wheelhouse; vessel control area
Leeward:	The downwind side; sheltered side
Windward:	Side facing into the wind; windy side
Galley:	Kitchen area
Head:	Restroom

Instructions:

1. Double-check to be sure you have all required equipment.
2. Board vessel at least one half hour prior to departure time.
3. Ask crew where and how to stow your gear.
4. Place clothes, cameras, lunch and all items to be kept dry inside, and all diving equipment outside on the deck.
5. Wait in the stern area for predeparture briefing.
6. Keep dockside rail clear during docking operations.
7. If susceptible to seasickness, take medication prior to departure.
8. If seasick, use the leeside rail, not the head.
9. Learn toilet operation and rules before using head.
10. Stay off the bow during anchoring operations.
11. Work out of your gear bag. No loose gear on deck.
12. Check out and check in with the Divemaster for all dives.
13. Pack and stow all gear before return trip.
14. Be available for *visual* roll call before boat is moved.
15. Check to be sure nothing is left behind when disembarking.

Rules:

1. No trash or litter overboard. Use trash cans.
2. Bridge and engine room are off limits.
3. Do not sit on the rails when underway.
4. Follow the instructions of the crew.

PADI OPEN WATER EQUIPMENT CHECKLIST

BASIC EQUIPMENT:

- ☐ Gear Bag
- ☐ Fins, Mask, Snorkel
  - Wet Suit:
  - ☐ Jacket
  - ☐ Pants
  - ☐ Vest
  - ☐ Hood
  - ☐ Boots
  - ☐ Gloves
- ☐ Weight Belt
- ☐ Buoyancy Compensator
- ☐ Tank (Filled)
- ☐ Backpack
- ☐ Regulator (with SPG)
- ☐ Compass
- ☐ Depth Gauge
- ☐ Knife
- ☐ Watch

ACCESSORY EQUIPMENT:

- ☐ Float & Flag
- ☐ Thermometer
- ☐ Game Bag
- ☐ Abalone Iron
- ☐ Measuring Device
- ☐ Dive Light
- ☐ Slate and Pencil
- ☐ Marker Buoy
- ☐ Buddy Line
- ☐ Camera, Film
- ☐ Spear
- ☐ Lift Bag

SPARE EQUIPMENT:

- ☐ Tanks
- ☐ Weights
- ☐ Straps
- ☐ O-Rings
- ☐ Tools
- ☐ CO_2 Cartridges
- ☐ Suit Cement
- ☐ Regulator HP Plug
- ☐ Bulbs, Batteries
- ☐ Nylon Line

PERSONAL ITEMS:

- ☐ Swimsuit
- ☐ Towel
- ☐ Jacket
- ☐ Extra Clothes
- ☐ Fishing License
- ☐ Tickets
- ☐ Money
- ☐ Certification Card
- ☐ Log Book
- ☐ Dive Tables
- ☐ Sunglasses
- ☐ Suntan Lotion
- ☐ Medications
- ☐ Toilet Articles
- ☐ Lunch, Thermos
- ☐ Cooler Chest
- ☐ Fileting Knife
- ☐ Eating Utensils
- ☐ Sleeping Bag

SAFE DIVING PRACTICES

1. BE WELL TRAINED. Be trained in scuba diving by a certified instructor of scuba diving and certified by a nationally recognized certifying organization.

2. NEVER DIVE ALONE. Always dive with a buddy who is completely familiar with you and your diving practices.

3. NEVER HOLD YOUR BREATH WHILE USING SCUBA. Breathe regularly. Exhale during emergency ascents. Do not hyperventilate excessively before breath-hold dives.

4. DON'T DIVE BEYOND YOUR LIMITS. Maintain good mental and physical condition for diving. Only dive when feeling well. Do not use any intoxicating liquor or dangerous drug before diving. Have a regular medical examination for diving. Be sure to exercise regularly, keep well rested, and maintain a well-balanced diet.

5. AVOID DEPTHS DEEPER THAN 100 FEET. This is the recommended sport diving limit.

6. USE PROPER EQUIPMENT. Use correct, complete, and proper diving equipment which is checked before each dive and well-maintained. Do not loan your scuba equipment to a non-certified diver. Have your scuba equipment regularly serviced by a qualified person. When scuba diving in open water, use flotation equipment (vest or buoyancy compensator) and a submersible pressure gauge and/or reserve warning mechanism.

7. PLAN YOUR DIVE. Know the area. Establish emergency procedures. Know the limitations of yourself, your buddy, and your equipment. Use the best possible judgement and common sense in planning and setting the limitations of each dive, allowing a margin of safety in order to be prepared for emergencies. Set reasonable limits for depth and time in the water. Always buddy dive—know each other's equipment, know hand signals, and stay in contact.

8. ALWAYS WEAR A BUOYANCY COMPENSATOR. Control your buoyancy to make diving as easy as possible. Be prepared to ditch your weight belt, make an emergency ascent, buddy breathe, clear your mask and mouthpiece, or take other emergency action if needed. In an emergency: stop and think; get control; take action.

9. PUT YOUR WEIGHT BELT ON LAST. Ditch your weight belt when a potential emergency arises. Be sure to unclasp it completely and throw it well away from your body.

10. USE A DIVER'S FLAG AND FLOAT. Make sure that your diving area is well-identified to avoid potential hazards from boats in the area.

11. HAVE YOUR TANKS VISUALLY INSPECTED AT LEAST ONCE A YEAR AND HYDROSTATICALLY TESTED EVERY FIVE YEARS. The hydrostat test every five years is required by law, but a visual inspection every year can head off trouble before it happens.

12. USE ONLY CLEAN, DRY, FILTERED AIR IN SCUBA TANKS. Be sure any source of compressed air always meets established standards for diving air.

13. NEVER USE EARPLUGS OR GOGGLES. Air pressure squeezes can cause damage in any area that cannot be vented.

14. DON'T CARRY KILLED GAME. Killed game can attract creatures that can become aggressive when they sense food.

15. CANCEL DIVES WHEN WATER AND WEATHER CONDITIONS ARE QUESTIONABLE. Too many unknowns can happen without aggravating the situation. It is far better to have everything in your favor which will make emergencies less serious.

16. BE FAMILIAR WITH THE AREA. Know your diving location. Avoid dangerous places and poor conditions. Take whatever special precautions are required.

17. ASCEND PROPERLY. When surfacing, look up and around, move slowly and listen, hold your hand up if any possible hazards exist. Do not hold your breath with scuba. Be sure to equalize pressure early and often both during ascent and descent.

18. KNOW DECOMPRESSION PROCE-DURES. Be familiar with decompression tables and emergency procedures. Make all possible dives "no-decompression" dives. Avoid stage decompression particularly on repetitive dives, at altitude, or when flying after the dive.

19. DON'T OVEREXTEND YOURSELF. If you are cold, tired, injured, out of air, or not feeling well, get out of the water. Diving is no longer fun or safe. If any abnormality persists, get medical attention.

20. AVOID TOUCHING UNKNOWN CREA-TURES UNDER WATER. Be especially careful of anything very beautiful or very ugly.

21. KNOW YOUR BOAT AND REGULA-TIONS. Be sure any boat used for diving is legally and adequately equipped for diving.

22. BE A GOOD CITIZEN DIVER AND SPORTSMAN. Comply with laws and regulations concerning diving. Be friendly and respect personal property. When diving have your certification card, diving log, and identification nearby.

23. BE AN ACTIVE DIVER. Keep actively diving and logging your dives with your buddy's signature by each logged dive. Try to dive no less than twelve times per year.

24. CONTINUE YOUR TRAINING. Continue your scuba diving training by taking advanced, open water, or specialty courses.

25. KNOW THE LOCATION OF YOUR NEAREST RECOMPRESSION CHAMBER. In case of emergency, the following numbers may be called twenty-four hours a day, seven days a week. Physicians are on call and consultation can be provided on air embolism or decompression sickness cases. Each maintains a worldwide listing of recompression chambers.

Brooks Air Force Base
LEO-FAST-Command Post
(512) 536-3278

Diving Accident Network (DAN)
(919) 684-8111

U.S. Navy Experimental Diving Unit
EDU Duty Phone
(904) 234-4353

GAS LAWS

Boyle's Law

If the temperature is kept constant, the volume of a gas will vary inversely as the ABSOLUTE pressure while the density will vary directly as the pressure. Since the pressure and volume of a gas are inversely related—the higher the pressure, the smaller the volume, and vice-versa. The formula for Boyle's Law is:

$$PV = C$$

Where P = absolute pressure
V = volume
C = a constant

Charles' Law

If the pressure is kept constant, the volume of a gas will vary directly as the AB-SOLUTE temperature. The amount of change in either volume or pressure is directly related to the change in absolute pressure. For example, if absolute temperature is doubled, then either the volume or the pressure is also doubled. The formula for Charles' Law is:

$$PV = RT \text{ or } \frac{PV = R}{T}$$

Where P = absolute pressure
V = volume
T = absolute temperature
R = a universal constant for all gases

General Gas Law

Boyle's Law illustrates pressure/volume relationships, and Charles' Law basically describes the effect of temperature changes on pressure and/or volume. The General Gas Law is a combination of these two laws. It is used to predict the behavior of a given quantity of gas when changes may be expected in any or all of the variables. The formula for the General Gas Law is:

$$\frac{P_1 V_1}{T_1} = \frac{P_2 V_2}{T_2}$$

Where P_1 = initial pressure (absolute)
V_1 = initial volume
T_1 = initial temperature (absolute)
P_2 = final pressure (absolute)
V_2 = final volume
T_2 = final temperature (absolute)

Dalton's Law

The total pressure exerted by a mixture of gases is equal to the sum of the pressures of each of the different gases making up the mixture—each gas acting as if it alone was present and occupied the total volume. The whole is equal to the sum of its parts and each part is not affected by any of the other parts. The pressure of any gas in the mixture is proportional to the number of molecules of that gas in the total volume. The pressure of each gas is called its partial pressure (pp), meaning its part of the whole. Dalton's Law is sometimes referred to as "the law of partial pressures." The formula for Dalton's Law is:

$$^P\text{Total} = \text{PPA} + \text{PP}_B + \text{PP}_C \cdots \cdots$$

and

$$\text{PP}_A = P_{\text{Total}} \times \frac{\%\text{Vol.}_A}{100\%}$$

Where P_{Total} = Total absolute pressure of gas mixture
PP_A = Partial pressure of gas A
PP_B = Partial pressure of gas B
PP_C = Partial pressure of gas C

Henry's Law

The amount of a gas that will dissolve in a liquid at a given temperature is almost directly proportional to the partial pressure of that gas. If one unit of gas dissolves in a liquid at one atmosphere, then two units will dissolve at two atmospheres, three units at three atmospheres, etc.

Air Consumption Formula

Knowing your air consumption rate is very important. By determining your consumption rate at the surface, it becomes a simple matter to calculate what it will be at any given depth. Since pressure gauges are calibrated in pounds per square inch (p.s.i.), your consumption rate must be in p.s.i. too. The formula is as follows:

$$\frac{\text{p.s.i.} \div \text{TIME}}{33/33 + \text{DEPTH}/33}$$

p.s.i. = p.s.i. consumed in timed swim at a constant depth.
TIME = Duration of timed swim.
DEPTH = Depth of timed swim.

EXAMPLE:

A diver swims at a depth of 10 feet for 10 minutes and consumes 300 p.s.i. of air. You want to determine his surface consumption expressed in p.s.i.

$$\frac{300 \text{ (p.s.i. used)} \div 10 \text{ (Time)} = 30}{33/33 + 10 \text{ (Depth)}/33 \quad = 43/33}$$

$$= \frac{30 \times 33}{43} = \frac{990}{43} = 23.02$$

23.02 p.s.i. = p.s.i. CONSUMED PER MINUTE AT SURFACE

NOTE: Consumption rate must be recalculated if tank size is changed.

DEPTH IN FEET

Surface	10	15	20	25	30	40	50	60	70	80	90	100	120	140	160
15	19.5	21.8	24.0	27.0	28.5	33.0	37.5	42.0	46.5	51	55.5	60	69	78	87
16	20.8	23.2	25.6	28.8	30.4	35.2	40.0	44.8	49.6	54.4	59.2	64	73.6	83.2	92.8
17	22.1	24.7	27.2	30.6	32.3	37.4	42.5	47.6	52.7	57.8	62.9	68	78.2	88.4	98.6
18	23.4	26.1	28.8	32.4	34.2	39.6	45.0	50.4	55.8	61.2	66.6	72	82.8	93.6	104.4
19	24.7	27.6	30.4	34.2	36.1	41.8	47.5	53.2	58.9	64.6	70.3	76	87.4	98.8	110.2
20	26	29.0	32.0	36.0	38.0	44.0	50.0	56.0	62.0	68.0	74.0	80	92	104	116
21	27.3	30.5	33.6	37.8	39.9	46.2	52.5	58.8	65.1	71.4	77.7	84	96.6	109.2	121.8
22	28.6	31.9	35.2	39.6	41.8	48.4	55.0	61.6	68.2	74.8	81.4	88	101.2	114.4	127.6
23	29.9	33.4	36.8	41.4	43.7	50.6	57.5	64.4	71.3	78.2	85.1	92	105.8	119.6	133.4
24	31.2	34.8	38.4	43.2	45.6	52.8	60	67.2	74.4	81.6	88.8	96	110.4	124.8	139.2
25	32.5	36.3	40.0	45.0	47.5	55.0	62.5	70.0	77.5	85.0	92.5	100	115	130	145
26	33.8	37.7	41.6	46.8	49.4	57.2	65.0	72.8	80.6	88.4	96.2	104	119.6	135.2	150.8
27	35.1	39.2	43.2	48.6	51.3	59.4	67.5	75.6	83.7	91.8	99.9	108	124.2	140.4	156.6
28	36.4	40.6	44.8	50.4	53.2	61.6	70	78.4	86.8	95.2	103.6	112	128.8	145.6	162.4
29	37.7	42.1	46.4	52.2	55.1	63.8	72.5	81.2	89.9	98.6	107.3	116	133.4	150.8	168.2
30	39	43.5	48.0	54	57.0	66.0	75.0	84.0	93.0	102.0	111.0	120	138	156	174
31	40.3	45.0	49.6	55.8	58.9	68.2	77.5	86.8	96.1	105.4	114.7	124	142.6	161.2	179.8
32	41.6	46.4	51.2	57.6	60.8	70.4	80.0	89.6	99.2	108.8	118.4	128	147.2	166.4	185.6
33	42.9	47.9	52.8	59.4	62.7	72.6	82.5	92.4	102.3	112.2	122.1	132	151.8	171.6	191.4
34	44.2	49.3	54.4	61.2	64.6	74.8	85.0	95.2	105.4	115.6	125.8	136	156.4	176.8	197.2
35	45.5	50.8	56.0	63.0	66.5	77.0	87.5	98.0	108.5	119.0	129.5	140	161	182	203
36	46.8	52.2	57.6	64.8	68.4	79.2	90.0	100.8	111.6	122.4	133.2	144	165.6	187.2	208.8
37	48.1	53.7	59.2	66.6	70.3	81.4	92.5	103.6	114.7	125.8	136.9	148	170.2	192.4	214.6
38	49.4	55.1	60.8	68.4	72.2	83.6	95.0	106.4	117.8	129.2	140.6	152	174.8	197.6	220.4
39	50.7	56.6	62.4	70.2	74.1	85.8	97.5	109.2	120.9	132.6	144.3	156	179.4	202.8	226.2
40	52	58	64.0	72.0	76.0	88.0	100	112.0	124.0	136	148.0	160	184	208	232

CONSUMPTION RATE AT SURFACE (p.s.i. PER MINUTE)

U.S. Navy

At some time or other, divers will find themselves struggling to convert cubic feet into cubic centimeters or something equally as irritating. The following figures will help you:

Length

1 inch	=	2.540 centimeters
1 foot	=	0.304 meters
1 yard	=	0.914 meters
1 fathom	=	1.828 meters or 6.0 feet
1 statute mile (5,280 feet)	=	1.609 kilometers
1 nautical mile (6,080 feet)	=	1.853 kilometers
1 centimeter	=	0.393 inches
1 meter	=	3.280 feet
1 meter	=	1.093 yards
1 meter	=	0.546 fathoms
1 kilometer	=	0.621 statute miles
1 kilometer	=	0.539 nautical miles

Capacity

1 cubic inch	=	16.378 cubic centimeters
1 cubic foot	=	0.028 cubic meters
1 cubic foot	=	28.317 liters
1 cubic yard	=	0.764 cubic meters
1 pint	=	0.568 liters
1 gallon	=	4.546 liters
1 cubic centimeter	=	0.061 cubic feet
1 cubic meter	=	35.314 cubic feet
1 cubic meter	=	1.308 cubic yards
1 liter (1,000 cc)	=	0.035 cubic feet
1 liter	=	0.220 gallons
1 liter	=	1.760 pints

Weight

1 ounce	=	28.349 grams
1 pound	=	0.454 kilograms
1 long ton	=	1.016 metric tons
1 long ton	=	1.016 kilograms
1 kilogram	=	2.205 pounds
1 metric ton	=	0.984 long tons
1 metric ton	=	2,205 pounds

PRESSURE

1 pound per square inch	= 0.073 kilograms per square centimeter
1 kilogram per square centimeter	= 14.223 pounds per square inch
1 atmosphere	= 14.7 pounds per square inch
1 atmosphere	= 1.033 kilograms per square centimeter

WATER

1 cubic foot of fresh water weighs 62.5 pounds approx.
1 cubic foot of average salt water weighs 64 pounds approx.
1 gallon of water weighs 8 pounds approx.

TEMPERATURE

To convert degrees Fahrenheit to degrees Centigrade, deduct 32 and multiply by 5/9.

To convert degrees Centigrade to degrees Fahrenheit, multiply by 9/5 and add 32.

CONVERSIONS (APPROXIMATE)

Miles to kilometers	multiply by 8/5
Kilometers to miles	multiply by 5/8
Statute miles to nautical miles	deduct 1/8
Nautical miles to statute miles	add 1/7
Pounds per square inch (p.s.i.) to atmospheres	divide by 14.7
Atmospheres or bars to kilos per square centimeter	nearly the same
Water depth (feet) to bars absolute	divide by 33 and add 1 bar
Water depth (meters) to bars absolute	divide by 10 and add 1 bar
Bars absolute to feet of water depth	subtract 1 bar and multiply by 33
Bars absolute to meters of water depth	subtract 1 bar and multiply by 10

WIND DIRECTION, SPEED, AND MEASUREMENT

Direction Wind direction is always specified as the direction from which the wind blows. (A westerly wind blows from west to east.)

Speed Wind speed is expressed in knots (a knot is a speed of one nautical mile per hour) by mariners and airmen and in miles per hour by landsmen and coastal navigators.

Conversions

1 knot	= 1.7 feet per second approx.
	= 0.51 meters per second approx.
1 mile per hour	= 1-1/2 feet per second approx.
	= 1.609 kilometers per hour approx.
1 foot per second	= 2/3 miles per hour approx.
	= 0.3 meters per second approx.
1 kilometer per hour	= 5/8 miles per hour approx.
1 meter per second	= 3-1/3 feet per second approx.

SOURCES OF FURTHER INFORMATION
ON DIVING

ACDE
(Assn. of Commercial Diving Education)
Box 36
Summerland, CA 93067

California Wreck Divers
Box 9922
Marina Del Rey, CA 90291

CBOA
(Charter Boat Owners Assn.)
Bud Wolfe
332 S. Bedford Drive
Beverly Hills, CA 90212

CNCA
(Council for National Cooperation in
   Aquatics)
220 Ashton Road
Ashton, MD 20702

CURO
(Council of Resort Operators)
Box 530173
Miami, FL 33153

DAN
Diving Accident Network
Duke University Medical Center
P.O. Box 3823
Durham, N.C. 27710

DEMA
(Diving Equipment Manufacturers
   Association)
P.O. Box 217
Tustin, CA 92680

Dive Canada (magazine)
559 Jarvis Street
Toronto, Ontario, Canada

IOF
(International Oceanographic Foundation)
3979 Rickenbacker Causeway
Virginia Key
Miami, FL 33149

NACD
(National Assn. of Cave Divers)
2900 N.W. 29th Avenue
Gainsville, FL 32605

NASAR
(National Assn. for Search and Recovery)
Box 2123
La Jolla, CA 92038

NOAA
(Sea Grant)
Division of Marine Resources
University of Washington HG-30
Seattle, WA 98195

Pacific Diver (magazine)
Seagraphic Publications Ltd.
1520 Alberni Street
Vancouver, B.C., Canada

Presidential Sports Award
Box 1412
Annex Station
Providence, R.I. 02904

Skin Diver (magazine)
8490 Sunset Boulevard
Los Angeles, CA 90069

UMS
(Undersea Medical Society)
9650 Rockville Pike
Bethesda, MD 20014

University of Rhode Island
National Underwater Accident Data Center
Box 68
Kingston, RI 02881

UPS
(Underwater Photographic Society)
Box 7088
Van Nuys, CA 91409

USA
(Underwater Society of America-Dive Club
   Information)
238 Sunset
Glen Ellyn, IL 60137

USGPO
(U.S. Government Printing Office)
Superintendent of Documents
Washington, D.C. 20402